PRINCIPLES
OF MRI

SELECTED TOPICS

PRINCIPLES

OF MRI

SELECTED TOPICS

John A. Markisz, MD, PhD
Associate Professor of Radiology
Cornell University Medical College
New York, New York

Joseph P. Whalen, MD, DSc
Professor of Radiology
College of Health Sciences
State University of New York
Syracuse, New York

Formerly
Dean, College of Health Sciences
State University of New York
Syracuse, New York

Formerly
Professor and Chairman
Department of Radiology
Cornell University Medical College
New York, New York

APPLETON & LANGE
Stamford, Connecticut

Copyright © 1998 by Appleton & Lange
A Simon & Schuster Company

98 99 00 01 02 / 10 9 8 7 6 5 4 3 2 1

Prentice Hall International (UK) Limited, *London*
Prentice Hall of Australia Pty. Limited, *Sydney*
Prentice Hall Canada, Inc., *Toronto*
Prentice Hall Hispanoamericana, S.A., *Mexico*
Prentice Hall of India Private Limited, *New Delhi*
Prentice Hall of Japan, Inc., *Tokyo*
Simon & Schuster Asia Pte. Ltd., *Singapore*
Editora Prentice Hall do Brasil Ltda., *Rio de Janeiro*
Prentice Hall, *Upper Saddle River, New Jersey*

Library of Congress Cataloging-in-Publication Data
Principles and practice of MRI : selected topics / [edited by] John A.
    Markisz, Joseph P. Whalen.
        p.   cm.
    Includes bibliographical references.
    ISBN 0-8385-8152-8 (pbk. : alk. paper)
    1. Magnetic resonance imaging.   I. Markisz, John A.   II. Whalen,
Joseph P.
    [DNLM: 1. Magnetic Resonance Imaging.   WN 185 P957 1997]
RC78.7.N83P746   1998
616.07'548—dc21
DNLM/DLC
for Library of Congress   97-42651
                                                                      CIP

ISBN 0-8385-8152-8

9 780838 581520

90000

Production Editor: Sondra Greenfield

CONTENTS

CONTRIBUTOR LIST

Patrick T. Cahill, PhD
Professor of Physics
Polytechnic Institute of New York
New York, New York
Chapter 4, "Quality Assurance for MRI"
Chapter 7, "Essentials of MR Angiography"

Zang Hee Cho, PhD
Professor of Radiology
University of California at Irvine
School of Medicine
Irvine, California
Chapter 5, "MRI Microscopy"

Joon-Young Chung, PhD
Department of Information and Communication
Korean Advanced Institute of Science and Technology
Seoul, Korea
Chapter 5, "MRI Microscopy"

Joseph P. Comunale, Jr., MD
Assistant Professor of Radiology
Cornell University Medical College
New York, New York
Chapter 7, "Essentials of MR Angiography"

Franklyn A. Howe, DPhil
Honorary Lecturer in Magnetic Resonance
CRC Biomedical Magnetic Research Group
Department of Cellular and Molecular Sciences
St. George's Hospital Medical School
London, England
Chapter 2, "Magnetic Resonance Spectroscopy in Vivo"

R. James R. Knowles, PhD
Formerly
Associate Professor of Physics in Radiology
Cornell University Medical College
New York, New York
Chapter 1, "Physics of MRI: A Modular Approach"
Chapter 4, "Quality Assurance for MRI"

Paul C. Lauterbur, PhD
Director, Biomedical Magnetic Resonance Laboratory
Distinguished University Professor, College of Medicine
Professor, Center for Advanced Study
Professor of Medical Information Science
Professor of Chemistry
Professor of Molecular and Integrative Physiology
University of Illinois at Urbana-Champaign
Urbana, Illinois
Chapter 6, "Reduced-Scan Imaging"

Soon-Chil Lee, PhD
Associate Professor
Department of Physics
Korean Advanced Institute of Science and Technology
Seoul, Korea
Chapter 5, "MRI Microscopy"

Zhi-Pei Liang, PhD
Assistant Professor
Department of Electrical and Computer Engineering
Beckman Institute for Advanced Science and Technology
University of Illinois at Urbana-Champaign
Urbana, Illinois
Chapter 6, "Reduced-Scan Imaging"

John A. Markisz, MD, PhD
Associate Professor of Radiology
Cornell University Medical College
New York, New York
Chapter 3, "Image Artifacts"
Chapter 7, "Essentials of MR Angiography"

Thomas Vullo, PhD
Multigon Industries
New York, New York
Chapter 4, "Quality Assurance for MRI"

Joseph P. Whalen, MD, DSc
Professor of Radiology
College of Health Sciences
State University of New York
Syracuse, New York

Formerly
Dean, College of Health Sciences
State University of New York
Syracuse, New York

Formerly
Professor and Chairman
Department of Radiology
Cornell University Medical College
New York, New York
Chapter 3, "Image Artifacts"

E. K. Wong, MD
Associate Professor
Department of Ophthalmology
University of California at Irvine
School of Medicine
Irvine, California
Chapter 5, "MRI Microscopy"

PREFACE

Clinical magnetic resonance is a rapidly expanding field, with major innovations in clinical techniques continuing to develop at a blistering pace. Investigation of clinical problems with magnetic resonance technology using such different applications as conventional imaging, fast scanning, angiography, and spectroscopy are now commonly available. These different methods take advantage of very different physical principles of magnetic resonance. Although a detailed knowledge of the fundamentals involved in these applications is not necessary to use them as a diagnostic tool, an appreciation of the generalized foundations will aid in more appropriate utilization in a clinical setting. This text presents a collection of articles for clinicians which will permit them to gain an understanding of the inherently different principles of these unique and vastly different techniques.

CHAPTER ONE

PHYSICS OF MRI: A MODULAR APPROACH

R. James R. Knowles

One of the most exciting aspects of magnetic resonance imaging (MRI) can also be one of its most frustrating. To a degree unprecedented in other medical imaging modalities, the significance of many image elements can be completely changed by simply altering the sequence of pulses used during the acquisition process. This has led to a wild proliferation of imaging sequences, many of which are denoted by tricky acronyms.[1]

To keep up with such an ever-changing field, it is necessary to be well grounded in the fundamentals of MRI. Certain basic components appear in various combinations to produce most imaging sequences. If one is familiar with these basic modules, one can infer a great deal about what to expect when these modules are strung together to form more complex sequences.

PRODUCING THE MAGNETIC RESONANCE IMAGE

All MRIs result from a complex interaction of constituents in the object (patient or phantom) with numerous instrumental factors. In the object, one must pay particular attention to the chemical state as well as the density of magnetic nuclei, relaxation times, and all physical movement including flow and diffusion. Similarly, instrumental factors such as magnetic field strength, radio frequency (RF), RF power, the timing of RF pulses, gradient strength, gradient direction, and gradient pulse timing are important.[1,2]

Magnetic Nuclei

Atomic nuclei are composed of various numbers of protons and neutrons. Both protons and neutrons carry intrinsic magnetic moments as well as intrinsic spins. If there are even numbers of protons or neutrons in a nucleus, these magnetic moments sum to zero because such nucleons tend to pair (two protons or two neutrons line up together with opposite orientations so that their magnetic moments just cancel each other out). Thus, nuclear magnetism results from unpaired protons or neutrons. For example, radioactive carbon-14 is not magnetic, but carbon-13 is. Although various magnetic nuclei are of biological interest, most of what follows will be primarily concerned with imaging the single unpaired proton of hydrogen-1, the most abundant magnetic nuclei in biological materials.

Static Magnetic Field

Nuclear magnetic moments behave like little bar magnets: They interact with all other magnetic fields. In particular, they tend to align with any applied external field. This alignment is statistical in nature and actually represents a competition between the strength of the applied field and thermal motion, which tends to randomize the orientations of the magnetic moments. Thus, more magnetic nuclei are aligned by a higher applied field and in a colder object.

In addition, this alignment with an external field cannot be exact because of quantum mechanical effects (the uncertainty principle). Thus, the magnetic moments actually precess about the external magnetic field much like a spinning gyroscope that is not perfectly aligned with gravity will precess about the local gravitational field. The frequency (f_0) of this precession is proportional to the applied magnetic field (B_0) and is given by Larmor's equation

$$f_0 = gB_0$$

where g is a constant that is different for each species of magnetic nuclei.

In MRI, the external field is commonly applied by either a superconducting magnet (in which case the field B_0 is usually directed horizontally along the length of the patient) or by a permanent magnet (in which case the field B_0 is often applied vertically or sideways to the patient). In MRI, B_0 typically varies from 0.3 to 1.5 T (where 1 tesla = 10,000 gauss, and the earth's magnetic field averages about 0.5 gauss). It is important to realize, however, that any magnetic field can affect the precessional frequency. In particular, unpaired electrons have magnetic moments some three orders of magnitude greater than nuclear magnetic moments, so that all electrons near the nucleus provide varying degrees of diamagnetic screening and any polar chemical bonds close to the nucleus can substantially shift its precessional frequency. Thus, the Larmor frequency is a function of external field strength, nuclear species, and local chemical environment. Changes in Larmor frequency due to chemical environment are known as chemical shifts.

Radio Frequency Input and Output

What makes the Larmor frequency especially important is that resonance phenomena cause a system of magnetic nuclei in a static external field to absorb RF energy at the Larmor frequency and radiate RF energy at this very same frequency. Such radio waves possess both electric and magnetic components. The magnetic component (*BI*) of the RF input is used to add energy in order to tip the precessing nuclei away from their alignment with the external magnetic field (B_0). When these nuclei eventually realign with the external field, they give up this added energy as radio waves, which can be detected and utilized to form MR images. For proton MRI, the Larmor frequency is typically in or below the VHF (very high frequency) television channels.

Aligning or realigning with the external magnetic field is an exponential process governed by the time constant T_1, termed the longitudinal or spin–lattice relaxation time. In the time T_1, about 63% of this realignment is completed. For biological materials, T_1 generally varies from a few seconds (pure water) down to a few hundred milliseconds. T_1 increases with the strength of the external magnetic field (B_0).[3,4] Conversely, T_1 may be shortened by using magnetic contrast agents.

There is a second relaxation time, the transverse or spin–spin relaxation time, which affects net magnetic moment.

When an RF pulse is used to tip the magnetic nuclei away from B_0, all the tipped nuclei start out precessing in their new alignment with the same phase (they all point in the same direction). Random fluctuations in the local magnetic field (eg, from other nuclei and from electrons) cause slight shifts in the Larmor frequency, both positive and negative. Eventually these stochastic effects randomize the phases of the precessing nuclei. With magnetic moments randomly pointing in all directions, the net magnetic moment cancels out. T_2 is the time constant for this statistical process and represents the time required for a dephasing of about 63%. T_2 must always be less than or equal to T_1. For biological materials, T_2 is usually a hundred milliseconds or less, and the variation with B_0 is generally small for the field strengths used in MRI.[3,4] Magnetic contrast agents can also be used to shorten T_2.

Tip angles measure how far the magnetic moments are rotated from their alignment with B_0 by the RF. Tip angles increase with applied RF power (RF pulse height × pulse duration). Three tip angles are particularly important. Ninety-degree pulses produce a net magnetic moment perpendicular to B_0. (MR signal strength is proportional to this transverse component of magnetization.) A tip angle of 180° causes the net magnetic moment to point in the direction opposite to B_0 and therefore precess in the opposite direction. The third tip angle is the Euler angle, which will be discussed in the section on gradient echoes. All three of these tip angles will recur in many different contexts.

Signal Localization by Magnetic Gradients

Once an RF signal has been produced, its point of origin in the object must be determined. This is accomplished by using magnetic gradients. Orthogonal linear gradients change the magnetic field strength in each of the three directions (x,y,z) proportional to the distance from the origin at the center of the magnet. By convention, B_0 is taken as the z-direction, and all magnetic gradients add to or subtract from this z-component magnetization. Thus, for example, an x-gradient does not imply a new magnetic field in the x-direction, but rather a systematic change in z-component magnetization as one moves along the x-axis. As a result of this gradient (B_{gx}), Larmor's equation predicts a corresponding change in frequency

$$f = g(B_0 + B_{gx})$$

If B_{gx} varies linearly with x, then the frequency shift $(f_0 - f)$ will also vary linearly with x. Thus, each x-position will correspond to a different frequency, and measuring the frequency shift will yield the x-coordinate of the RF signal. This method of localization is termed a frequency-encoding gradient, and resolution along this gradient is equal to the number of frequency measurements made while the gradient is turned on.

Slice-selective gradients comprise a slight variant on this frequency-encoding strategy. By using an RF pulse with a very narrow frequency range while a frequency-encoding gradient is active, only a narrow plane of magnetic nuclei perpendicular to the gradient direction will be excited by the RF because only these nuclei will have a Larmor frequency matched to the frequency range of the RF pulse. Thus, one localization can occur during the RF excitation itself.

Frequency encoding persists only as long as the gradient is turned on; but even after the gradient has been turned off, phase differences remain. Those nuclei that experienced a higher magnetic field have precessed faster and gotten ahead of those nuclei that experienced a lower magnetic field. A phase-encoding gradient can be used to establish such phase differences, which are then measured at some time after the gradient has been turned off. Unfortunately, one cannot measure local phase differences but only the summed phase of all the signals combined. To determine local phases, one must repeatedly turn on and off the phase-encoding gradient with different amplitudes and measure the resulting summed phases. By turning on and off the phase-encoding gradient n times, one can algebraically determine n local phases along this gradient, corresponding to n localizations. Thus, resolution along a phase-encoding direction is equal to the number of phase-encoding gradient steps used.

Frequency- and phase-encoding gradients are generally combined in most imaging sequences. If there were three frequency-encoding gradients, for example, the signal would come from a single voxel (volume element), and the SNR (signal-to-noise ratio) would be very poor. Phase-encoding gradients improve the SNR by measuring a summed signal from a whole string of such voxels (while the electronic noise in a well-designed system remains essentially the same as for measuring a single voxel). On the other hand, phase encoding takes much more time than frequency encoding because of the many gradient steps required. Hence, the practical compromise is to use a combination of the frequency-encoding and phase-encoding gradients in the same sequence. One of the most common combinations (the so-called spin–warp gradient) includes a slice-selective gradient, an orthogonal phase-encoding gradient, and an orthogonal frequency-encoding read gradient.

COMPUTER CONTROL AND RECONSTRUCTION

Controlling all these RF and gradient pulses with microsecond timing is accomplished by electronic logic under computer control. Data acquisition can be ordered to reduce artifacts and achieve physiological gating. In addition to controlling imaging sequences and data acquisition, computers are required for image reconstruction. The input to the computer is in the form of signal intensity as a function of frequency and phase. In order to produce an image of signal intensity as a function of spatial location, the most natural choice is a reconstruction method that is some variant on the Fourier transform, because this transform links the commonplace spatial domain (x,y,z,t) with the more exotic frequency or K-space domain (Kx,Ky,Kz,W), and vice versa. It is fortuitous for MRI that much attention has been given in the recent past to optimizing FFTs (fast-Fourier transforms) for other computer applications. Special image processors can now routinely reconstruct images as fast as they can be displayed.

One aspect of image reconstruction that deserves some special consideration is whether the method preserves the difference between positive and negative phase or only reconstructs the magnitude of the signal. Phase-sensitive reconstructions become important in studying flow as well as in some imaging sequences such as inversion recovery.

Image Displays

Image reconstruction yields arrays of numbers representing signal strength as a function of position. These arrays can be two, three, or even four dimensional. The optimal way of presenting this information remains a subject of some debate. For example, is it useful to assign different colors to different ranges of numbers for visual display, or is color just another distraction? Is the ultimate presentation an electronic display of a three-dimensional data set that allows the viewer to arbitrarily change angle and depth of view as well as gray scale, or does this demand too much time and effort from the viewer? In practice, most MR images are presented as small sequential images on large sheets of film, even though less information is available than in an electronic image with gray scale controls.

In what follows, the main focus will be on relating image-intensity variations to variations in the imaged object and to choices of imaging sequences. How do chemistry, density, relaxation times, and motion combine in a given sequence to produce a particular signal intensity?

Basic Imaging Sequences

Two imaging sequences, the basic spin echo and the basic gradient echo, demonstrate most of the modules needed to understand the more complex examples. Both of these sequences are also among the most common in current clinical practice.[1,2,5]

Spin Echo
One very basic problem in MRI is that kilowatts of RF power are applied to the input excitations, but only microwatts of power are obtained in the output signals. To produce a reasonable SNR, the signals must be measured sufficiently long after the excitation pulses to allow the input pulse to decay through some 10 orders of magnitude. During this waiting time after the 90° pulse, however, the initial signal or FID (free induction decay) is itself decaying away. Intrinsic dephasing (represented by T_2) is supplemented by dephasing from magnetic inhomogeneities or gradients (B_g), from macroscopic magnetic susceptibility differences or magnetic materials (B_m) such as decomposing hemoglobin in a hemorrhage and from complex diffusion effects:

$$1 + gB_g + gB_m + \text{diffusion } T_2^*T_2$$

T_2^* (T_2-star) is always shorter than T_2 and generally very much shorter. To obtain a reasonable signal, these effects must be reversed, and in fact T_2^* can be reduced to T_2 (the unavoidable minimum) by using a 180° pulse at a time $TE/2$ after a 90° excitation pulse. The 180° pulse inverts the magnetic nuclei so that they spin in the opposite direction with respect to all nonrandom magnetic fields like B_g and B_m. This reversal acts to rephase the nuclei, because those nuclei in higher fields (and therefore precessing faster, ahead of nuclei in lower fields) are retarded more than the nuclei in lower fields now that they are spinning in the opposite direction with respect to this same higher field. The net result is that fast and slow precessors rephase at a time $TE/2$ after the 180° pulse and at a time TE after the 90° pulse. This rephased signal is termed a spin echo, and the time TE is the echo time. One can even introduce a second 180° pulse after this spin echo and produce a second echo, and so on. Each of these echoes will be reduced by progressive T_2 decay plus any diffusion along gradients (although for typical MRI gradient strengths, diffusion loss will be minimal), because the second law of thermodynamics does not allow even a 180° pulse to reverse such microscopic random effects. To locate the origin of this spin echo signal, it is common to employ slice-selective gradients during the RF pulses, followed by an orthogonal phase-encoding gradient, with a frequency-encoding gradient active during the reading of the spin echo to determine the third coordinate. All the gradients in this spin–warp sequence produce different phase shifts at different spatial locations, and these phase shifts attenuate the summed signal. When the phase shifts are not being used to determine location (ie, with all frequency encoding gradients), the signal strength can be improved by eliminating these phase shifts with rephasing gradients. A rephasing or compensatory gradient should be equal in magnitude and opposite in sign to the gradient causing the phase shifts. A 180° pulse effectively changes the sign of any gradient following it because the magnetic moments have been reversed by the pulse. After a time TR (the repetition time), all these RF and gradient pulses are repeated for the next phase-encoding step. During the time TR, T_1 decay mechanisms realign the magnetic moments with B_0. If TR is short with respect to T_1, the next 90° pulse will find little magnetization aligned along B_0 to tip into the transverse plane and therefore produce little signal. On the other hand, if TR is long with respect to T_1, a much larger signal will be generated. In the limit of a very long TR, all T_1 values will recover more or less fully, and signal intensity will depend only on the density of magnetic nuclei (spin density). Thus, short TR values produce maximum T_1 contrast.

Conversely, a short TE allows less T_2 decay and hence generates more signal. Long TE values, however, allow all short T_2

values to decay to nearly zero and therefore produce maximum T_2 contrast. In classical spin echo sequences, TR values are relatively long, and much time is spent waiting for T_1 recovery. This makes for acquisition times of order minutes

$$T = anTR$$

where a is the number of signal averages and n is the number of phase-encoding gradient steps. Multislice techniques use this time to excite and read other slices. Thus, one can acquire as many slices during T as can be fitted between the reading of the first slice and its reexcitation after time TR.[6] Usually, small gaps are left between these slices, and the order of slice excitation is carefully chosen so as to minimize the leakage of RF excitation between adjacent slices. Of course, multislice sequences can also be made multi-echo, even though this may reduce the number of slices that can be scanned during T.

As a final variant on the basic spin echo sequence, consider the effects of placing another 180° pulse at time T_1 before the 90° pulse. During T_1 (the inversion time), magnetic moments will rotate back toward B_0 so that at the time of the 90° pulse, magnetic moments will be spread out with tip angles between zero (short T_1 values) and 180° (long T_1 values). After the 90° tip, some values of T_1 will have positive phase, others will have negative phase, and still others will make no contribution to the image at all. This spin echo version of inversion recovery thus increases T_1 contrast but demands more time and requires a phase-sensitive reconstruction plus display in order to gain maximum benefit from it.

Gradient Echo
Another approach to moving the signal away from the excitation pulse is to apply a dephasing gradient during the FID and then reverse this gradient to rephase and read the signal. Such a gradient-recalled echo differs from a spin echo in that a gradient reversal removes only the gradient term from T_2^*. Without the 180° pulse of the spin echo, though, a gradient echo can be read much closer to the 90° pulse and thus suffers from far less T_2^* decay.

With all its other gradients the same as in the spin echo sequence, this gradient echo sequence is very compact in time. If one attempts to capitalize on this compactness by reducing TR to produce a fast-imaging sequence, one soon discovers that 90°

pulses do not produce the maximum signal. As TR approaches the average T_1 value, it becomes possible to increase the signal by tipping to less than 90°. The tip angle that produces the maximum signal for given values of T_1, T_2, TR, and TE is termed the Euler angle. Longer T_1 values produce more signal with a smaller tip angle, while shorter T_1 values can tolerate a tip angle closer to 90°. Thus, tip angle becomes another way of manipulating T_1 contrast. When TR approaches the average T_2 value, tip angles also become a way of manipulating T_2 contrast.[5]

To obtain still more signal, the dephasing effects of the phase-encoding gradient can be eliminated by installing a rewinder gradient before the next RF pulse. Such a gradient is simply a phase-encoding gradient run in reverse: If the phase-encoding gradient starts large and negative, then the rewinder starts large and positive. Both gradients run through zero and then increase in opposite directions. Gradient echo fast-scan techniques can reduce slice acquisition time to the order of seconds. This alleviates many problems from motion artifacts, especially respiration.

In addition (as we will see later in the section on flow imaging), these gradient echo sequences tend to accentuate flow. Such fast scans, however, do not permit multislice techniques.[5,7]

Some Hybrid Imaging Techniques

We have seen how a simple spin echo sequence can be easily elaborated into a multislice multi-echo technique. Similarly, a fast-scan technique was developed from the basic gradient echo sequence. Both spin echoes and gradient echoes have inversion recovery forms. We will now expand this elaboration process to illustrate the usefulness of our basic modules in understanding still more complex imaging sequences.

Echo-Planar Imaging

It is possible to reduce scan time to the order of tens of milliseconds and thereby remove even cardiac motion artifacts. This is achieved in echo-planar imaging (EPI) by following a single slice-selective 90° pulse with long series of gradient reversals so as to produce a large number (64 or 128) of gradient echoes. Between each of these echoes, the phase is advanced (eg, by an orthogonal gradient that stays on all the time or by one that just blips on before each echo). Therefore each echo will be phase encoded, and one set of coordinates can be calculated from them.[7,8]

In this simple form, echo-planar resolution in the phase-encoding direction is limited by the number of echoes, which are in turn limited by T_2 decay. To maximize signal, EPI is generally done at the highest available field strength, which then increases all chemical shifts. Larger-than-normal gradient pulses are also required by this technique.

With only a single 90° excitation pulse, there is no T_1 recovery and hence no T_1 contrast. Such images are essentially spin-density images. It is possible, however, to produce T_1 contrast by introducing additional RF pulses. An inversion recovery variant with a 180° pulse before the 90° one is probably the simplest example of this sort of approach.

T_2 contrast is even more complex because the various phase-encoded echoes exhibit differing amounts of $T_2{}^*$ decay, and reconstruction redistributes these effects throughout the image. One may, however, follow the 90° pulse with a 180° pulse to produce a spin echo–like T_2 contrast. This T_2 contrast applies only to broad image features (because only the center of K-space is completely rephased by the 180° pulse), while in regions of fine detail and at edges, $T_2{}^*$ decay continues to act to limit resolution and generate artifacts, including large chemical shifts.

Fast-Spin Echo Imaging

One may also phase encode the multiple echoes produced by 180° pulses in a spin echo sequence. In fast-spin echo (FSE) imaging, the object is not so much a fast acquisition time as it is acquiring a great deal of information in one acquisition. Thus, 4, 8, or 16 phase-encoded echoes are common, and multislice techniques are generally used to make efficient use of the long TR values required for recovery.[7,8]

Once the acquisition is complete, some tricks of reconstruction can be employed to generate images with any T_2 contrast available from any of the echoes. This is possible because all the echoes are true spin echoes, and any one of them can be made the center of K-space by simply scrolling the origin of K-space to the desired echo. As in the echo-planar case, this produces a T_2 weighting for the broad contrast features of the image, but in the fine detail and edges of the image, T_2 weighting of the components of the point-spread function can generate blur and artifacts. Moreover, some aspects of FSE, such as the high-intensity signal from fat at long TE values, are difficult to explain.[8]

Volume (3-D) Imaging

There are many ways to image an entire volume. For example, one could simply use two multislice acquisitions, positioned so that the second acquisition filled in the gaps of the first. One could also simply stack together many single slices acquired by a fast-scan technique. To allow an arbitrary plane to be reconstructed in any direction from such data sets, however, requires that the slices be very thin (to maintain more or less the same resolution in all directions) and therefore very low in signal.

One of the most common ways of achieving equal resolution in all directions while overcoming this low signal problem is to use phase-encoding gradients for two orthogonal directions. This pattern of gradients slows down the acquisition a great deal, but fast-scan techniques can still produce tolerable scan times with this technique:

$$T = anmTR$$

where a is the number of signal averages, n is the number of phase-encoding steps along one axis, m is the number of phase-encoding steps along an orthogonal axis, and TR is a short repetition time.[2,5]

Spectral (4-D) Imaging

Increasing the number of phase-encoding gradients can be generalized to all three spatial axes. This greatly inflates the acquisition time

$$T = anm1TR$$

where n, m, and 1 are the number of phase-encoding steps on each of the three orthogonal gradients. Such a technique produces a four-dimensional data set, because the read gradient is now phase encoded so that different chemical shifts each have their own associated phases. Furthermore, such a phase-encoding gradient pulse generates far less dephasing than a frequency-encoding read gradient would, so the signals from the different chemical shifts are better separated and less blurred into one another. Proton chemical shifts, however, remain relatively small compared to those of other biologically interesting magnetic nuclei. For example, the fat–water shift is only about 3.5 ppm (parts per million), with the absolute value of this frequency shift increasing with field strength. Therefore a very homogeneous high magnetic field is required to effectively separate these chemical shifts.[9]

Magnetic field requirements have proven less of a practical deterrent to 4-D imaging than have the acquisition time requirements. Various 2-D approaches have used either frequency shifts or relaxation time differences to eliminate one component. A chemical component can be selectively excited before the general excitation pulse so that this component makes no contribution at echo time. An inversion recovery technique can null out the unwanted component, or a highly selective saturation pulse plus dephasing gradients (spoilers) can suppress the component. In addition, TE can be varied by shifting the 180° pulse in time to alter the phase between signals at two frequencies and thereby obtain two images with opposite phase differences, which can be added and subtracted to yield pure images of the two components. The most common candidates for such separate imaging have been water and fat.[9,10]

Flow and Diffusion Imaging

Flow can produce changes in both signal intensity and signal phase. Flow into an imaging slice can increase signal by bringing in unequilibrated spins that are not limited by T_1 recovery (because they have not experienced previous RF pulses). Such a wash-in of signal is all that is seen with a gradient echo technique, because a nucleus can contribute to the image even if it has moved out of the slice after being excited. But in a spin echo sequence, flow may produce either a wash-in or a wash-out effect because there are two slice-selective RF pulses, and spins with sufficiently high velocity may escape from the slice between the two pulses and not contribute to the signal (ie, a gradient can refocus excited nuclei both inside and outside the slice, but a slice-selective 180° pulse is limited exclusively to the inside). For a multislice acquisition, wash-in is at a maximum where the flow first enters the stack of slices and has not yet experienced any excitations. In addition, one can tag flowing spins with an excitation pulse and then measure displacement of the resulting signal after a selected interval of time to determine the flow velocity. Conversely, one can suppress the signal from flow into an imaging volume by applying a 90° pulse to the regions bordering this volume and then exciting the volume itself. Flow into the imaging volume will then have no longitudinal magnetization to be excited and consequently make no contribution to the image.[2,5]

Flow along a gradient also produces phase shifts. These phase shifts reduce the amplitude of odd-numbered echoes in a spin echo sequence, but not the amplitude of even-numbered echoes (because an even number of 180° reversals cancels out the shift). Moreover, one can use a bipolar gradient with two equal but opposed parts to induce a phase shift in nuclei moving along that gradient but not in nuclei stationary with respect to the gradient. This phase shift can then be imaged by phase-sensitive methods and can even be quantitatively measured to determine the velocity of the flow. Conversely, gradient moment nulling uses combinations of gradients to eliminate motion artifacts resulting from flow by cancelling out phase shifts in constant velocity, accelerated flow, or both. Because of the time involved, one must generally make do with only a constant-velocity nulling gradient such as a triplet with areas in the ratio 1:–2:1.[2,5]

During recent years, MR angiography has become increasingly popular because no injected contrast material is needed. MR angiography is a conceptual reversal of the gradient moment nulling technique discussed previously. In MR angiography, the stationary tissue signal is suppressed, and flow is selectively excited to generate the majority of the image. Projected views can be acquired very rapidly, and three-dimensional views with rotations are possible if more time is available.[11,12]

In addition to coherent flow, there is also the random flow of diffusion and microscopic perfusion. With the magnitude of gradients typically used for spin echo sequences, these effects are generally minimal in all echoes. Thus, one could compare the signal produced by the second echo of standard spin echo sequence with the signal produced by the first echo of a sequence with much larger gradients added.[13,14] The TE of the second sequence must be exactly double the TE of the first, and the large gradients in the second sequence could either be bipolar or arranged symmetrically around its 180° pulse. The signal of this second sequence would then be reduced with respect to the signal from the first sequence by the effects of the dephasing caused by an effective diffusion (consisting of both true diffusion and some microscopic perfusion) along the large gradient. Other variants of large gradients may be used to distinguish apparent or effective diffusion from nonrandom flow.[15,16] An increase in this effective diffusion may indicate cell damage earlier than T_2-weighted or other more traditional techniques.[17]

Magnetization Transfer Imaging

Hydrogen nuclei associated with macromolecules (including perhaps even some of their water of hydration) have short T_2 values with broad resonance peaks (behaving somewhat like solids), while hydrogen nuclei associated with small molecules have much longer T_2 values with narrow resonance peaks (behaving like typical liquids). One can study the transfer of magnetization between these two pools of hydrogen nuclei by selectively exciting one pool and observing the loss of magnetization when the other pool has been previously saturated and when it has not been.[18] Because of its narrow resonance peak, the liquid-like pool is generally selectively excited, while the solid-like pool is either presaturated with an off-resonance pulse or not. The differing rates of disappearance of magnetization from the liquid-like pool in the two cases thus provide some measure of content and order in the imaged tissues, and may be particularly sensitive to disruptions of this order and/or changes in macromolecular content.[18]

CONCLUSION

Many more imaging sequences exist than can be covered here, and more are being invented all the time. It is hoped that the modular development of imaging elements presented here will allow the reader to gain some insight into these sequences without resort to calculations, K-space maps, or phase diagrams. On the other hand, some details do demand such precision, and many particulars of the newer pulse sequences have not yet been fully worked out. Thus the future may provide all of us with a few surprises.

REFERENCES

1. Rink PA (ed): *An Introduction to Magnetic Resonance in Medicine: The Basic Textbook of the European Workshop on Magnetic Resonance in Medicine.* New York: Thieme Medical Publishers, 1990.
2. Wehrli FW, Shaw D, Kneeland JB (eds): *Biomedical Magnetic Resonance Imaging: Principles, Methodology, and Applications.* New York: VCH Publishers, 1988.
3. Bottomley PA, Foster TH, Argersinger RE, Pfeifer LM: A review of normal tissue hydrogen NMR relaxation times and relaxation mechanisms from 1–100 Mhz:

Dependence on tissue type, NMR frequency, temperature, species, excision, and age. *Med Physics* 1984;11:425–448.

4. Bottomley PA, Hardy CJ, Argersinger RE, Allen-Moore G: A review of H-1 nuclear magnetic resonance relaxation in pathology: Are T1 and T2 diagnostic? *Med Physics* 1987;14:1–37.

5. Wehrli FW: *Fast-Scan Magnetic Resonance: Principles and Applications.* New York: Raven Press, 1991.

6. Kneeland JB, Knowles RJR, Cahill PT: Multi-section multi-echo pulse magnetic resonance techniques: Optimization in a clinical setting. *Radiology* 1985;155: 159–162.

7. Cohen MS, Weisskoff RM: Ultra-fast imaging. *Magn Reson Imaging* 1991; 9,1:1–37.

8. Listerud J, Einstein S, Outwater E, Kressel HY: First principles of fast spin echo. *Magn Reson Q* 1992;8,4:199–244.

9. Brateman L: Chemical shift imaging: A review. *AJR* 1986;146:971–980.

10. Tien RD: Fat-suppression MR imaging in neuroradiology: Techniques and clinical application. *AJR* 1992;156:369–379. Review.

11. Edelman RR, Mattle HP, Atkinson DJ, Hoogewoud HM: MR angiography. *AJR* 1990;154:937–946. Review.

12. Bosmans H, Marchal G, Van Hecke P, Vanhoenacker P: MRA review. *Clin Imaging* 1992;16:152–167.

13. Le Bihan D, Breton E, Lallemand D, et al: MR imaging of intravoxel incoherent motions: Application to diffusion and perfusion in neurologic disorders. *Radiology* 1986;161:401–407.

14. Le Bihan D, Breton E, Lallemand D, et al: Separation of diffusion and perfusion in intravoxel incoherent motion MR imaging. *Radiology* 1988;168:497–505.

15. Harada K, Fujita N, Sakurai K, et al: Diffusion imaging of the human brain: A new pulse sequence application for a 1.5-T standard MR system. *AJNR* 1991;12:1143–1148.

16. Moseley ME, Kucharczyk J, Asgari HS, Norman D: Anisotropy in diffusion-weighted MRI. *Magn Reson Med* 1991;19:321–326.

17. Moseley ME, Kucharczyk J, Mintorovitch J, et al: Diffusion weighted MR imaging of acute stroke: Correlation with T2 weighted and magnetic susceptibility enhanced MR imaging in cats. *AJNR* 1990;11:423–429.

18. Santyr GE, Mulkem RV: Magnetization transfer in MR imaging. *J Magn Reson Imaging* 1995;5:121–124.

CHAPTER TWO

MAGNETIC RESONANCE SPECTROSCOPY IN VIVO

Franklyn A. Howe

In this chapter, the type of data that can be acquired by magnetic resonance spectroscopy (MRS) and localized MRS techniques currently in routine use are described, and the research and clinical applications of in vivo MRS are reviewed. A bibliography of MRS texts, including a list of review articles, is also included. Magnetic resonance spectroscopy is unique in that it allows for the noninvasive investigation of the biochemistry of specific tissue. For example, in the ^1H spectrum (Fig. 2–1) there are peaks from metabolites such as N-acetyl aspartate (NAA), total creatines (tCr, comprising creatine and phosphocreatine), total choline (tCho, contributions from choline, phosphorylcholine, and glycerophosphorylcholine), *myo*-Inositol (mI, which may also have underlying components from inositol monophosphates and glycine), and complex overlapping peaks from amino acids such as glutamate and glutamine (Glx). The phosphorus-31 (^{31}P) spectrum (Fig. 2–2) has peaks from phosphocreatine (PCr), inorganic phosphate (P_i), and nucleoside triphosphates (NTP). The pioneering in vivo MRS studies[1] used small surface coils to restrict the sensitive volume (approximately a hemisphere with the same diameter as the coil) to a particular tissue of interest.[2] For example, ^{31}P spectra were acquired from surface tumors,[3] muscle,[4] and pediatric brain.[5] In the last decade, there have been significant advances in localized MRS techniques. The major or-

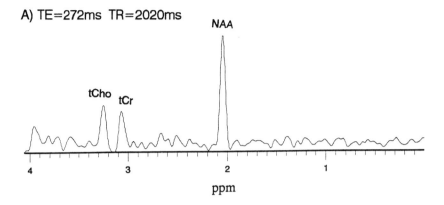

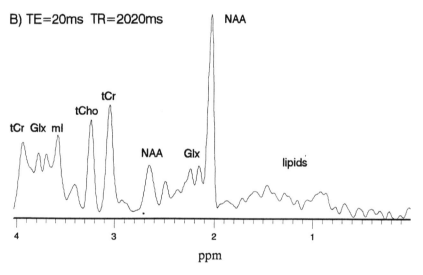

Figure 2–1. Hydrogen-1 spectra (processed with Lorentz-Gauss weighting for resolution enhancement and baseline removal [60]) acquired with the STEAM technique from an 8-cm³ voxel in parietal white matter of normal brain. Note the reversal of the relative amplitudes of the tCr and tCho peaks at the longer echo time due to differential T_2 weighting. *Abbreviations: TE* = echo time; *TR* = repetition time; tCho = total choline; tCr = total creatine; NAA = *N*-acetyl aspartate; Glx = glutamate and glutamine; ml = *myo*-inositol; STEAM = stimulated echo acquisition mode. *(Unpublished data, St. George's Hospital Medical School.)*

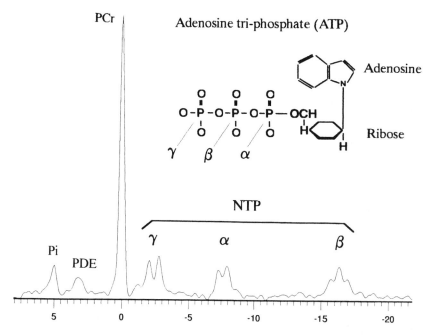

Figure 2–2. Phosphorus-31 spectrum from human gastrocnemius muscle. The structure of adenosine triphosphate (ATP) has three nonequivalent phosphorus nuclei that produce the three multiplets, labeled α, β, and γ. In muscle, adenosine diphosphate (ADP) is bound to myosin and as such is NMR-"invisible." The three multiplets are therefore solely from ATP. *Abbreviations:* P_i = inorganic phosphate; PDE = phosphodiester; PCr = phosphocreatine; NTP = nucleoside triphosphates; NMR = nuclear magnetic resonance. *(Unpublished data, St. George's Hospital Medical School.)*

gans, such as brain, heart, kidney, liver, and other regions, such as muscle and breast, are now amenable to localized MRS of a variety of nuclei in both normal and pathological states. Magnetic resonance spectroscopy thus has the ability to provide basic biochemical information of normal tissue function and the potential to provide diagnostic information in disease.

To acquire an MR spectrum from a well-defined region of tissue, a combination of radio frequency (RF) pulses and switched magnetic field gradients is used: the same technique as that used for slice selection in magnetic resonance imaging (MRI). A pulse sequence containing three orthogonal slice-selective pulses produces a signal from a cuboid volume of interest (VOI). An important point is that, for MRS, the nuclear magnetic resonance (NMR) signal must be acquired with all gradients switched off so that the chemical shift information of the spectrum is preserved. In MRS, there is a compromise between voxel size and examination time in order to acquire spectral data with a good enough signal-to-noise ratio (SNR). The NMR signal in MRI arises from protons in water or lipid, which in human tissue are typically at concentrations of 80 and 4 M, respectively. These concentrations provide enough signal to allow acquisition of MR images of high spatial resolution and a voxel size as small as 1 mm^3 in less than a minute. The metabolites observed by MRS are only at millimolar concentrations, hence the necessity for more prolonged signal averaging and much larger voxel sizes. Typically, an ^{1}H spectrum from an 8-cm^3 volume in the brain can be acquired in 10 min at a field strength of 1.5 T. For the lower-sensitivity ^{31}P nucleus, a 30-min acquisition time is not unusual to acquire a spectrum from a 27-cm^3 volume.

The hardware requirements for ^{1}H MRS are essentially the same as for MRI. Other nuclei, such as ^{19}F, ^{31}P, and ^{13}C, resonate at progressively lower frequencies than ^{1}H, and additional RF coils and amplifiers are therefore needed. Dual-tuned ^{1}H/^{31}P volume head coils are available, but generally, for observation of other nuclei, surface coils are used. To obtain the maximum SNR and resolution of the spectral peaks, the highest possible field strength is needed. This is 1.5 T for clinical systems, up to 4 T for whole-body research systems, and for in vivo animal studies field strengths up to 11 T are available. The requirement of good magnetic field homogeneity is higher for MRS than MRI, and it is usual to optimize this over the region of interest (ROI) for each individual MRS examination. For volume-localized spectroscopy, gradient strengths stronger than the usual 10 mT/m are ideally used to minimize the chemical shift displacement artifact (this is discussed in the Artifacts section under Localization Techniques). Fast gradient risetimes (0.5 ms or less) with generation of minimal eddy currents (by using shielded gradients), which are now necessary for some fast-imaging techniques, are required to obtain the best short echo time ^{1}H spectra.

THE NMR SPECTRUM

As will have been discussed in other chapters on MRI, the MR signal arises from nuclei that have a small magnetic moment. Magnetic resonance imaging uses the magnetic moment of the proton of the hydrogen nuclei of water and lipid molecules. Although these protons both come from the ^{1}H nucleus, the frequency at which they resonate is different. It is this shift in resonance frequency that enables NMR to differentiate between chemical species. For a totally isolated nucleus, the resonance frequency is directly proportional to the external magnetic field strength, and a single peak at this frequency is observed in the spectrum. For a nucleus in an atom, which is part of a molecular structure, the surrounding electrons shield[a] the nucleus very slightly from the external magnetic field. The resonance frequencies are shifted by an amount that is measured in parts per million (ppm). The Larmor equation is then written

$$\bar{\omega} = 2\pi f = \gamma(1 - \sigma)B_0 \qquad (1)$$

where σ is the shielding constant, or when expressed as a multiple of 10^{-6}, the chemical shift in parts per million. The signal acquired in an MRS experiment arises from many chemical species, all resonating at slightly different frequencies according to Equation 1. By applying the process of Fourier transformation to this data, a spectrum is produced (see Figs. 2–1 and 2–2). The axis is the resonance frequency, and the area under each peak is proportional to the number of nuclei resonating at that frequency. Spectra are usually displayed with a horizontal scale in parts per million based on the chemical shift in Equation 1. Although the absolute resonance frequency increases with increasing magnetic field strength, the value of σ generally does not change. The advantage of a relative scale in parts per million, rather than absolute frequency, is that spectra acquired at different field strengths can be directly compared. The scale origin is arbitrary, and in the ^{1}H spectrum 0 ppm is defined to be at the resonance of tetramethylsilane (TMS). This puts the water peak at 4.7 ppm and the lipid peaks at approximately 0.9 and 1.3 ppm. Figure 2–1 shows a typical ^{1}H spectrum taken from a normal brain with the major metabolite peaks labeled. In ^{31}P, the PCr resonance is usually set at 0 ppm. A typical in vivo ^{31}P spectrum from the calf muscles of a healthy volunteer is shown in Figure 2–2. The inset shows the molecular structure of adenosine triphosphate (ATP). The peaks, labeled α, β, and γ, are from the three phosphate nuclei whose resonance frequencies are dif-

---

[a] More precisely, the electrons, which have a magnetic moment 1860 times that of protons, interact strongly with the external magnetic field, and their orbitals are modified. The effect of this is to create a magnetic field at the nucleus, which can oppose the externally applied field.

ferent due to different degrees of shielding by the surrounding bond electrons. These peaks also demonstrate the effects of spin coupling.[b] The β-ATP peak is split into a triplet, with peak amplitudes in the ratio 1:2:1, by the spin-coupling interaction with the other two adjacent ^{31}P nuclei. The γ-ATP and α-ATP peaks are split into a closely spaced doublet because of the interaction with the one adjacent ^{31}P nucleus. Adenosine diphosphate (ADP), which has a similar molecular structure to ATP, produces resonance peaks very close to the γ-ATP and α-ATP peaks. The ATP and ADP resonances cannot be easily distinguished in vivo and are sometimes labeled as NTP.

The fact that, in a spectrum, the resonant peaks of a molecule can be split into complex patterns by the effects of spin coupling can be both an advantage and a disadvantage. For example, in the ^{1}H spectrum the lactate signal is a doublet centered at 1.33 ppm with a constant peak separation of ≈7 Hz. This may enable it to be distinguished from lipid resonances that also occur at ≈1.3 ppm (see Fig. 2–8 for an example). The splitting of peaks can be a disadvantage in that it reduces the amplitude and hence the visibility of the resonance peak above the noise. The complex peak structures of glutamate (Glu) and glutamine (Gln) overlap considerably, and, at 1.5 T, it is almost impossible to distinguish them. They are frequently labeled as Glx over a spectral region rather than as individual peaks (see Fig. 2–1).

Although the majority of biological chemicals contain one or more of the NMR-accessible nuclei, such as ^{1}H, ^{31}P, or ^{13}C, not

---

[b] All nuclei that generate an NMR signal do so by virtue of their magnetic moment. The small magnetic field generated by one nucleus can extend spatially to affect the magnetic field at an adjacent nucleus. Depending on the relative orientation of these two nuclei, either parallel or antiparallel, this can increase or decrease the local magnetic field, and hence the nuclear resonance frequency, by a small amount. This mutual interaction has the effect of splitting a single resonance peak into two closely spaced peaks. If three nuclei are involved then three closely spaced peaks, with amplitudes in the ratio 1:2:1 are observed. If nuclei of the same species are involved, this effect is known as homonuclear coupling, and for nuclei of different species, such as ^{31}P and ^{1}H, as heteronuclear coupling. A technique known as decoupling is often used in ^{13}C and ^{31}P spectroscopy. Some peaks are split by spin coupling with ^{1}H nuclei and so are reduced in intensity, also the spectrum becomes more complex. By irradiating at the ^{1}H frequency the coupling is eliminated, thus simplifying the spectrum and increasing the SNR of the peaks. For in vivo work precautions must be taken to avoid using excessive power at the ^{1}H frequency. A general text on NMR should be consulted for more details on these phenomena.

TABLE 2–1. HYDROGEN-1 METABOLITES IN WHITE MATTER OF NORMAL ADULT BRAIN.

Metabolite	Concentration Shift (ppm)	(mmol/kg)	T_1 (ms)	T_2 (ms)
NAA	2.02	8–17	1400	400
tCr	3.03	5–11	1200	200
tCho	3.24	1.6–1.9	1300	330
ml	3.53	4–7	1200	180

Abbreviations: NAA = *N*-acetyl aspartate; tCr = total creatine; tCho = total creatine; ml = *myo*-Inositol.
Relaxation time data are the average from references 62–64 and 74. The concentration data are from the same references and show the range of values obtained by using different assumptions and methods of quantitation. Using any one technique gives a much smaller variability.

all chemical species are visible by NMR. One reason is that there is a minimum concentration (typically 1 mmol/L at 1.5 T) below which a large enough signal cannot be acquired in a reasonable length of time. A second reason is that nuclei become NMR "invisible" if they are compartmentalized, bound, or are part of a large macromolecule, and so become relatively immobile. This causes a reduction in T_2 to such an extent that the resonance line broadens out to become an unidentifiable part of the spectral baseline. This is true for the P_i peak for which less than 60% of the total physiological phosphate, as measured by chemical assay, appears in the ^{31}P spectrum. The nature of the NMR-invisible P_i is unknown, but it could be sequestered in vesicles or bound to macromolecules.[6] A third reason for invisibility is that the resonance falls close to or at the same frequency

TABLE 2–2. PHOSPHORUS-31 METABOLITE T_1 RELAXATION TIMES (S) IN HUMAN TISSUE.

Metabolite	Brain[a]	Calf Muscle[b]	Liver[b]	Heart[c]
PME			1.5	
P_i	1.45	4.7	0.7	
PDE			2.0	
PCr	3.14	6.5		3.98
α-ATP	0.85	4.2	0.8	
β-ATP	0.86	4.1	0.6	1.86
γ-ATP	0.65	3.9	0.6	

From references [a]: (75); [b]: average of (76), (78), (79); [c]: (77).
Abbreviations: PME = phosphomonoesters; P_i = inorganic phosphates; PDE = phosphodiesters; PCr = phosphocreatine; ATP = adenosine triphosphate.

as a more concentrated compound. It is a particular problem for in vivo NMR that the spectral resolution is ultimately limited by the microscopic homogeneity of the magnetic field within the tissue at the cellular level. The problem of peak identification is an exciting challenge to the in vivo spectroscopist and may require the use of high-resolution one- (1-D) and two-dimensional (2-D) NMR of tissue extracts and other traditional biochemical techniques such as high-pressure liquid chromatography (HPLC).[7-9] Although the origins of the major peaks have now been determined in ^{1}H and ^{31}P spectra, it would not be surprising if there were new discoveries still to be made, especially from the relatively unexplored area of in vivo ^{13}C MRS. Tables 2–1 and 2–2 list the major metabolites observed in ^{31}P and ^{1}H spectroscopy with some of their MR parameters.

MRS BY NUCLEUS

Several nuclei have been of interest to in vivo MR spectroscopists, including ^{1}H, ^{31}P, ^{13}C, ^{19}F, ^{14}N, ^{15}N, and ^{23}Na. In the next section, the type of information that can be obtained from MR spectra of some of these nuclei is briefly discussed.

Hydrogen-1

Although the proton is the most sensitive stable nucleus for MRS (ie, it is 100% naturally abundant and resonates at the highest frequency, thus giving the strongest NMR signal), ^{1}H MRS studies have been mainly confined to the brain for two reasons. First, very good field homogeneity is necessary to permit resolution of the metabolite peaks, which span a small chemical shift range of about 3.5 ppm. Second, to observe the small metabolite signals, the very large water signal must be suppressed (or not excited), which requires both excellent magnetic field homogeneity and minimal motion of the tissue region under investigation. The major resonance in normal brain is from NAA (at a concentration of $\approx$1/5000th that of water), which is predominantly found within neurons and so has been used as a marker for neuronal loss. Two other prominent resonances arise from tCho and tCr. Lactate (Lac), which is usually a result of abnormal anaerobic glycolysis, is observed in many pathological conditions. These four compounds have long T_2s (see Table 2–1) and can still be observed with acquisitions at long echo times (typically with TE = 136 or 272 milliseconds), conditions under which good water suppression and a flat baseline are more easily achieved. The lactate doublet at 1.33 ppm occurs in a region of the ^{1}H spectrum where, at short TE acquisitions, there are often large peaks from mobile lipids. In this case, it is often difficult to distinguish an elevation in lactate from an increase in lipid. At TE = 136 milliseconds, spin-coupling effects (see footnote b) produce inversion of the lactate doublet relative to other peaks, and this effect can be used to distinguish lactate from lipid. By acquiring spectra with short TEs, of the order of 20–30 milliseconds, resonances from amino acids such as Glu and Gln,[10,11] from mI, *scyllo*-inositol,[12] and glucose (Glc)[13,14] can be observed. The increased information found in short TE spectra is offset by the increased difficulty in accurately analyzing these data, which now contain a large background of low-intensity resonances from a plethora of macromolecules.

Phosphorus-31

Phosphorus-31 MRS can yield important information on cellular bioenergetics from monitoring the high-energy phosphates that have resonance peaks from P_i, phosphocreatine (PCr), and the NTP. There are two ionic states of phosphate, $H_2PO_4^{1-}$ and HPO_4^{2-}, which exist in equilibrium within the cell but have distinct resonance frequencies separated by approximately 3 ppm. There is rapid exchange of ^{31}P nuclei between these two ionic states, and a single average resonance frequency is observed. Intracellular pH is obtained by measuring the chemical shift difference between the P_i and PCr or α-NTP peaks and reading the pH from a standard calibration curve.[6,15] The chemical shifts of the β-NTP and γ-NTP peaks are dependent on the Mg^{2+} concentration, thus the intracellular concentration of this ion may also be determined.[16] The phosphomonoester (PME) and phosphodiester (PDE) resonances provide information on the synthesis and degradation of cellular membranes, which is of particular relevance to the study of rapidly proliferating tissue such as a cancer.[17] Typical areas of ^{31}P studies are of muscle (including the heart) energetics,[18] tumor biochemistry,[17] and maturation/degeneration and pathology in the brain.[19]

Carbon-13

Despite the ubiquity of carbon in organic molecules, only the ^{13}C isotope has a nucleus with a magnetic moment. The natural abundance of ^{13}C is only 1%, which combined with the lower resonant frequency makes ^{13}C NMR about 1/6000 the sensitivity of ^{1}H NMR. The ^{13}C spectrum is complex and has a large chemical shift range of 200 ppm. The use of ^{1}H decoupling, to remove the ^{1}H–^{13}C multiplet splittings, enables the resolution of many resonances. Because of the large chemical shift range, localization for in vivo studies has been mainly achieved by the use of small surface coils or with chemical shift imaging (CSI). When using gradient techniques such as image-selected in vivo spectroscopy (ISIS), the effects of the chemical shift displacement artifact must be considered.[20] Techniques for in vivo ^{13}C MRS are reviewed in Beckman.[21] The ^{13}C spectrum is dominated by the signals from the $-CH_2-$ groups in fatty acids. This can be a problem when adipose tissue overlies the tissue being studied. Other resonances arise from triglyceride lipids, glycogen, creatine, amino acids, carnosine, and taurine. Of these, glycogen is a polymer with a molecular mass of $\geqslant 10^8$ Da, so it was surprising that it was visible by NMR at all.[22] Natural abundance ^{1}H-decoupled ^{13}C spectra from gastrocnemius muscle, liver, and adipose tissue have been obtained from normal volunteers.[23] In a single tumor study of a histiocytoma, the main ^{13}C intensities were reduced, but additional ^{13}C resonances were also observed compared with normal muscle.[24] Studies using an infusate of a ^{13}C-enriched substrate can provide information on metabolic processes, such as the tricarboxylic acid (TCA) cycle, as the ^{13}C label is transferred to intermediates.[21] Resonances from glutamate and glutamine have recently been detected in the human brain (Fig. 2–3) after infusion of [1-^{13}C] glucose.[20] Although this is an exciting area of research, the expense of isotopically enriched glucose is currently prohibitive for general use.

Fluorine-19

In contrast to ^{1}H, ^{13}C, and ^{31}P, no naturally occurring chemicals containing ^{19}F nuclei are found in vivo. The NMR sensitivity of the ^{19}F nucleus is very high (83% that of ^{1}H), and the lack of any background signal makes ^{19}F MRS ideal for monitoring the up-

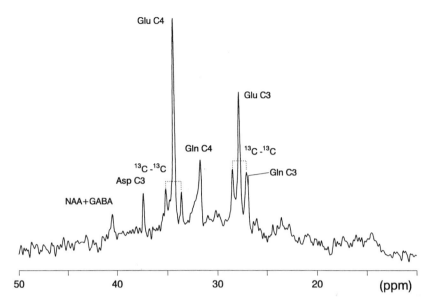

Figure 2–3. A proton-decoupled ^{13}C spectrum from the human brain after infusion of D-[1-^{13}C] glucose. The ISIS technique was used to localize to a 144-cm^3 voxel in the occipital–parietal region of the brain, and the spectrum is from data accumulated between 120 and 180 minutes after the infusion started. The main resonances are from glutamate (Glu), glutamine (Gln), aspartate (Asp), and γ-aminobutyric acid (GABA). Homonuclear splitting (^{13}C–^{13}C) of the glutamate peaks is observed. By measuring the rate at which the ^{13}C label from glucose is incorporated into glutamate and then glutamine enables the study of amino acid metabolism in vivo. *Abbreviations:* ISIS = image-selected in vivo spectroscopy; NAA = *N*-acetyl aspartate. *(Reproduced, with permission, from: Gruetter R, Novotny EJ, Boulware SD, et al: Localised ^{13}C NMR in the human brain of amino acid labelling from D-[1-^{13}C] glucose. J Neurochem. 1994;63:1377–1385.)*

take and metabolism of fluorinated drugs. Although many animal studies have been made,[25] issues of toxicity and the quantity of the drug needed to provide a strong enough MRS signal have limited human studies. 5-Fluorouracil (5FU) is a well-established anticancer drug that is given in large enough doses to enable MRS monitoring. The kinetics of 5FU uptake and formation of its main catabolite, α-fluoro-β-alanine (FBAL), have been measured in the liver of tumor patients undergoing chemotherapy.[26,27] Modulation of 5FU by interferon-α has recently been observed in patients with colorectal cancer.[28]

LOCALIZATION TECHNIQUES

Two types of techniques exist for obtaining in vivo spectra: those that produce signals from a single cuboid volume such as STEAM (*stimulated* echo *acquisition* mode),[29,30] PRESS (*point-resolved* spectroscopy),[31] and ISIS (*image-selected* in vivo spectroscopy)[32,33]; and CSI (chemical shift imaging, also termed SI for spectroscopic imaging),[34,35] which acquires data from the whole sample so as to produce low-resolution images for each metabolite peak in the spectrum. Chemical shift imaging is often used in conjunction with a single voxel method to produce images of metabolite distributions from single slices or columns.[36] A recent echo-planar SI technique allows 0.75-cm^3 spatial resolution metabolite maps at short echo time.[37]

ISIS

The basic sequence is shown in Figure 2–4. A series of gradient pulses is applied along each axis in combination with frequency-selective inversion pulses. The slice thickness along each axis is independently variable by changing the gradient strengths. After a short delay, a nonselective 90° excitation pulse generates the free induction decay (FID). To acquire a signal from a cuboid volume, a cycle of eight experiments is performed in which all possible combinations of the three slice-selective pulses are used. Since the FID is acquired immediately after the excitation, there is no T_2 weighting of the signal. This makes the ISIS technique ideal for acquiring data from metabolites that contain nuclei with short T_2 and has led to its widespread use in ^{31}P spectroscopy. The delay time between the switched gradients and the acquisition of the data (typically 100 ms) allows any eddy currents produced by the switched gradients to die away and only causes a slight T_1 weighting of the NMR signal. To simplify the explanation of this method, we consider the 1-D case in which just the z-gradient is used to acquire data from a single slice. In acquisition I, the 180° pulse is omitted, and, after the 90° pulse, an FID is acquired from the whole sample. In acquisition II, the selective 180° pulse first inverts the magnetization in a slice. After the 90° excitation pulse, the acquired FID now contains a signal from the central slice, which has the polarity opposite to the outer volume signal. The difference, I − II, between these two acquisitions yields a signal from just the central slice. The main disadvantage of the full 3-D

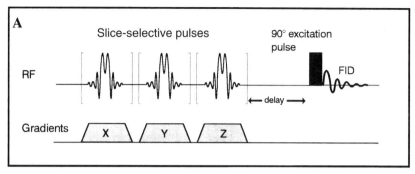

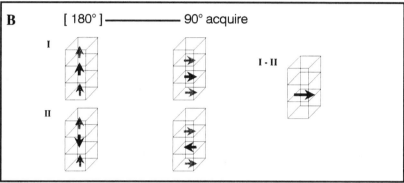

Figure 2–4. *A.* The combination of slice-selective inversion pulses and switched magnetic field gradients used in the ISIS localization technique. The 90° excitation could be with either a hard or an adiabatic pulse. In the full 3-D localization experiment, multiples of eight acquisitions are necessary. This covers all eight possible combinations of inversion pulses, that is {ON ON ON}, {ON ON OFF}, {ON OFF ON}, {OFF ON ON}, {ON OFF OFF}, {OFF ON OFF}, {OFF OFF ON}, {OFF OFF OFF}. ***B.*** The manipulation of nuclear magnetization for a 1-D ISIS experiment. In acquisition I, the inversion pulse is omitted and all the magnetization is in phase. In acquisition II, the magnetization in the central slice is inverted prior to excitation. The difference between these two acquisitions is a signal from the central slice. *Abbreviations:* ISIS = image-selected in vivo spectroscopy; 3-D = three-dimensional; 1-D = one-dimensional.

ISIS localization technique is the necessity for multiples of eight acquisitions before a localized signal can be reconstructed. Since the VOI is generally much smaller than the whole sample, the effects of patient motion between individual acquisitions can severely degrade the accuracy of the localization and lead to contamination of the "localized" spectrum by signals from outside the chosen VOI. An advantage of ISIS is that it is relatively insensitive to the actual flip angles used, and, since no echo is being formed, adiabatic inversion and excitation pulses can be used. This overcomes the limitations of RF homogeneity when surface coils are used for RF transmission. Refinements to the ISIS technique are conformal ISIS, which employs oblique slice selection to more closely match the localized voxel to the shape of a lesion,[38] and outer volume suppressed image-related in vivo spectroscopy (OSIRIS).[39]

STEAM and PRESS

These two methods are generally used for ^1H spectroscopy. They are often called "single-shot" techniques since a localized signal is obtained from one acquisition. In both methods an echo signal is acquired, and the delay between excitation and acquisition produces T_2 weighting of the peak amplitudes in the spectrum. The STEAM and PRESS sequences are shown in Figure 2–5. After the initial 90° pulse, the magnetization within a slice lies in the transverse plane. This generates the usual decaying FID due to T_2 relaxation and the dephasing effect of B_0 inhomogeneity. In STEAM, the second slice-selective 90° pulse rotates the magnetization within a column (the intersection of two slices) back to the z-axis. While the magnetization is aligned along the z-axis, there is no T_2 decay. The third slice-selective 90° then rotates the magnetization within a cube (the intersection of three slices) back into the transverse plane. For the spins in this cube, the dephasing effects of B_0 inhomogeneity are now reversed and a stimulated echo signal is formed. The PRESS sequence (sometimes referred to as a double spin echo sequence) performs localization in a similar fashion to STEAM, but two slice-selective 180° pulses follow the initial 90° excitation. A spin echo signal is acquired that arises from magnetization within the cube formed by the intersection of all three slices. In both STEAM and PRESS, the magnetization outside of this cubic volume is incompletely refocused and dephases. The routinely implemented sequences, however, must have additional gradient pulses, known as "crushers." These are necessary to completely destroy any remaining signals from the three excited slices that lie outside the much smaller central VOI. The stimulated echo in STEAM produces only half the maximum signal that would be acquired from a spin echo using the PRESS sequence. But by using only 90° pulses, STEAM has the advantage of sharper slice profiles, which leads to more precise localization.[40] There is no T_2 weighting in the middle TM period for the STEAM

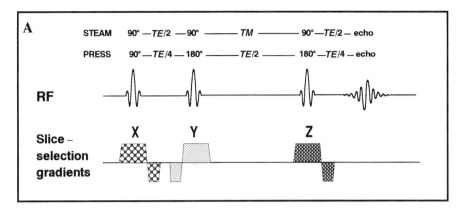

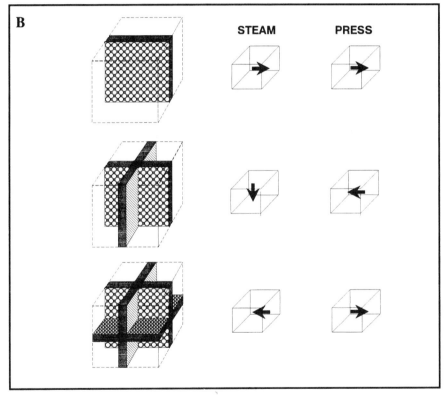

Figure 2–5. *A.* The combination of slice-selective RF pulses and switched magnetic field gradients used in the STEAM and PRESS sequences. In STEAM, negative lobes in all the gradient pulses compensate for spin dephasing during slice selection. In PRESS, refocusing lobes are not necessary for the y- and z-gradients because 180° RF pulses are used. ***B.*** The intersection of three orthogonal slices produces a signal from the central cube. The orientation of the magnetization in the central cube is shown diagrammatically for STEAM and PRESS after each RF pulse. *Abbreviations:* RF = radio frequency; STEAM = stimulated echo acquisition mode; PRESS = point-resolved spectroscopy.

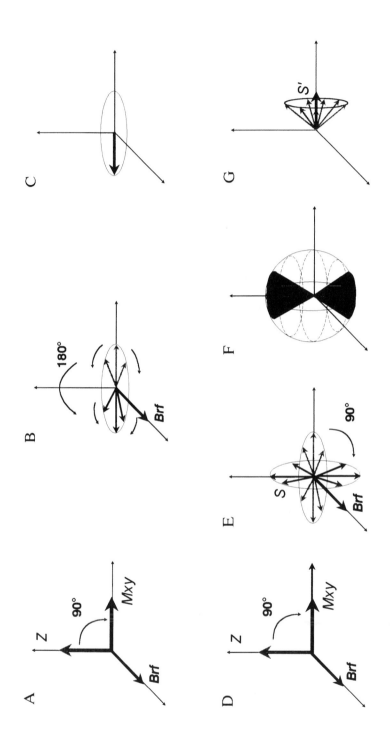

sequence, hence a shorter echo time (minimum $TE \approx 10$ ms) can be achieved than with PRESS (minimum $TE \approx 40$ ms). A more detailed description of the difference between spin echo and stimulated echo formation is given in Figure 2–6.

CSI

In CSI, the raw data are acquired using the phase-encoding technique familiar from imaging. An excitation pulse is followed by a short gradient pulse that produces a linear variation in the phase of the magnetization across the sample or patient. The FID signal, which is from magnetization in the whole sample, is either acquired immediately after the gradient pulse, if short T_2 nuclei such as ^{31}P are being observed or an additional 180° pulse can be used and an echo signal is acquired. A recent development in RF pulse design now allows the acquisition of ^{31}P CSI data with a spin echo pulse and a very short TE of 2.5 ms.[41] To obtain spectral data from n voxels along one spatial dimension, n FIDS (or multiples thereof if signal averaging is needed to increase the SNR) must be acquired. The phase-encoding gradient is incremented in n equal steps from a negative to a positive value. The reconstruction of these data with a 2-D Fourier trans-

---

Figure 2–6. Comparison of the formation of a spin echo (SE) and stimulated echo (STE). The B_0 field is along z, T_1 and T_2 relaxation are assumed to be negligible. **A.** Z-magnetization rotated into the xy-plane. **B.** After a $TE/2$, the spins have dephased due to the effects of inhomogeneities in the magnetic field. A 180° pulse is now applied. **C.** After a further $TE/2$, the spins come back into phase and produce a spin echo. Since the spins always dephase and rephase in the xy-plane, they all contribute to the final SE signal. **D.** Z-magnetization rotated into the xy-plane. **E.** After a $TE/2$, when the spins have dephased in the xy-plane, a second 90° RF pulse is applied. The spins are now in the xz-plane and precess around the z-axis. We shall consider just one set of spins S that are at an angle to the z-axis. **F.** After the mixing time (TM), the spins S are spread out on the surface of a cone. **G.** A third 90° pulse rotates the axis of the cone to the y-axis. It is possible to imagine that at least one spin, S', is in the xy-plane with the appropriate phase to realign exactly along the y-axis after a further $TE/2$. This spin contributes fully to the STE, but all the other spins lie tilted out of the xy-plane and can only contribute a component along y that must be less than maximum. In fact, the sum of all spin components along y is exactly half the maximum possible, hence the STE signal is only half the SE signal. The mathematically inclined can find the original description of echo formation in Hahn EL: Spin echoes. *Phys Rev* 1950;80:580–594.

form produces a spectrum for each of the *n* locations. For simplification, we discuss the 1-D CSI sequence shown in Figure 2–7A. In Figure 2–7B, we consider voxel A, which is at the magnet center, and voxel B, which is off center. We also choose different res-

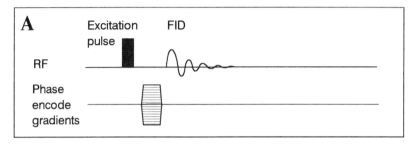

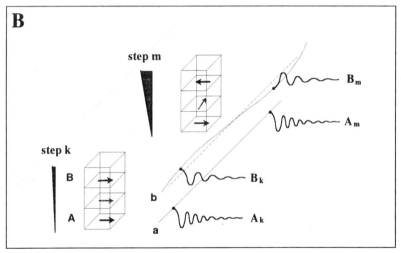

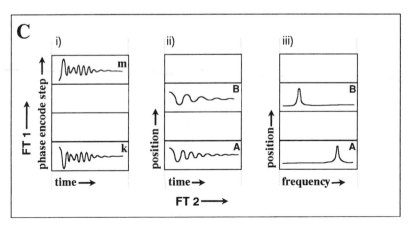

onance frequencies (ie, different chemical species) for the nuclei in the two voxels to demonstrate the CSI principle. After an excitation pulse, the magnetization of the whole sample is aligned in the transverse plane. In step k, the zero-amplitude phase-encoded gradient pulse has been applied. The signals from these two voxels produce FIDs A_k and B_k, which are in phase and, for this example, at different frequencies. In step m, the phase-encoding gradient pulse now has a significant amplitude. The phase-encoding gradient produces no increase in the B_0 field at the magnet's center, hence the phase of the magnetization in voxel A is unchanged. Off center, in voxel B, the phase-encoded gradient pulse has produced a momentary increase in the B_0 field. Over the period of the gradient pulse, the magnetization in voxel B precesses at a faster rate, which we have chosen to produce a 180° increment in phase. After the phase-encoding gradient pulse is switched off, the FID signals from across the sample now have different phases. The size of this phase difference varies linearly with spatial position, but the frequency information is preserved. The signal acquired at each step is the sum of FIDs from the whole sample. Now consider all the phase-encoded steps. For the first point of FID A, the amplitude remains constant as shown by line a for all phase-encoding steps. For the first point of FID B, the amplitude oscillates sinusoidally

---

Figure 2–7. *A.* The 1-D CSI sequence. An excitation pulse is immediately followed by a phase-encoding gradient pulse, after which the FID is acquired. For ^{1}H MRS, for which the metabolites have a long T_2, a 180° pulse follows the gradient and an echo signal is acquired. The excitation (and inversion) pulse can be slice selective if CSI within a slice (or column) is required. *B.* Voxel A is at the magnet isocenter and voxel B is off center. The wedges indicate the amplitudes of the phase-encoded gradient pulse as a function of distance from the isocenter for two of the phase-encoded steps. The FIDs A and B show the NMR signal generated by the magnetization in the two voxels depicted. (N.B. They are at different frequencies because they depict different chemical species, *not* because they are in different spatial positions.) Lines a and b depict how the first real point of the FID varies as a function of the phase-encoded gradient. *C.* (i) A data array depicting the total NMR signal acquired from voxels A and B at phase-encoded steps k and m. (ii) After the first Fourier transformation the data array contains the raw FIDs that originate from each voxel. (iii) After the second Fourier transform, the data array displays the localized spectra with chemical shift information preserved. *Abbreviations:* FID = free induction decay; NMR = nuclear magnetic resonance.

with the phase-encoding step (also known as "pseudo-time") as depicted by line b. Just considering these first points of the FIDs, it can be seen that the frequency of this oscillation in amplitude increases linearly with distance from the magnet's center. The spatial position has now been encoded by the frequency of the amplitude oscillations (this is entirely equivalent to the technique of frequency encoding using the read-out gradient in MRI, but in pseudo-time rather than real time). If there were 16 phase-encoded steps, a Fourier transform of the first point of the 16 FIDs would produce the first 16 points of the FIDs arising from the 16 voxels. This is depicted in Figure 2–7C, where the sum of the FIDs A and B is shown for the two steps k and m. There would in fact be 16 of these in total. The first Fourier transform, FT 1, is made along the phase-encoding data dimension, and the result, shown in the next set of boxes, is the two FIDs from voxels A and B. A second Fourier transform, FT 2, of each FID then yields the spectrum associated with each voxel. A 1-D CSI data set of ^1H spectra from the brain of a stroke patient is shown in Figure 2–8.

For a full 3-D image, a total of $L \times M \times N$ acquisitions, in which all possible combinations of gradient steps in the three orthogonal axes are used, gives an array of $L \times M \times N$ spectra. There is thus a serious time penalty for performing a full 3-D CSI experiment. Since the FID arises from the whole volume at each acquisition, however, the advantage of signal averaging is still maintained. It can be shown that the SNR per unit time for a single voxel experiment is the same as for a CSI experiment if the voxel size in the CSI data is the same as in the single voxel acquisition.[42] Chemical shift imaging has the advantages of creating no chemical shift displacement artifact and acquiring a set of spectra covering the whole sample. Furthermore, the grid of spectra can be retrospectively shifted to optimize the alignment of voxels to the lesion or tissue geometry. For studying focal disease in the brain, CSI provides data from both normal and pathological tissue in the same acquisition.[43–46] Metabolite maps from 2-D CSI data are shown in Figure 2–9 for ^{31}P MRS of normal brain and Figure 2–10 for ^1H MRS in a patient with adrenoleukodystrophy.

Water Suppression

In ^1H spectroscopy, the water resonance is the dominant signal, more than 50,000 times stronger than that of the metabolites.

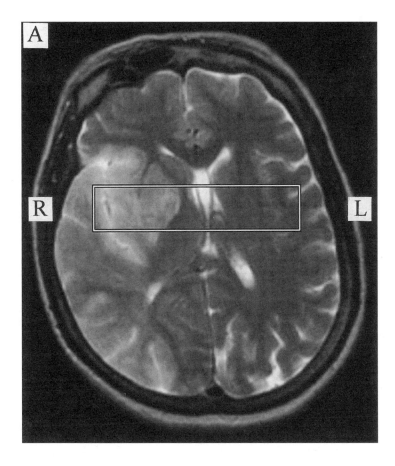

Figure 2–8A. Hydrogen-1 1-D CSI data from a stroke patient (female, age 61). **A.** T_2-weighted image showing the VOI chosen for spectroscopy. A region smaller than the width of the brain is chosen to avoid exciting signal from the high concentrations of lipid in the scalp.

This signal must be suppressed prior to data acquisition so that the full dynamic range of the receiver can be used to capture the much weaker metabolite signal. The most common technique is to use chemical shift-selective (CHESS)[47,48] pulses prior to the localization sequence. These pulses only excite a small region of the spectrum centered at the water resonance. The excited water signal is then dephased with a strong gradient pulse, leaving the metabolite resonances unaffected. (This technique is sometimes used for fat suppression in MRI.)

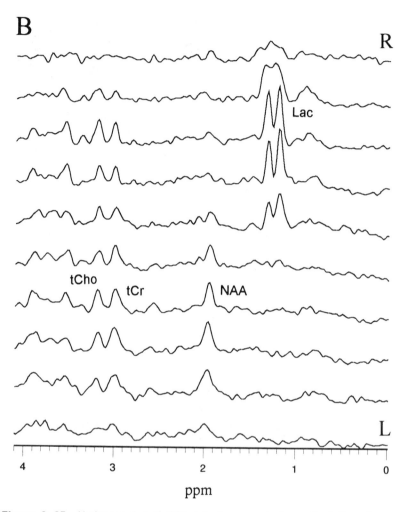

Figure 2–8B. Hydrogen-1 1-D CSI data from a stroke patient (female, age 61). *B.* Hydrogen-1 spectra from 1-cm thick slices across the VOI. Lactate is present and NAA reduced in the infarct. Spectroscopy acquisition parameters were: STEAM localization, *TE* = 30 ms, *TR* = 1000 ms, 16 averages, 10-cm × 2-cm × 1.5-cm thick voxel, 32 phase-encoding steps, 32-cm FOV. First-order phase and lineshape correction of the spectra was performed using a water signal reference. *(Data acquired in collaboration with Drs A Pereira and MM Brown, St. George's Hospital Medical School.) Abbreviations:* 1-D = one-dimensional; CSI = chemical shift imaging; VOI = volume of interest; NAA = *N*-acetyl aspartate; STEAM = stimulated echo acquisition mode; FOV = field of view.

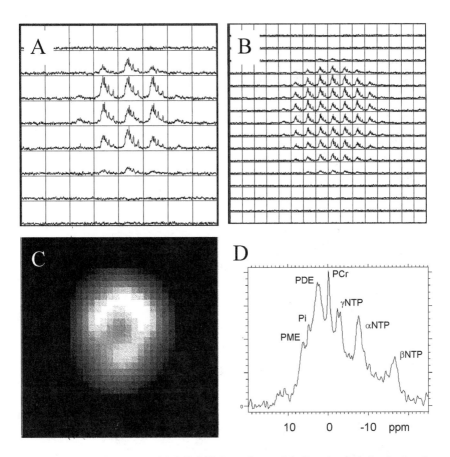

Figure 2–9. Phosphorus-31 2-D CSI data of an axial slice through the brain of a normal volunteer (female, age 25) acquired using the echo CSI sequence of reference.[41] **A.** Grid showing spectra from each 64-cm³ voxel. **B.** Data after interpolation to a 16 × 16 matrix. (Raw data zero-filled once prior to Fourier transformation.) **C.** Phosphorus-31 metabolite map created after interpolation of the data to a 32 × 32 matrix. (Raw data zero-filled twice prior to Fourier transformation.) The image intensity is proportional to the total phosphorus signal in each voxel. The low-intensity central region corresponds to the ventricles. **D.** Typical spectra from the data set in **B.** Spectroscopy acquisition parameters: TR = 1000 ms, TE = 2.5 ms, 8 × 8 phase encodes, 24-cm FOV, 4-cm slice thickness. *(Unpublished data, St. George's Hospital Medical School.) Abbreviations:* PME = phosphomonoester; P_i = inorganic phosphate; PDE = phosphodiester; PCr = phosphocreatine; γ-NTP = gamma-nucleoside triphosphate; α-NTP = alpha-nucleoside triphosphate; β-NTP = beta-nucleoside triphosphate.

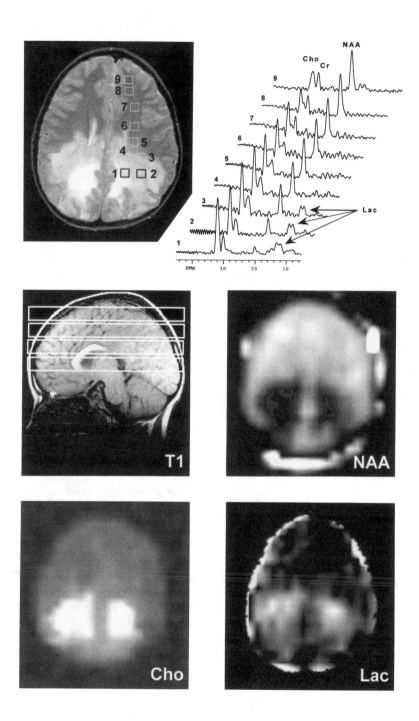

Artifacts

There are two major sources of artifacts in MRS: distortions of the MR spectrum itself and inaccuracies in the definition of the localized volume.

PEAK LINESHAPE DISTORTION. These can arise from poor B_0 homogeneity or the presence of residual eddy currents during data acquisition. In ^{1}H MRS, these distortions can be partially corrected for by using a water signal acquired from the same voxel, with the same acquisition parameters as the metabolite spectrum, as a reference.[49,50] Another effect arises in ^{31}P CSI. The short T_2s of ^{31}P metabolites usually preclude the acquisition of a spin echo. Instead, the FID is acquired directly after the phase-encoded gradients. Typically, the first four data points of the FID are missing. This produces a rolling baseline in the spectrum, which makes calculation of the peak areas difficult. But, as discussed later, time domain analysis techniques overcome this problem.

OUTER VOLUME CONTAMINATION. With the STEAM and PRESS techniques, only the signals from nuclei in the chosen VOI are supposed to be received, but it is possible that some signal from outside of this volume is also generated. Since the VOI is generally a lot smaller than the whole sample, there is the possibility of acquiring a spectrum with substantial contamination from unwanted tissue.[51] The ISIS technique is particularly prone to this since the required signal is formed from the subtraction of large signals. Tissue motion further aggravates this form of artifact. For single-voxel techniques, slice profiles, which define the sensitive

---

Figure 2–10. Two-dimensional ^{1}H CSI from a 5-year-old male patient with adrenoleukodystrophy. ***Top:*** T_2-weighted axial image with corresponding ^{1}H spectra from selected voxels. There is loss of NAA and increased tCho and lactate in the regions of demyelination (hyperintensities in the image). Voxels 5–7 come from normal-appearing white matter but still have spectroscopic abnormalities (reduced NAA and increased tCho). ***Middle and bottom:*** T_1-weighted sagittal localizer, spectral data come from the second slice down. The NAA, tCho, and tCr metabolite maps correspond with the axial image above. Spectroscopy acquisition parameters: $TR = 2300$ ms, $TE = 272$ ms, 32×32 phase encodes, 15-mm slice thickness, nominal voxel size 0.8 mL. *(Reproduced, with permission, from Kruse B, Barker PB, van Zijl PCM, et al: Multislice proton magnetic resonance spectroscopic imaging in X-linked adrenoleukodystrophy. Ann Neurol 1994;36:596–608.)* Abbreviations: NAA = N-acetyl aspartate; tCho = total choline; tCr = total creatine; Lac = lactate.

volume, can be measured using either an imaging technique or a phantom.[52,53] In ^{1}H MRS, it can be particularly important to know the size and sensitivity of the VOI if it is placed in outer regions of the brain. If the slice profiles are broader than expected, the spectrum can easily be contaminated with large signals arising from the high concentrations of lipid in the scalp. This problem can be alleviated by the use of saturation pulses for outer volume suppression.[54]

CHEMICAL SHIFT DISPLACEMENT. When frequency-selective (ie, slice-selective) pulses are used in the presence of a field gradient, a linear displacement of the excited VOI takes place, with chemical shift offset within the acquired spectrum.[55]

$$\text{Displacement (cm)} = 0.1 \times \text{Shift (ppm)} \times \frac{B_0(\text{T})}{\text{Gradient (mT/m)}} \qquad (2)$$

This displacement is most severe for nuclei that have a very large range of chemical shifts, such as ^{31}P and [13]C. Since this displacement occurs simultaneously along all three axes, the overlap of the VOI for peaks at the extremes of the spectrum can become quite small. For ^{31}P MRS at 1.5 T, with a 27-cm^3 cubical ISIS volume selected with a 5-mT/m gradient strength, the voxels from which the P_i and β-NTP signals arise are displaced relative to each other by 0.6 cm along each direction. The selected VOIs for these peaks only overlap by 50%.

FOURIER BLEED. This artifact occurs in CSI. Although most of the spectral signal in a given voxel arises from tissue within the voxel's spatial dimensions, there are also contributions to the spectrum from the rest of the sample. The size of this unwanted signal oscillates in magnitude and diminishes with distance from the voxel's center. This mathematical artifact is known as the "point spread function"[35,56] and also occurs for phase encoding in MRI. It is more severe for CSI because far fewer phase-encoding steps are used. The spectrum for each voxel from a CSI data set is magnetization from the whole sample, which is weighted in proportion to this point spread function. Artifacts occur when there are local regions of high-intensity signals, such as PCr in muscle or lipids in the scalp. These signals can "bleed" across the whole of the CSI data set and appear as contaminating signals in voxels where these metabolites should not be present.[57] This bleed can be minimized to just the adjacent voxels by weighting the data prior to Fourier transformation[56] and by using outer volume suppression.[37,54,58] Since each acquisition in CSI contains data from the whole sensitive volume of the receive coil, patient motion can also produce "bleed" artifacts over all of the reconstructed spectra. Fourier bleed is observed in MRI along the phase-encoded axis.

Interpreting a localized spectrum requires an awareness of the spectral characteristics of tissue adjacent to the chosen VOI and an assessment of the proportion of "background" signal from contaminating signals originating from this adjacent tissue. In view of these problems, it is important to perform regular quality-control measurements, to check on gradient and RF performance, and to use phantoms to assess the efficiency of localization.[53,59]

SPECTRUM QUANTITATION

Many studies use one peak in the spectrum as a reference, and biochemical differences between normal and pathological tissue are interpreted from changes in peak area ratios. The disadvantage to this method is that it is not always clear whether one peak is elevated or the other is decreased. Peak area ratios are also insensitive to an overall reduction or increase of all metabolite concentrations. An alternative technique is to obtain a control spectrum from normal tissue, and then subtract the control from the spectrum obtained from pathological tissue, this process gives a "difference" spectrum.[60] Comparison of the "difference" spectrum with spectra from metabolite solutions enables the determination of which metabolites are elevated and which are decreased by the pathology. The analysis of MRS data to give absolute metabolite concentrations is also possible. Assuming the signal from a peak in a spectrum arises from just one chemical species, the peak area is proportional to the number of molecules of that chemical in the localized volume. Three stages are involved in converting a resonance peak area into metabolite concentrations. First, the spectrometer sensitivity must be calibrated so that the received MR signal intensity can be related to the number of nuclei contributing to the signal. The second, and sometimes most difficult step, is to calculate the area of the peak. Finally, the peak areas should be corrected for the effects of T_2 relaxation and T_1 saturation during the data acquisition, and for partial volume due to tissue heterogeneity.

Spectrometer calibration can be performed in one of two ways.[61] An endogenous reference, such as the tCr or the water peak in ^{1}H MRS, can be used, providing that a value of its concentration may be assumed.[62-64] This has the advantage that the reference signal comes from the same tissue volume as the spectrum, and variations in coil loading and sensitivity are automatically taken into account. (N.B. In some cases, chemical shift displacement may need to be accounted for.) A major disadvantage is the possibility that the reference signal may not be constant. For focal pathology in the brain, such as stroke or tumor, a reference spectrum from the uninvolved contralateral side may be more reliable. A second technique is to use an external reference. This requires that a second experiment be performed, using a phantom, with the same localization technique. The phantom can simply be a sphere containing doped water for ^{1}H MRS, or a known concentration of a stable chemical such as sodium dihydrogen phosphate for ^{31}P MRS. An advantage of this second method is that the calibration can be performed without the patient, thus reducing total examination time. Disadvantages are the need to correct for coil loading, and if surface coils are used, their inhomogeneous RF sensitivity must be carefully accounted for.[65]

In vivo spectra often consist of many overlapping peaks, which, for ^{1}H spectra at short *TE*s and some ^{31}P spectra, sit on top of a large, broad baseline hump. The calculation of peak areas by simple integration or triangulation is very dependent on the choice of baseline, which may introduce large variability in the analysis. An exception is for long echo time ^{1}H spectra in which there is a flat baseline and only the three peaks of tCr, tCho, and NAA (plus lactate in some pathologies). A more sophisticated approach is to assume that the shape of each peak in the spectrum, or the FID signal in the time domain, can be described by a "model function." The data are then fitted to a sum of model functions (one for each resonance signal) using an algorithm that minimizes the difference between the model and the raw data. In the frequency domain, the individual peaks can be fitted to a specified lineshape, such as a lorentzian or gaussian,[11] or an experimentally determined model function[66]; in the time domain, the FID may be fitted to a sum of decaying exponential signals.[67,68] Time domain techniques have the advantage that it does not matter if a delay occurs between the excitation and the acquisition of the FID (eg, due to the phase-encoding time in ^{31}P CSI).

This has a significant advantage over analysis in the frequency domain, since the effects of an acquisition delay can cause severe distortion of the peak lineshape and the baseline in the frequency spectrum. Even if there is no delay, the first few points of the FID can be deliberately ignored. This has the effect of omitting the rapidly decaying components of the signal (which produce the broad background in the spectrum), and errors in peak fitting due

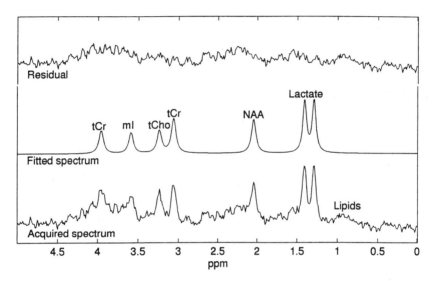

Figure 2–11. *Lower trace:* Short echo time ¹H spectra from an 8-cm³ voxel in an infarct following stroke. STEAM localization: $TE = 30$ ms, $TR = 2020$ ms, 256 acquisitions. The unprocessed spectrum is shown and contains broad spectral components, such as lipids (0.5–1.8 ppm), Glx and macromolecules (2–2.8 ppm). *Middle trace:* Time domain analysis with VARPRO using the following constraints: 1) First three points omitted; 2) The linewidths of tCr, ml, tCho, and NAA were assumed to be dominated by B_0 homogeneity and thus equal; 3) Lactate signal a doublet with separation 7 Hz. *Upper trace:* Residual signal (the difference between the fitted spectrum and acquired spectrum) comprising lipids, macromolecules, and unresolved signals such as Glx. By constraining the fit parameters, the main resonance signals can be resolved from these other components. Quantitation, without relaxation time corrections and assuming a water reference signal of 41.7 M, gives: ml = 7.9; tCho = 1.9; tCr = 8.8; NAA = 8.7; Lactate = 21 mM. (N.B. The data are shown as frequency domain, but all processing was performed on the time domain FID.) *(Unpublished data, St. George's Hospital Medical School.)* Abbreviations: STEAM = stimulated echo acquisition mode; Glx = glutamate and glutamine; VARPRO = variable projection; tCr = total creatine; ml = *myo*-Inositol; tCho = total choline; NAA = *N*-acetyl aspartate.

to the presence of a baseline hump can be reduced. Figure 2–11 shows a fit to the main peaks of a ^{1}H spectrum from the brain of a stroke patient using the variable projection time domain algorithm. (*Note:* Although the analysis was of the time domain signal, the data are displayed after Fourier transformation as a spectrum.) The residual contains the broad baseline components such as lipids and the complex peaks such as Glx.

There is a delay between excitation of the magnetization and the acquisition of an echo signal, hence all the peaks in a spectrum are T_2 weighted. Because of SNR considerations, most spectra are not acquired fully relaxed so that there is also T_1 weighting. These effects are not the same for all peaks, and knowledge of their individual relaxation times is needed for proper quantitation. Both metabolite concentrations and relaxation times have been shown to vary with the subject's age.[69,70] It is not practical to acquire enough data for relaxation time measurements in each patient. Values calculated from studies on normal volunteers are a useful starting point. But these could be significantly different in pathology, such as in multiple sclerosis lesions[71] or where there is edema, as in stroke.[72] Some degree of tissue heterogeneity occurs within any voxel from which a localized spectrum has been acquired. At the most basic level, water is compartmentalized into intra- and extracellular components. Within focal pathology, edema, necrosis, and hemorrhage can occur, as well as viable normal tissue. Absolute quantitation requires corrections to account for these partial volumes.[73,74] In practice, this is very difficult, and interpretation of the biochemical significance of spectral changes must therefore take into account the fact that the MR spectrum is generally an average of several tissue types. Metabolite relaxation times and concentrations for some normal tissue are given in Tables 2–1 and 2–2 (data taken from references[62–64, 74–79]).

THE PRACTICALITIES OF THE MRS EXAMINATION

We briefly detail below some of the basic requirements and procedures necessary when embarking on an MRS study.

1. **Safety.** Safety considerations are the same as for MRI as regards B_0 field strength, RF power deposition, and gradient switching rates. Generally, MRS sequences play out RF pulses at a slower rate so that RF heating is not a problem.

The exception to this is for advanced techniques such as ^{1}H decoupling in ^{31}P and ^{13}C spectroscopy, in which case power deposition calculations must be performed, bearing in mind that some avascular tissues are very sensitive to heating.

2. **Patient comfort.** The total examination time for MRS is much longer than for MRI. At 1.5 T, a minimum time of 20–30 min for a single-voxel ^{1}H STEAM acquisition and between 60–90 min for ^{31}P 2-D/3-D CSI are typical. This is due to the need for good-quality MR images in addition to the spectroscopy data acquisition and the additional time needed for shimming and setting up the acquisition parameters. Physical comfort is important not only to the patient, but also because patient motion can more seriously degrade the quality of MR spectra than MR images. If longitudinal studies are required, full patient compliance for follow-up studies is vital.

3. **RF coils.** For MRS in regions other than the brain, surface coils are generally used. Although it may seem obvious, precise and reproducible positioning of the coil over the anatomical region of interest is very important. Use of MRI-visible fiducial markers attached to the coil enables the relative position of coil and the organ, tissue, or lesion of interest to be determined. Corrections for spatial variations in receive sensitivity, excitation flip angle, and localization artifacts can then be made.[61]

4. **Examination protocol.** Ideally, a database of spectra from age-matched normal volunteers should be available. These should be acquired using identical acquisition parameters, voxel size and position, and RF coil as for the patient studies. The use of phantom experiments to initially optimize the acquisition parameters and check on the quality of the localization technique is recommended. Keeping the acquisition parameters identical throughout a study is desirable from considerations of artifacts caused by eddy currents and voxel definition. This is also necessary to allow valid inter- and intrasubject comparison of spectra since most spectra are acquired with some degree of T_1 and T_2 weighting.

5. **The MRS examination.** Prior to acquiring spectroscopic data, "localizer" images are required that have the contrast necessary to show any focal pathology, such as multiple sclerosis plaques, an infarct, or a tumor. From these images, the size and position of the region for localized spectroscopy can be chosen. Additional information, such as computed tomogra-

phy (CT) images (for stroke and brain tumors) or mammo-grams (for breast tumors), can often be useful in determining the extent and position of lesions if the MR contrast is low. Once a region of interest has been chosen, the field homo-geneity over this region must be optimized by using the tis-sue water signal. The transmitter power for the nucleus of in-terest for MRS must then be set to produce the required flip angle at the VOI (eg, 90° pulses for STEAM or a lower flip an-gle for acquisition of a ^{31}P spectrum at optimum SNR). For lo-calized ^{1}H spectroscopy, the water signal, as acquired with the localization sequence, can be used. For other nuclei, a nonlocalized signal may be needed to provide enough SNR in a reasonable time. Alternatively, the transmitter power can be set on the basis of phantom calibrations or by using a ref-erence sample attached to the receive coil. For ^{1}H spec-troscopy, the water resonance frequency must also be accu-rately determined and the RF power of the CHESS pulses adjusted for optimum water suppression. To some extent, these procedures can be automated in the same way as with the MRI prescan.[80]

CLINICAL SPECTROSCOPY

A review of clinical MRS research and the potential clinical ap-plications of MRS are given in this section. This is not meant to be an exhaustive list but rather a selection to demonstrate the broad application of in vivo MRS and the wealth of information available by this noninvasive technique.

SKELETAL MUSCLE

Many of the first human in vivo MRS studies were performed on skeletal muscle. This is in part due to the particular course of technical development of in vivo MRS systems. The first mag-nets for human studies were only suitable for limbs, and before more sophisticated methods of localization were available sim-ple surface coils were used. By this method, ^{31}P spectra could be obtained from arm and leg muscles. (*Note:* The adipose tissue overlying muscle does not produce a ^{31}P signal in vivo.) The ^{31}P spectrum provides information on P_i and the high-energy phos-phates (HEPs) of PCr and ATP. In addition, the chemical shift difference between P_i and PCr provides a measure of intracellular pH (pH_i), and there are small contributions to the spectrum from PME and PDE. During muscle contraction, the hydrolysis of ATP ($ATP + H_2O \rightleftarrows ADP + P_i$) is the immediate source of energy. This ATP would be used up quickly if there were not a reservoir of energy in the form of PCr. The enzyme creatine kinase catalyzes the reaction of $PCr + ADP + H^+ \rightleftarrows ATP + Cr$, which can replenish ATP as fast as it is broken down. During nonexhaustive aerobic exercise, the level of ATP in the ^{31}P spectrum remains constant, P_i increases, and PCr decreases, as demonstrated in Figure 2–12 for the quadriceps muscle. There is also a decrease in pH_i as measured by the change in chemical shift of the P_i peak. Because the creatine kinase reaction is near equilibrium, during steady-state exercise, the P_i/PCr ratio can be used to calculate the cytosolic free ADP concentration, which is micromolar in concentration and thus too low to be directly detectable by ^{31}P MRS.[81] MRS is therefore useful for studying muscle bioenergetics. The absolute change and rates of change of these metabolite levels and pH_i can be monitored noninvasively at rest, during controlled exercise (using a magnet-compatible ergometer and the MRS data acquisition gated to the exercise periodicity), and during recovery. For example, the steady-state value of P_i/PCr human calf muscle during exercise depends on the kinetics of the installation of the exercise.[82] When an incremental exercise protocol is used during steady-state exercise, the P_i/PCr ratio is 2.13, and there is less intracellular acidification compared with a P_i/PCr ratio of 1.34 when exercising from cold. The calculated value of ADP was not found to be significantly different. Separate measurements of tissue oxygenation showed that exercise from cold produced a far greater degree of tissue deoxygenation, suggesting the difference in the kinetics of the P_i/PCr and pH_i changes reflects an initial limitation in oxygen delivery before circulatory adjustments have established a new level of blood oxygenation. Recent muscle activity and diet may alter the appearance of ^{31}P spectra in studies of both exercising and resting muscle.[83] The quantitative interpretation of ^{31}P MRS spectra and the metabolic relationships that must be assumed are discussed in current readings.[84]

Phosphorus-31 MRS has been used extensively for physiological investigations of normal muscle bioenergetics[85] as well as studies on impairment of muscle function and metabolism in

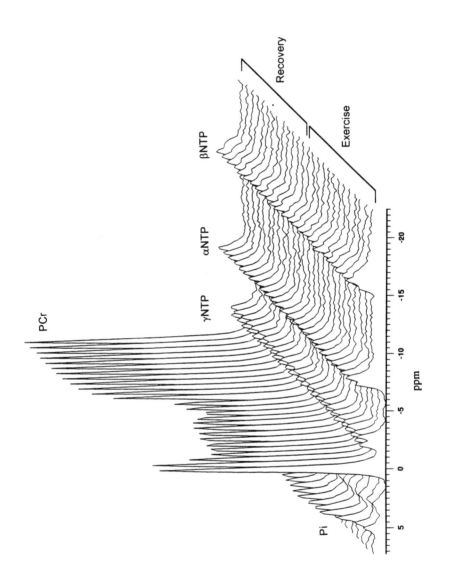

various disease states. One of the first successes was with the diagnosis of McArdle's syndrome,[86] which is caused by a deficiency in the enzyme glycogen phosphorylase. During exercise, the usual conversion of stored glycogen in muscle to lactic acid is blocked, resulting in a lack of the usual intracellular acidification observed by ^{31}P MRS. In resting muscle of patients with muscular dystrophies, all metabolite levels are altered (elevated P_i, PDE, PME, and decreased PCr relative to ATP), compared with normals.[87] A greater elevation of pH_i was observed in Duchenne's than in Becker's muscular dystrophy compared with normals or carriers. In response to aerobic exercise, carriers showed a more rapid depletion of PCr than normals. Patients with mitochondrial myopathies also demonstrate a more rapid depletion of PCr during exercise as well as slower recovery than normal,[88] whereas Parkinson's disease patients showed no significant differences in MRS parameters from normal.[89] Phosphorus-31 MRS has recently been used in conjunction with near-infrared (NIR) spectroscopy, which measures hemoglobin deoxygenation, in a clinical protocol to detect mitochondrial defects.[90] Two-dimensional CSI has been used to demonstrate differences in both the kinetics and magnitude of ^{31}P metabolite changes in different muscle groups in the human arm during exercise.[91]

Hydrogen-1 and Carbon-13 MRS in Skeletal Muscle

Hydrogen-1 MRS has been used to measure lactate formation and pH during anaerobic exercise, but editing techniques are necessary to distinguish the lactate from the large lipid signals arising from fat depots in muscle.[92] In short echo time ($TE = 20$ ms) studies of human quadriceps muscle at rest, the T_1 and T_2 relaxation times of carnosine, betaines, creatines, and lipids were measured.[93] Metabolites were found to have T_2 in the

---

Figure 2–12. Phosphorus-31 spectra acquired from the quadriceps muscle in a 28-year-old normal volunteer. During exercise, the NTP levels remain constant, PCr falls, and P_i rises. Spectroscopy acquisition parameters: $TR = 1875$ ms (leg exercise was performed in synchrony with the ^{31}P acquisition), 32 averages acquired per spectrum with a 12-cm diameter surface coil. *(Data acquired in collaboration with Prof B Whipp and MA McLean, St. George's Hospital Medical School.) Abbreviations:* NTP = nucleoside triphosphate; PCr = phosphocreatine; P_i = inorganic phosphate.

range 100–200 ms compared with a water T_2 of 30 ms. Recent short echo time-localized ^{1}H MRS studies of normal muscle have shown that due to the highly ordered structure of muscle fibers the creatine resonance exhibits similar anisotropy to liquid crystals.[94] The creatine CH_2 resonance is a singlet for only one orientation of the muscle fibers with respect to the static magnetic field (ie, when the fibers are at the "magic angle" of 54.7°). Generally, the resonance is split into two peaks whose separation is a function of fiber orientation to the magnetic field. Although this clearly complicates the acquisition and interpretation of ^{1}H spectra from muscle, applications can arise in the study of inflammation and degenerative muscle diseases in which alterations occur in the molecular structures of membranes and fibers.

There has been recent interest in the determination of muscle lipid content. In adipose tissue, the $-CH_2-$ and $-CH_3-$ groups of lipids have single resonances in vivo at 0.9 and 1.3 ppm, respectively. In muscle at long echo times ($TE > 150$ ms), these two peaks are split and have been tentatively assigned to intracellular and extracellular components of triglycerides and fatty acids.[95] An example $TE = 350$ ms ^{1}H spectrum from the soleus muscle of a healthy volunteer is shown in Figure 2–13. The extracellular lipid intensities are likely to vary between individuals on the basis of fitness, age, sex, and race. Future accurate resolution of the intracellular triglyceride and fatty acid components of muscle may provide a tool for investigating muscle energy storage and pathological lipid metabolism,[96] but unequivocal assignments of these peaks are yet to be determined.

Carbon-13 MRS was used previously to study glycogen storage in muscle,[22] and quantitative measurements now show that glycogen synthesis in skeletal muscle provides a dynamic buffer for postprandial glucose homeostasis.[97] In a study of glycogen storage disease, a patient was demonstrated to have muscle glycogen levels two to three times higher than normal.[98]

HEART

Most in vivo MRS studies of the human heart have used the ^{31}P nucleus; this is the obvious choice for studying cardiac energy metabolism and suffers fewer technical difficulties than other

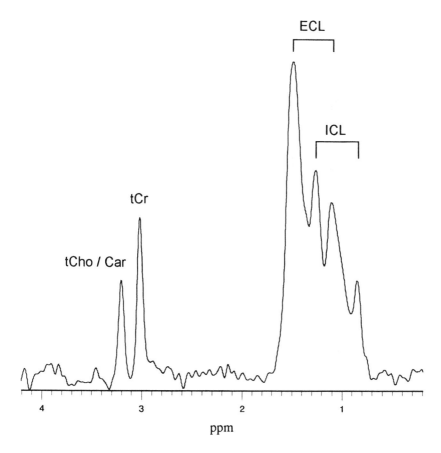

Figure 2–13. Long echo time ^{1}H spectrum from the soleus muscle of a healthy 24-year-old male volunteer. Peak assignments as in reference 95. Cholines (tCho), carnosine (Car), extracellular lipids (ECL), and intracellular lipids (ICL). Spectroscopy acquisition parameters: PRESS, *TE* = 350 ms, *TR* = 3000 ms, 8-cm[3] voxel, 128 acquisitions. *(Unpublished data, St. George's Hospital Medical School.)*

nuclei (ie, poor field homogeneity and very high lipid content in ^{1}H studies and low SNR in ^{13}C studies). Cardiac ^{31}P spectra contain predominantly PCr and ATP resonances, a small P_i peak being usually obscured by the strong 2,3-diphosphoglycerate (2,3-DPG) from blood in the heart chambers. Spectral localization is needed to discriminate the cardiac signal from that from the overlying skeletal muscle in the chest wall. The simplest technique used the spatial localization afforded by a surface coil in combination with a single slice-selective excitation pulse.[18] Subsequently, 1-D CSI was used to obtain ^{31}P spectra (see Fig. 2–14A) from a series of contiguous 10-mm thick slices (localized

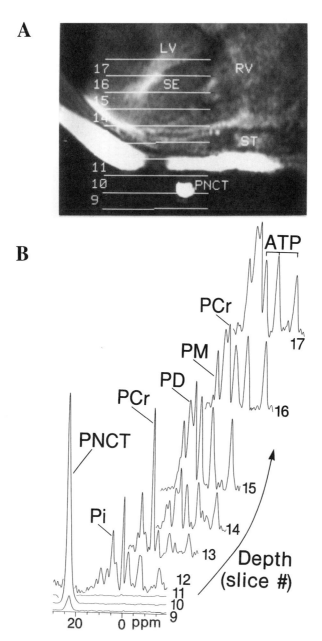

Figure 2–14. **A.** Hydrogen-1 image and **B.** corresponding ³¹P spectra from a 1-D CSI data set from the heart of a patient with coronary heart disease. LV denotes left ventricle; RV, right ventricle; SE, septum; ST, sternum; PNCT, phosphonitrilic trimer reference marker. *(Reproduced, with permission, from Weiss RG, Bottomley PA, Hardy CJ, et al: Regional myocardial metabolism of high-energy phosphates during isometric exercise in patients with coronary artery disease.* N Engl J Med *1990;323:1593–1600.)*

with a 6.5-cm diameter surface coil) at increasing depth (and consequently decreasing SNR) from chest wall, epicardium, and endocardium in a 9-min gated acquisition.[99] An alternative method of spectroscopic imaging of human heart is the so-called rotating frame technique.[100] Examples of ^{31}P spectra, obtained from normal and ischemic heart using the phase-modulated rotating frame-imaging (PMRFI) technique are given in Figure 2–14c. This uses the spatial inhomogeneity of the RF field of surface coils and involves modulation of the RF pulse to acquire a series of data that can be processed to give spectra at different depths. An advantage of this technique is that no gradients are involved. The sensitive volume of surface coils is a poorly defined hemisphere and does not give good localization lateral to the coil. A combination of 2-D gradient localization and 1-D spectroscopic imaging performed at 4 T uses the greater SNR at higher field strength to reduce the voxel size to 1-cm slices along a 5-cm square column.[101] Spectra localized exclusively to the myocardium, with no contaminating signal from blood, were obtained. Alternatively, 2-D CSI techniques can improve spatial selectivity and low spatial resolution maps ($2 \times 2 \times 4$ cm^3 voxels) of ^{31}P metabolites over the heart can be created.[102]

In cardiac studies, data are ideally acquired in synchrony with the cardiac cycle. For spectroscopic imaging studies and those involving exercise protocols, maximal SNR is obtained in a reasonable examination time by gating the acquisition to the base heart rate, giving a *TR* of around 1 s. At this repetition time, all the metabolite peaks suffer some degree of T_1 saturation, and the PCr/ATP ratio must be corrected to compare results from different studies.[103] The saturation factors can be estimated by acquiring nonlocalized spectra at both short (one cardiac cycle) and long (six or more cardiac cycles) *TR*, but this gives an average factor for skeletal muscle, cardiac tissue, and blood. In a study of normal volunteers, in which spectroscopic images were acquired at 1.5 T at both long and short *TR*, a mean T_1 of 6.8 s for PCr in chest wall muscle was calculated, substantially longer than the 4.3 s calculated for heart; for β-ATP the T_1 in heart was 3 s compared with 3.4 s in muscle.[104] The saturation correction factor for the PCr/ATP ratio is thus significantly different between heart and muscle at short *TR*. In contrast, however, a study at 4 T showed no significant difference.[101]

In other studies,[99] it was observed that the mean PCr/ATP ratio of 1.72 ± 0.15 measured in normal subjects did not change

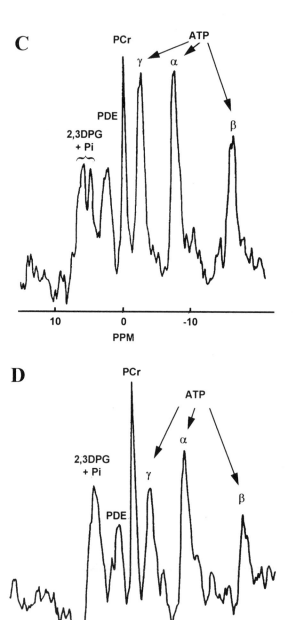

during isometric hand grip exercise. In patients with coronary artery disease, it decreased by 37%, from 1.59 ± 0.31 at rest to 0.91 ± 0.24 during exercise. A decrease in the PCr/ATP ratio during exercise has also been observed, indicating a role for ^{31}P MRS in diagnosis of myocardial ischemia.[105] Technical considerations, analysis of spectra, and the clinical significance of cardiac MRS are discussed in a recent review.[103]

LIVER

A ^{31}P spectrum from normal liver is compared with that from a tumorous liver in Figure 2–15. The α-ATP resonance peak contains a small contribution from nicotinamide adenine dinucleotides (NAD) and α-ADP, and the γ-ATP peak contains contributions from β-ADP. Unlike heart, brain, and muscle, the liver lacks the enzyme creatine kinase, so the PCr resonance is absent. This provides a useful marker for the efficiency of spectral localization; the presence of a PCr peak in a "liver" spectrum indicates contamination by ^{31}P signals from body wall muscle. Spectra are acquired with a surface coil for optimum SNR, although a separate whole-body transmit coil can be used to give uniform excitation, and localization is commonly achieved using the CSI technique.[106] At a typical *TR* of under 1 s for CSI acquisitions, each peak is saturated by an amount dependent on its T_1. Relaxation time changes with pathology can significantly change the appearance of the ^{31}P spectrum in addition to the effects of any metabolite concentration changes.[107]

Figure 2–14. *C.* and *D.* Phosphorus-31 spectra acquired from patients using the PMRFI technique. *C.* A patient with aortic stenosis and symptoms of heart failure. *D.* A patient with aortic stenosis and no symptoms of heart failure. The PCr/ATP ratio for patients with symptoms of heart failure is lower than that for patients without symptoms. The 2,3-diphosphoglycerate (2,3-DPG) resonance (from a metabolite found in red blood cells) comes from blood in the chambers of the heart and overlaps the P$_i$ resonance. *(Adapted, with permission, from Conway MA, Allis J, Ouwerkerk R, et al: Detection of low phosphocreatine to ATP ratio in failing hypertrophied human myocardium by ^{31}P magnetic resonance spectroscopy. Lancet 1991;338:973–976.) Abbreviations:* ATP = adenosine triphosphate; PCr = phosphocreatine; PM = phosphomonoester; PD = phosphodiester; PCr = phosphocreatine; P$_i$ = inorganic phosphate.

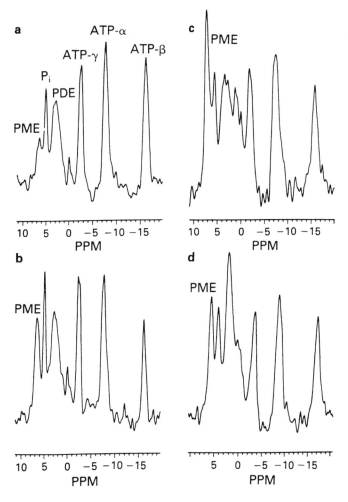

Figure 2–15. Phosphorus-31 spectra from PMRFI data of the liver acquired at 1.9 T. **A.** Normal liver. There is only a very small PCr contribution, confirming that the spectrum is well localized to the liver. **B.** and **C.** Increased PME in patients with hepatic lymphoma. **D.** Patient **C.** after chemotherapy. *(Reproduced, with permission, from Dixon RM, Angus PW, Rajagopalan B, et al: Abnormal phosphomonoester signals in ³¹P MR spectra from patients with hepatic lymphoma. A possible marker of liver infiltration and response to chemotherapy. Br J Cancer 1991;63:953–958.)* Abbreviations: PMRFI = phase modulated rotating frame imaging; PCr = phosphocreatine; PME = phosphomonoester.

Quantitative measurements made in normal liver using ISIS localization give T_1 relaxation times (see Table 2–2) of PME, PDE, and P_i up to three times longer than that of ATP, hence the relative size of the peaks depend greatly on the acquisition parameters.[78,79] Age-related differences are also likely to occur in liver spectra. It has been observed that PME/ATP in neonates is higher than in adults, which may be due to an elevated rate of membrane synthesis in the developing liver, but further studies are still needed.[108]

In ^{31}P in vivo studies, a diversity of metabolic patterns is seen in diseased liver compared with normal liver: raised PME in alcoholic hepatitis and liver tumors; reduced P_i in biliary cirrhosis; raised PME and low PDE in acute viral hepatitis.[109] A detailed study has shown that the PME/P_i ratio shows a significant positive correlation with the severity of alcoholic hepatitis as assessed from biopsy samples.[110] No difference in P_i/ATP between patients and controls was observed, suggesting cellular energetics were not impaired, but this does not preclude a reduction in both P_i and ATP or an accumulation of "invisible" mitochondrial P_i. In patients with fatty change or cirrhosis, there was no change in PME/P_i, but in another study a relative elevation of PME signal was observed, which increased with the severity of cirrhosis.[111] In this study, it was confirmed that T_1 was not shortened, suggesting a real increase in PME, perhaps due to phosphorylcholine and phosphorylethanolamine, which are precursors in membrane synthesis. A recent study has distinguished the effects of alcohol-related liver injury on the ^{31}P spectrum from the acute effects of alcohol ingestion.[112]

The dynamic study of biochemical processes in the liver is readily accessible by MRS. In normal volunteers after an overnight fast, ^{31}P spectra were acquired over a period of 70 min after a bolus infusion of L-alanine (2.8 mmol/kg body weight).[113] Maximal changes of PME/ATP (+98%) and P_i/ATP (−33%) relative to the preinfusion baseline value, occurred at approximately 40 min after infusion, no change in pH$_i$ was observed. L-Alanine is a key precursor of gluconeogenesis and is cleared rapidly by the liver. With supporting evidence from studies in rat liver, it was proposed that the rise in PDE is due to elevated concentrations of 3-phosphoglycerate, a gluconeogenic intermediate. Hepatic glycogen concentration can be directly determined using ^{13}C MRS,[114] thus allowing the direct study of carbohydrate metabolism.[115] Subjects with insulin-dependent diabetes mellitus (IDDM) were studied throughout the day following three "mixed meals" of carbohydrate, protein, and fat.[116] Hepatic glycogen was observed to increase over the course of the day, but in IDDM patients was only 30% of that in the control group. It was concluded that low levels of hepatic glycogen may therefore be a factor predisposing IDDM patients to severe hypoglycemia.

KIDNEY

Very few in vivo studies of the human kidney have been made. It is smaller and situated deeper, than such organs as the liver and heart, hence the SNR is poorer. The effects of respiration and abdominal motion are also worse. Despite these drawbacks, it has been demonstrated in normal volunteers that both ^1H and ^{31}P MRS of kidney in situ are possible. Using respiratory-gated ^1H STEAM, coupled resonances between 3.2 and 4 ppm have been observed.[117] These signals increased after dehydration and decreased after rehydration, suggesting they are "osmotically active metabolites." Spectroscopic imaging was used to compare normal and transplanted kidney.[118] Quantitative ^{31}P spectra from a volume containing 55% cortex and 45% medulla have been obtained using ISIS localization.[79] Metabolite concentrations of PME 2.6 ± 0.9; P_i 1.6 ± 0.4; PDE 4.9 ± 1.1; and NTP 2.0 ± 0.3 mmol/L were determined. The importance of patient positioning to minimize contamination from body wall muscle and maximize SNR is discussed.

BRAIN

The normal and pathological brain have been studied extensively using MRS,[19,119] but particularly using ^1H and ^{31}P nuclei, although ^1H MRS has gained predominance because of the ability to acquire data from smaller voxels. Many spectral changes are not specific to a particular disease; for example, in ^1H MRS, lactate is observed in both stroke and tumors, and all neurodegenerative diseases are accompanied by a reduction in NAA. Magnetic resonance spectroscopy may still provide an index of the severity of a disease, however, and a prognostic indicator of the response to therapy. In brain tumors and metabolic diseases such as hepatic encephalopathy (HE), there appear to be very specific patterns of spectral change that are diagnostically useful. In chronic HE, systemic lupus erythematosis (SLE), and stroke ^1H spectra have shown abnormalities from regions of the brain that appear normal by MRI. Hydrogen-1 MRS data can be acquired within the context of routine neuroimaging and have recently been shown to significantly improve diagnosis for a range of pathologies.[120] Results from selected MRS studies of the brain are reviewed in the following seven sections.

Normal Brain

The ^{1}H spectra in Figure 2–1 and data in Table 2–1 are for normal white matter in the adult brain. Quantitative studies have shown that significant regional variations occur in both relaxation times[121] and metabolite concentrations.[62,121] In one study,[62] the total NA signal (the combined contribution of NAA and N-acetyl aspartate glutamate [NAAG]) showed little regional variation, with a mean concentration of 11.4 mmol/kg. NAAG was undetectable in gray matter but contributed 22% to the NA peak in white matter. Total creatine was 6.1 mmol/kg in white matter, 8.2 mmol/kg in gray, and 9.1 mmol/kg in the cerebellum. Total cholines showed the largest percentage variability: 1.4 mmol/kg in gray matter; 1.8 mmol/kg in white matter; and 2.9 mmol/kg in the pons. Quantitative data have shown that marked alterations occur in ^{1}H spectra until age 5.[70] At birth, mI dominates the brain spectrum; thereafter, the absolute mI concentration decreases, as do tCho, brain water content, and water T_2. The NAA concentration at birth was found to be only 50% that of adults. In normal aging, metabolite concentrations in parietal white and occipital gray matter have been reported constant up to age 80.[122] A 13% reduction of NAA concentration has been observed in the occipital lobes of a group aged 60–80 (compared with a group aged 20–30), with no other significant changes of metabolites or relaxation times in basal ganglia or temporal or frontal lobes.[123]

Two-dimensional CSI has been used to create ^{31}P metabolite maps of the normal brain.[124,125,126] At a spatial resolution of 27 cm[3], examination times of between 40 and 80 min are necessary for adequate SNR, but there is the advantage in studies of focal disease that both normal and pathological tissue spectra can be directly compared.[125] Typical values for ^{31}P metabolite concentrations measured in central white matter of normal adults are 3 mM for PME, PCr, and ATP; 11 mM for PDE; and 0.7 mM for P_i.[126] In nonlocalized spectra, which have no acquisition delays, 80% of the ^{31}P signal consists of a large broad resonance from phosphate in bone and immobile membrane phospholipids.[127] In localized ^{31}P spectra, a significant proportion of phospholipid signal may still arise from membrane phospholipids. A technique employing off-resonance saturation can be used to create metabolite maps of mobile phospholipids, which may have applications in studying demyelinating diseases.[127]

Cerebral Ischemia

The potential of ^{1}H MRS as a clinical tool to investigate the extent of neuronal injury in ischemia and to monitor the metabolic effects of therapeutic intervention was realized early on with the observation in a human brain infarct of a dramatic loss of NAA and tCr and the appearance of lactate.[72] Visualization of ischemia-induced changes in the brain can be obtained using T_2-weighted MR images and, more recently, using diffusion-weighted images for the acute stage.[128] Successful therapeutic intervention (using agents such as N-methyl-D-aspartate antagonists and thrombolytics) requires the early identification of viable neuronal tissue within the infarct or of compromised, but viable, peripheral tissue. This potentially salvageable tissue has been called the "ischemic penumbra,"[129] and its detection is one goal of MRS.[130] In ^{1}H MRS studies using animal models, a reduction in NAA and tCr and the appearance of lactate occurs at between 10 min and 1 h after ischemia.[131,132] Such early observations are not routinely possible in human studies for logistic reasons, and most MRS data in "acute" stroke are of patients observed within 6–36 h.

Reduced NAA and elevated lactate are routinely observed in human infarcts.[133–136] Within 24 h of infarction, NAA is typically reduced by 30% compared with normals and lactate observed at concentrations up to 30 mmol/L.[135] Reductions of NAA, tCr, and tCho concentrations have also been observed in the contralateral hemisphere.[136] A spectroscopic imaging study has shown the presence of lactate in acute stroke prior to changes visible by T_2-weighted MRI.[137] Similarly, reduced NAA/tCho ratios and, in some cases, elevated lactate were observed in noninfarcted brain tissue of patients with cerebral hypoperfusion caused by carotid artery stenosis.[138] At 4.1 T, high spatial resolution spectroscopic imaging (0.5-cm[3] voxel size) demonstrated elevated lactate in the peri-infarct of a 6-week-old stroke.[139] Continuous reductions in NAA, tCr, tCho are observed for up to 2 weeks after infarct[135,140,141]; the ongoing loss of NAA suggests the presence of viable cells within the is-chemic region. Lactate also decreases over this period but has been observed to persist for several months.[133] The lactate peak at 1.33 ppm coincides with those from lipids and macromole-cules, making the unequivocal detection of low lactate concen-tration difficult. Lactate can be distinguished from lipids and macromolecules on the basis of their T_1 differences (typically 100–200 ms for lipids and macromolecules and 1400 ms for lac-tate), by the so-called metabolite nulling technique.[142] Using this technique with spectroscopic imaging, coincident elevation of both lactate and lipid are observed in regions of infarct in cases of subacute stroke.[143] In patients studied from 1 day to 6 weeks after infarct, a continual reduction in lactate concentration was accompanied by an increase in the lipid/macromolecule peaks at 0.9 and 1.3 ppm, as shown in Figure 2–16.[144] Beyond 7 days after infarct, increases in both tCho and tCr concentrations have been observed,[135] which may arise from proliferating glial cells during tissue repair.

T_1 and T_2 relaxation times of NAA, tCr, and tCho display a trend for higher values in the infarct but are not significantly different from those in normal brain tissue.[145,146] The T_2 of water, which may be as high as 290 ms in the chronic stage compared with 100 ms in normal white matter[135] and lactate T_2 (780 ± 257 ms), is longer than that of other metabolites.[146] These observa-tions may indicate that the intracellular relaxation mechanisms for NAA, tCr, and tCho are relatively unaltered by cellular edema or that normal tissue is within the spectroscopy voxel. Water and lactate (which diffuse into the extracellular space) have an average T_2 contributed from both intra- and extracellu-lar spaces.

Energy metabolism during cerebral ischemia has been stud-ied by ^{31}P MRS. In the acute stage of infarction, there is an in-crease in P_i and decrease in the PCr and ATP signal intensities,[147] and the infarcted tissue becomes acidotic (pH < 6.9) with a con-comitant increase in intracellular Mg^{2+} concentration.[148] Intracel-lular pH returns to normal at about 3 days after the ischemic in-sult, and metabolite ratios return to normal after 10 days, by which time the infarcted tissue has become significantly alka-lotic.[147,148] Using a combined ^{31}P and ^1H MRS study, a reciprocal relationship of lactate concentration and pH_i changes has been demonstrated in the cat brain after transient ischemia, consistent with lactic acidosis due to anaerobic glycolysis.[149] In chronic infarcts,

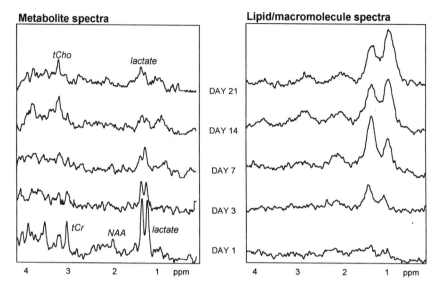

Figure 2–16. Longitudinal study of an infarct in a 35-year-old female stroke patient. The ¹H spectra are localized to the core of the infarct. *Left:* "Metabolite only" spectra created by taking the difference between a "standard" acquisition and a "metabolite-nulled" acquisition. *Right:* Metabolite-nulled spectra showing only lipid and macromolecule resonances. The day 1 lactate concentration was 20 mM. By day 21, there were very high lipid signals but only 3 mM lactate. Note the return of the tCho resonance by day 14. "Standard" spectra acquisition parameters: STEAM, $TE = 30$ ms, $TR = 2020$ ms, 8 cm³ voxel, 256 acquisitions. "Metabolite-nulled" spectra acquisition parameters; as for the "standard" but with an inversion pulse at TI = 700 ms prior to the acquisition. *(Data acquired in collaboration with Drs DE Saunders and MM Brown, SGHMS.) Abbreviations:* tCho = total choline; tCr = total creatine; NAA = *N*-acetyl aspartate; STEAM = stimulated echo acquisition mode.

a reduction in absolute phosphorus signal intensity has been observed despite a normal PCr/P_i ratio, implying a reduction in the number of active cells in the infarcted region.[150] A ¹H and ³¹P spectroscopic imaging study in humans found elevated lactate and alkalosis in six chronic infarcts.[151] After infusion of ¹³C-labeled glucose, it was demonstrated by ¹H MRS that the lactate in a patient with a 32-day-old infarct was derived from blood glucose.[152] Further studies are needed to demonstrate that this conversion occurs in active neuronal tissue in the "penumbra," rather than in anaerobically respiring macrophages or glial cells.

In infants who had suffered birth asphyxia, on the first day, the ^{31}P spectra were no different to those of normals; subsequently there was a significant reduction in PCr/P$_i$, and those infants whose PCr/P$_i$ ratio fell below 0.8 had a poor prognosis for survival or normal neuro-development.[153] In a study of 61 premature newborn infants, those with a PCr/P$_i$ ratio below the 95% confidence limits of the normal group, suffered neurological impairment or death; of the 12 who had ATP/P$_i$ below the 95% confidence limit for normals, 11 died.[154] Similarly, in a ^{1}H MRS study of infants following perinatal hypoxia-ischemia, a high Lac/NAA ratio was prognostic for impaired neurological development and poor chances of survival.[155]

In six patients with acute brain damage (four with demyelinating lesions and two with mitochondrial encephalopathy, lactoacidosis, and stroke-like episodes [MELAS]), NAA in the lesion was initially reduced to between 20 and 72% compared with contralateral NAA, but a significant increase in NAA was observed as their clinical condition improved.[156] Taking into account the possibility of partial volume and corrections for relaxation time changes, these investigators conclude that a recovery in NAA had occurred and suggest that reduced NAA could be due to a reversible impairment of the mitochondrial processes from which NAA is synthesized. The hypothesis of NAA recovery,[156] the continued loss of NAA in the subacute stage of stroke,[135] the appearance of lactate before MRI changes,[137] and metabolic changes observed when MRI is normal[136,138] suggest that ^{1}H MRS and ^{31}P MRS may be useful in monitoring metabolic changes that occur in a variety of conditions relating to cerebral ischemia. This information will be important in the development of appropriate treatment and management of conditions like stroke.

Acquired Immunodeficiency Syndrome

Concentrations of ^{31}P-detectable metabolites (PCr, NTP, etc) were decreased by 30% in patients with mild-to-moderate acquired immunodeficiency syndrome (AIDS) dementia complex, independent of the severity of brain atrophy,[157] although it was not clear whether this was due to cellular loss or metabolic dysfunction. Several studies now show that abnormalities in ^{1}H MRS occur in regions of the brain that appear normal by MRI[158,159] and that NAA levels may indicate the degree of CNS involvement.[160] Serial studies of patients with human immunodeficiency virus (HIV)-

induced neurological disease have demonstrated decreasing NAA levels correlated with the severity of neurological impairment,[161] and the NAA/Cho ratio has been reported as the most significant indicator of central nervous system involvement.[162] An apparent T_2 of 493 ± 199 ms for NAA was found in white matter of HIV-seropositive patients with diffuse MRI abnormalities, compared with 292 ± 118 ms for controls.[163] No other significant changes in metabolite relaxation times were observed. These data suggest that although reduced NAA in AIDS indicates neuronal loss, the relative reductions observed in long echo time spectra may not accurately reflect the degree of loss. A short echo time 1-D CSI study of the frontal lobe showed no change in NAA/Cr but elevated mI/Cr in white matter of patients without AIDS dementia complex, and a significant reduction in NAA/Cr in the gray matter of patients with AIDS dementia complex.[164] This raises the possibility of therapeutic intervention before irreversible neuronal damage occurs. Focal brain lesions are common in patients with AIDS, but unequivocal diagnosis is not always possible by MRI. The ¹H MRS spectra of lesions from toxoplasmosis, lymphoma, progressive multifocal leukoencephalopathy, and cryptococcosis were found to be distinctly different ($p = 0.0001$) with regard to NA, tCr, tCho, mI, and lactate levels.[165] Differentiation of the four groups was achieved with 94% accuracy by MRS alone, hence MRS may provide an important adjunct to MRI in clinical diagnosis and selection of appropriate therapy.

Hepatic Encephalopathy

Hepatic encephalopathy, which frequently occurs as a result of cirrhosis or other severe liver diseases, may produce a variety of neuropsychiatric abnormalities. Magnetic resonance spectroscopy has been used to investigate the underlying biochemical changes in the brain as a result of HE and as a potential method for the early diagnosis of this condition. Patients with biopsy-proven cirrhosis have been examined by ³¹P MRS.[166] PME/ATP and PDE/ATP ratios were significantly lower in patients with subclinical or overt encephalopathy than in the control group, but no consistent changes in P_i and PCr were seen. The researchers note that PME and PDE peaks contain contributions from phosphocholine and glycerophosphocholine, respectively, and reductions of the choline resonance in ¹H spectra are also found in HE, suggesting that cerebral phospholipid metabolism is altered in these patients.

In ^{1}H spectra, a triad of changes are observed: elevated glutamine, decreased mI, and decreased choline.[167] Elevated glutamine is expected as a consequence of hyperammonemia due to reduced liver function; ammonia and glutamate are then converted in astrocytes to glutamine by glutamine synthetase.[19] Confirmation that Gln not Glu was elevated (signals from these two amino acids overlap at clinical field strengths), required an elegant analysis using a comparison of spectra from normals, patients, and model solutions of glutamate and glutamine.[60] In a study of 20 patients with HE, spectroscopic changes showed 94% concordance with neuropsychiatric test results; furthermore, MRS was shown to distinguish HE from subclinical HE.[168] In order of clinical severity of HE, Cho depletion precedes reductions in mI, both of which occur prior to MRS-observable elevations in Glx (Fig. 2–17). These changes are reversed following successful liver transplantation.[169] It has been proposed that the cerebral mI signal is predominantly from an osmolarity-sensitive pool of inositol,[170] hence mI and Cho depletion may be the result of osmotic stress caused by the accumulation of glutamine.[169,170] The use of MRS, which is quantifiable, to detect subclinical HE may improve the staging of liver transplants and drug intervention, thereby reducing the chances of neuropsychological impairment.[168]

Multiple Sclerosis

N-acetyl aspartate concentrations are generally found to be depressed in sclerotic lesions,[171–173] but more interestingly, reduced NAA has also been reported in regions of the brain that appear normal by MRI.[174,175] In a study of gadolinium (Gd)-enhancing plaques, a reduced NAA/tCho ratio was found that was independent of the percentage of the lesion that it enhanced or the percentage of the spectroscopy volume that was occupied by the lesion.[176] Another study[177] also suggests that neurochemical changes can occur in the normal-appearing white matter surrounding a lesion. Elevated tCho is frequently observed in lesions[173,178] and mI/tCr has been reported elevated[173,178] as well as unchanged in Gd-enhancing lesions.[176] Changes in both tCho and mI in focal lesions may be related to alterations in membrane synthesis and turnover. Using ^{31}P MRS, abnormal phospholipid peaks have been observed in both lesions and normal-appearing white matter of multiple sclerosis patients.[175,179] Ex vivo ^{1}H NMR

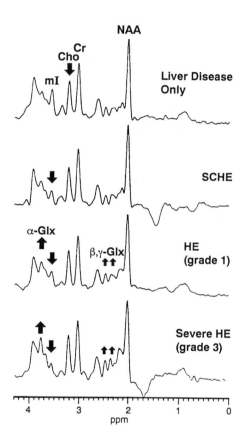

Figure 2–17. Hydrogen-1 spectra from four different patients showing representative spectra in the progression of hepatic encephalopathy (HE). From top to bottom, the spectra represent liver disease (no HE), subclinical HE (SCHE), grade 1 HE, and grade 3 HE. Spectroscopy acquisition parameters: STEAM *TE* = 30 ms. *(Reproduced, with permission, from Ross BD, Jacobson S, Villamil F, et al: Subclinical hepatic encephalopathy: Proton MR spectroscopic abnormalities.* Radiology *1994;193:457–463.) Abbreviation:* STEAM = stimulated echo acquisition mode.

analysis of plaques from postmortem multiple sclerosis brain tissue demonstrated a 34% reduction in NAA and a 42% reduction in total creatine compared with normals, but no changes in total choline or mI.[180] These results support the interpretation of relative reductions of NAA in vivo as neuronal loss but suggest neuronal loss may be underestimated if tCr is used as a reference, and changes of mI/tCr must likewise be interpreted with this in mind. Using short echo ¹H MRS, large resonances at 0.9 and 1.3 ppm have been observed in acute lesions that enhance with Gd, and these resonances have been assigned to products of myelin breakdown in the initial inflammatory stage of lesion development.[174,178] Progressive neuronal impairment has been associated with further reduction in NAA/tCr in a group of patients with both clinical and MRI abnormalities,[171] supporting the hypothesis that permanent clinical disability is a result of axonal loss.[177] Current data strongly suggest that the sensitivity of ^{1}H MRS to multiple sclerosis-induced neurochemical changes, which are not observable by MRI, will be of particular importance in developing and assessing effective therapies.

Alzheimer's Disease

In patients with suspected Alzheimer's dementia (AD), the NAA/tCr ratio is reduced as might be expected,[181,182] but, unexpectedly, an elevation of mI/tCr has also been observed.[183] Quantitative measurements have now shown a 50% increase in mI in AD patients compared with age-matched controls; NAA is decreased and metabolite relaxation times are unchanged.[73] In a study of over 100 patients with dementia, the mI/tCr ratio distinguished AD from frontal lobe or occipital cortex dementia, with 82% sensitivity and 64% specificity.[184] Studies using ^{31}P MRS are so far inconclusive. Alterations in both high-energy phosphate and phospholipid metabolism have been shown, suggesting "the AD brain is under energetic stress."[185] Another study measured reduced glucose metabolism but observed no change in phosphorus metabolite levels with severity of AD.[186] Perchloric acid extracts of AD brain tissue, however, exhibit elevated PMEs and PDEs.[182] A recent study observed a significant increase in PME-to-total-phosphorus signal in patients with mild AD but no correlation with neuropsychological status and suggested discrepancies with other studies may be due to different patient populations.[187] The biochemical significance of increased mI in AD is yet to be determined, and interpretation of in vivo studies is confounded by a diagnosis that can only be confirmed postmortem. Nevertheless, MRS looks like a promising tool in the diagnosis and management of dementias.[188]

Other Neurological Conditions

Magnetic resonance spectroscopy studies in some other neurological conditions are reviewed very briefly in this section. In epilepsy, NAA concentrations are reduced in the epileptogenic focus.[189] Lateralization of temporal lobe epilepsy is deducible from reduced NAA levels in the lobe ipsilateral to the seizure focus.[190,191] In a review of ^{1}H and ^{31}P spectroscopic imaging studies of patients with epilepsy, it was noted that the focus tissue is alkalotic, with reduced PME and increased P_i.[192] Spectroscopic editing techniques have been used to detect elevated levels of GABA in the cerebrum of patients treated with the antiepileptic drug vigabatrin.[193] Recent studies of schizophrenic patients have shown reduced β-ATP levels in the basal ganglia[194] and elevated ATP levels in the dorsal prefrontal cortex[195]; reduced PME and elevated PDE in the prefrontal cortex[195,196]; asymmetry in ^{31}P metabolite distributions in the temporal lobes[197]; and reduced NAA levels as in the frontal cortex[198] and in the right hippocampal region.[199] These studies indicate that alterations in membrane phospholipid and energy metabolism and neuronal loss in schizophrenia can be monitored by MRS. If these changes precede clinical symptoms and structural changes in the brain, MRS may aid in understanding the pathogenesis of this disease and in its treatment.[200] In SLE, reductions in NAA/tCr have been shown to correlate with atrophy.[201] Similarities of ^{1}H spectra in SLE to those found in stroke, seizures, and inflammatory changes have been noted, along with reductions of NAA/tCr in normal-appearing white matter.[202] Reduced NAA/tCr and elevated tCho/Cr in patients with adrenoleukodystrophy have been observed in ^{1}H spectroscopic images.[203] Spectra in regions of abnormal MRI were most affected, but MRS changes were also observed when the MRI was normal, suggesting MRSI (MR spectroscopic imaging) is a sensitive indicator of neurological involvement in this disease. Neuronal loss, determined by reduced NAA, was detected in normal-appearing white matter of a patient with Creutzfeldt-Jakob disease and mI was also elevated.[204] With inborn errors of metabolism, phenylalanine has been quantitated in patients with phenylketonuria[205] and elevated glycine observed in infants with nonketotic hyperglycinemia,[206] and in Canavan's disease, an inborn error of NAA metabolism, NAA is elevated.[207,208]

CANCER

Magnetic resonance spectroscopy can provide a powerful tool in the study of human cancer. Clearly, human tumors can be studied only within the context of some treatment regimens, but the wealth of information obtained from in vivo MRS studies of animal models,[209,210] in vitro studies of human tumor biopsies, and cell cultures may be used in the interpretation of the results. Biochemical information obtained by MRS may be used to ask how the metabolism of tumors differs from normal tissue; whether there are spectral characteristics that provide diagnostic information on tumor type and grading; and whether there are changes in the tumor spectrum that can be used to monitor the efficacy of anticancer treatments.[211] The first in vivo ^{31}P tumor spectrum was obtained from a sarcoma in a hand in 1983.[3] Spectra from other tumors revealed a diversity of patterns, but common features were neutral-to-alkaline pH in all tumors and elevated PME in nonbrain tumors.[212] A thorough review of the typical metabolic characteristics of the many human cancers that have now been studied by ^{31}P and ^{1}H spectroscopy is given in reference 17, and articles covering various aspects of in vivo MRS in cancer can be found in references 213–216.

Tumor pH

A classic feature of tumor metabolism is the production of lactic acid by aerobic glycolysis,[217] from which it was originally assumed that tumors would be acidic.[218] Phosphorus-31 MRS, which can measure pH_i, has shown the surprising result that pH_i is close to neutral or slightly alkaline in animal[6] and human[17] (and references therein) tumors. Regulation of tumor pH_i in the steady state is to the same physiological level as in normal tissue, it is the extracellular space (as sampled in microelectrode measurements), which is more acidic by typically 0.5 pH units. Low pH_e has been confirmed by MRS in animal tumor models using 3-aminopropyl phosphonate (APP), which has a pH-sensitive ^{31}P resonance but only accesses the extracellular space.[219] Reversal of the intracellular–extracellular pH gradient compared with normal tissue may have consequences for the linked equilibria of other ions and may explain the buildup of Ca^{2+} and calcification associated with many tumors.[220]

Phosphorus-31 MRS in Tumors (Nonbrain) and Response to Therapy

Several points must be born in mind when comparing tumor spectra. In vivo ^{31}P spectra are acquired with a short *TR* of between 0.5 and 3 s to optimize the SNR. Changes in metabolite T_1, either between tumor type or in response to treatment, contribute to any observed spectral variation. Tumors are more heterogeneous than many other tissues studied by MRS, and this heterogeneity has been observed spectroscopically in soft tissue sarcomas.[221] When surface coils are used for excitation, since they produce spatially dependent T_1 saturation, the relative contributions of each metabolite peak to the spectrum are distorted if there is spatial heterogeneity in the metabolite concentrations. Last, spectra may be contaminated by signal from adjacent non-malignant tissue such as muscle, particularly if just a simple surface coil is used for superficial tumors, but also even if a gradient localization scheme is used.[17,55] Partial volume effects on ^{31}P spectra have been studied for patients with superficial liver tumors.[222] Nevertheless, a survey of nonbrain cancers shows that different tumor types at different locations in fact have many similarities in their ^{31}P spectra: 89% had high PME, 75% high PDE, 82% low PCr, and all had neutral-to-alkaline pH.[17]

Changes in the ^{31}P spectra of tumors have been observed as a result of successful or partial response to therapy[17]: increased PDE/PME in sarcoma[223]; increased PME/ATP[224] and increased PDE/β-ATP[225] in non-Hodgkin's lymphoma; and increased P_i/PME in lymphoma.[226] A study using surface coil localization of 28 patients with a variety of musculoskeletal tumors found the following characteristics: PME, PDE, and P_i significantly elevated; PCr decreased; ATPs unchanged; and pH alkaline compared with thigh muscle.[227] After chemotherapy, a reduction in PDE correlated with high levels of necrosis at surgery, indicating successful therapy even though tumor volume was not significantly reduced.

Elevated PME is a feature of malignant breast tissue,[228,229] and, in a limited number of patient studies, a reduction in the level of PME has been observed in response to therapy.[230–232] A significant association of the PME/γ-ATP ratio measured in vivo, with S-phase fraction of aneuploid tumors, suggests that elevated PME reflects a demand for increased phospholipid metabolism by rapidly proliferating cells.[231] High-resolution ^{31}P MRS of biopsy samples shows that the PME region contains predominantly phosphoethanolamine (PE) with a small contribution from phosphocholine (PC), but the PE and PC content does not correlate with S-phase fraction.[231,232] Multivariate analysis of phospholipid profiles from high-resolution ^{31}P spectra of human breast tumor extracts has been used to distinguish among malignant, benign, and noninvolved tissue.[233] The PDE peak, observed in vivo at low field strength (clinical 1.5 T), arises from membrane phospholipids, but at the much higher field strength (8.4 T) used for in vitro spectroscopy; PDE is invisible due to line-broadening from chemical shift anisotropy, and direct comparison of in vivo and in vitro results may not be valid.[234] Although most breast cancers occur after menopause, a study of normal breast in premenopausal normal volunteers demonstrated elevated PME during lactation.[235] This study also showed that the relative PME intensity varies with menstrual cycle (lowest in week 2), and, after menopause, the whole ^{31}P spectrum has poorer SNR, but the relative metabolite levels are unchanged. Phosphocreatine does not contribute to breast spectra except artifactually. This can occur with simple surface coil localization, which can still elicit signals from the very high levels of PCr in underlying chest wall muscle.[231,235] This is demonstrated in Figure 2–18, which compares a breast tumor spectrum with spectra from muscle and normal breast using [31]P 3-D CSI.[236]

Heterogeneous distributions of ^{31}P metabolites in the liver of a patient with carcinoid metastases compared with a normal volunteer have been observed using CSI.[237] Phosphomonoester/β-ATP is significantly elevated in malignant tumors[238,239] and in metastases[239] in comparison with normal liver (see Fig. 2–15 for example), but primary and secondary neoplasms could not be distinguished from their spectral characteristics. Elevated levels of PE and PC were observed in high-resolution ^{31}P spectra of histologically normal tissue obtained from tumor-bearing human liver,[240] suggesting altered membrane metabolism in the host liver. A systemic effect of altered lipid metabolism of host liver may have already been indirectly obtained from in vivo studies, with abnormal spectra being observed even when <50% of the selected spectroscopy volume is filled by the tumor.[222,239] Successful chemotherapy or chemoembolization produced an elevation of P_i within 24 h and increased PME/ATP after 3 days, changes that were not observed in the one patient who showed continued tumor growth.[241] Another study observed acute reductions of most metabolite concentrations except P_i, which remained constant or increased, and a long-term decrease in PME/ATP.[242] These opposing results may be due to the different localization techniques used and methods of data analysis. Importantly, changes in the

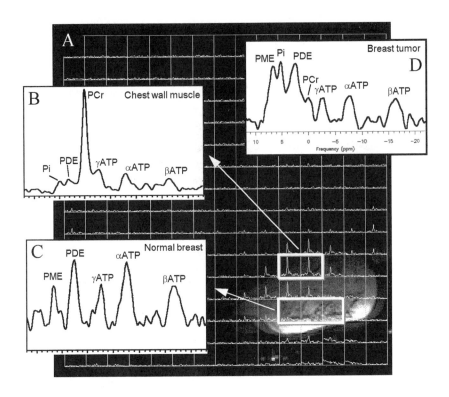

Figure 2–18. Phosphorus-31 spectra of breast tissue taken from 3-D CSI data sets. **A.** The central grid of ^{31}P spectra from the breast of a normal volunteer (56 yr) overlaid on a GRE image. The data have been interpolated to a 16 × 16 matrix. **B.** Spectrum from chest wall muscle (data summed from two voxels as shown). Although the chest wall muscle is twice as far from the coil as the breast, the muscle PCr signal is five times the intensity of the ATP signals from the breast. **C.** Spectrum from normal breast (data summed from three voxels as shown). **D.** Breast tumor spectrum of a 44-year-old patient with an infiltrative ductal carcinoma showing elevated PME and P$_i$ peaks (data summed from four voxels in a 3-D CSI data set). Spectroscopy acquisition parameters: 12-cm diameter surface coil, *TR* = 1000 ms, 45° excitation pulse at coil center, 8 × 8 × 8 phase encodes, 32-cm FOV. *(Data acquired in collaboration with Drs H Gogas and J Mansi, St. George's Hospital Medical School.) Abbreviations:* CSI = chemical shift imaging; GRE = gradient echo; PCr = phosphocreatine; ATP = adenosine triphosphate; PME = phosphomonoester; P$_i$ = inorganic phosphate; PDE = phosphodiester; FOV = field of view.

[31]P spectrum were not paralleled by alterations in standard MRI or CT,[242] and, although there were large differences in ^{31}P spectra among individuals, each patient showed a similar pattern of change following successful treatment.[241]

A demonstration of the possible prognostic value of ^{31}P MRS for monitoring efficient therapy has recently been given for soft tissue sarcomas treated with combined fractionated radiation and hyperthermia.[243,244] In a study of 20 patients, those with ≥95% necrosis after therapy had a mean pretherapy pH of 7.3 ± 0.14, whereas those with <95% necrosis had a pH of 7.17 ± 0.13 (P 0.0001). Furthermore, in a combined analysis with T_2 measured by MRI, pretherapy values of $T_2 \geq 100$ ms or pH ≥ 7.3, predict with 90% sensitivity that a tumor will achieve 95% necrosis. A decrease in ATP/P_i following the first treatment is also associated with a greater chance of high necrosis.[245]

A recent advance for human in vivo studies is the use of ^{1}H-decoupled ^{31}P MRS; this will significantly improve studies on tumors for which phospholipid metabolism is altered. An in vivo study of non-Hodgkin's lymphoma has now demonstrated that the raised PME signal is predominantly PE with only a small PC contribution, and that there is no glycerophosphoryl-choline (GPC) or glycerophosphorylethanolamine (GPE) but only a broad signal from membrane phospholipids in the PDE region.[246] Previously, these components were not resolvable in vivo.

Hydrogen-1 MRS in Peripheral Tumors

Few in vivo ^{1}H MRS studies of nonbrain cancers have been conducted due to technical difficulties associated with motion, field homogeneity, and high lipid concentrations. Tumorous regions in the breast are characterized by higher water/fat ratios (1.2–5.0) than in normal breast tissue (0.2–0.4).[228] Musculoskeletal tumors have been shown to have different spectral characteristics from normal muscle, although the high lipid peak intensity makes deconvolution of metabolite peaks difficult.[24,247] Malignant prostate tissue is characterized by low citrate levels[248,249] and elevated tCho.[250] Both normal and malignant prostate tissue have heterogeneous metabolite distributions.[249,250] A combined ^{31}P/^{1}H MRS study also showed low PCr and high PME content in malignant prostate tissue.[251]

Phosphorus-31 of Brain Tumors

Compared with normal brain tissue, average characteristics of tumor ^{31}P spectra are elevated PME, reduced PDE, and alkaline

pH_i. In one study of different tumor types, meningiomas were the most distinctive, with decreased PDE and PCr reduced below the level of ATP; malignant gliomas showed reduced PDE, which was sometimes split; and nonmalignant astrocytomas could not be distinguished from normal brain tissue.[252] With combined ^{1}H and ^{31}P MRS, both high lactate and alkaline pH_i were observed in astrocytomas.[253] It must be remembered, however, that pH measured by ^{31}P MRS is intracellular, whereas lactate is also present in the extracellular space. Reduced ATP levels in both an astrocytoma and its surrounding edema were observed using 2-D CSI.[254] With quantitative single-voxel spectroscopy, it was shown that a 20 to 70% reduction in total phosphorus signal occurs in tumors.[255] Reduced ^{31}P metabolites have been deduced from 2-D CSI[256] and 3-D CSI[257] data in which tissue from noninvolved brain tissue acted as a control. In making these comparisons, it should be noted that abnormalities in localized ^{31}P spectra of uninfiltrated tissue of brain tumor patients may be possible.[257] Increased free Mg^{2+} was associated with reduced ATP for a variety of tumors.[258]

Several studies show changes in tumor ^{31}P spectra following therapy.[255,259,260] In 1,3-bis-(2-chloroethyl)-1-nitrosourea (BCNU) treatment of gliomas, an acute transient reduction of 0.15 pH units followed intravenous administration of BCNU, whereas a 0.15-pH increase occurred following super-selective intra-arterial infusion.[261] Further studies are still needed to clarify the mechanisms producing these spectral changes, but potentially they may provide information on improving therapy and evaluating the effectiveness of treatment.

Hydrogen-1 MRS of Brain Tumors

Hydrogen-1 spectra from brain tumors are distinctly different from normal brain tissue and have the following typical characteristics: elevated tCho; reduced tCr; reduced NAA; and the presence of lactate, alanine, or lipids.[17,262,263] Tumor cells, which are nonneuronal in origin (most tumors and all metastases), lack NAA but may contain other N-acetyl compounds. When present, NAA is most likely to come from residual normal brain tissue within an infiltrative tumor.[264,265] Observations for specific tumor types from in vivo studies include no NAA, very low tCr, elevated tCho, and sometimes alanine in meningiomas;[260,263-265] elevated tCho, reduced tCr, and frequently lactate in astrocytomas[265–268]; or reduced NAA/tCho, NAA/tCr, tCr/tCho, and the presence of lactate or lipids was observed in four different types of metastases; there was high variability of ratios within groups and no differences between groups.[269]

High-resolution spectra from perchloric acid (PCA) extracts of tumor biopsies[270–273] and cultures of human tumor cells[274] can provide a basis for interpreting in vivo tumor spectra and a better understanding of their metabolism. An example of in vivo and in vitro ^{1}H spectra from the same meningioma is given in Figure 2–19. Most tumor extracts contain negligible NAA, low Cr, and elevated tCho.[271,272] A significantly higher in vitro tCho/Cr ratio was observed in grade IV astrocytomas compared with other grades and normal brain tissue.[270] In vitro ^{1}H MRS[273] and ^{31}P MRS[275] show that relative proportions of GPC and PC in the tCho peaks may be significant in distinguishing between tumor type and grade. A shift in the glutamate/glutamine ratio toward glutamine was observed in astrocytomas and meningiomas,[271] and high levels of glutamate were seen in cultured meningioma cells.[273] Significant amounts of alanine were observed in meningioma (thereby confirming the in vivo assignment) as well as in glioblastoma and pituitary adenoma[272] and metastatic tumors.[264] The presence of high alanine in some tumors suggests their metabolism may involve transamination pathways and partial oxidation of glutamine rather than glycolysis.[267]

Lipid peaks at 0.9, 1.3, and 2 ppm are frequently observed in vivo, particularly at short TEs[264,267] but also at long TEs.[265,276] These signals must arise from mobile lipids rather than lipid bilayers in intact membrane. The mobile lipid content of whole biopsy samples from high-grade astrocytomas, measured by high-resolution ^{1}H spectroscopy, has been found to correlate with the histologically determined extent of necrosis.[277] Tumor biopsies, which gave mobile lipid signals in ^{1}H MRS, when examined by electron microscopy revealed lipid droplets of approximately 1 µm in diameter.[278] The droplets were most abundant in the necrotic core of the tumors and suggest that the pattern of mobile lipid signals may be a marker for highly aggressive brain tumors.

In vivo ^{1}H spectra from patients with brain abscesses were shown to be clearly distinguishable from those for brain tumor. In addition to the lactate, alanine, and lipid peaks, which are frequently found in tumors, there were also peaks from acetate

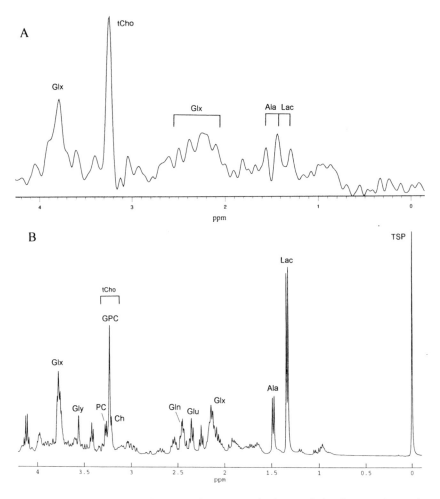

Figure 2–19. Hydrogen-1 spectra from a meningioma. ***A.*** In vivo spectrum at 1.5 T. Peaks from glutamate and glutamine (Glx), cholines (tCho), alanine (Ala), and lactate (Lac) are visible. Spectroscopy acquisition parameters: STEAM, *TE* = 30 ms, *TR* = 2020 ms, 256 acquisitions, 4-cm³ voxel. ***B.*** In vitro spectrum at 9.4 T (400 MHz) of a PCA extract from a sample of the resected tumor. The individual choline (Ch), glycerophosphocholine (GPC), and phosphocholine (PC) peaks are resolved, as are the complex peak structures of glutamate (Glu) and glutamine (Gln). The lactate doublet is artificially high as a result of anaerobic glycolysis in the tumor that occurs between surgical excision and "snap" freezing. The peak at 0 ppm is from TSP, which is added to the extract as a chemical shift reference and standard for quantitation. Peak assignments taken from reference 274. *(Data acquired in collaboration with A Maini and Prof BA Bell, St. George's Hospital Medical School.) Abbreviations:* STEAM = stimulated echo acquisition mode; TSP = 3-trimethylsilylpropanoic acid.

(1.89 ppm), succinate (2.38 ppm), and amino acids, which are known end products of bacterial metabolism.[279] In vitro 1-D and 2-D ^{1}H spectroscopy of the aspirated pus was used to confirm peak assignments; it also contained resonances from other amino acids, and NAA, tCr, and tCho were absent in both in vivo and in vitro spectra.

Quantitative in vivo studies confirm some of the trends observed from metabolite ratios. Up to 50% reductions in tCr and up to 50% elevation in tCho is observed for astrocytomas and meningiomas,[267,280] although another study shows that tCho in astrocytomas does not differ from normal brain tissue.[275] T_2 of tCr in tumors was found to be not significantly different from normal brain tissue.[267,280] The T_2 of tCho was elevated in tumors compared with normal brain tissue,[267] which may be due to changes in phospholipid metabolism and also explains the relative prominence of tCho in long echo time data. Absolute quantitation of lactate and alanine is frequently hampered by the high lipid signals present in short echo time spectra. Metabolite nulling techniques can be used to overcome this, and concentrations of between 5 and 10 mmol/L have been observed.[268]

Although lactate may arise from active anaerobically respiring tumor cells (the classic feature of tumors[217]), the steady-state level depends on the balance between production rate and clearance. High lactate levels may be the result of accumulation in cysts or necrotic regions where there is poor clearance,[265] and an in vitro study recently demonstrated that macrophages could also be a source of lactate.[281] Evidence for pooled lactate is given by the lack of correlation between glucose utilization rates (GUR), measured by ^{18}F fluorodeoxyglucose positron emission tomography (PET), and lactate levels measured by single-voxel ^{1}H MRS in gliomas.[282] Because of the heterogeneous nature of most tumors, the characteristics of its spectrum may vary if the voxel size and placement within the tumor changes.[263] A four-compartment model was suggested to describe long echo time spectral characteristics of tissue within a single voxel: normal brain tissue (NAA, tCr, tCho); vital tumor tissue (tCr, tCho); anaerobically respiring cells (Lac); and necrotic cells and breakdown products (cholines and lipids).[276] A clearer picture of tumor heterogeneity is now emerging from in vivo ^{1}H spectroscopic imaging measurements[43,45,283] and histological and detailed ex vivo ^{1}H MRS studies of biopsies.[284,285]

In 2-D MRSI studies, high lactate levels were not spatially correlated with regions of high tCho,[43,283] and, as in single-voxel studies, the presence of lactate was not a reliable indicator of malignancy in gliomas.[283] Comparing ^{1}H MRSI with PET, tumors in which lactate was observed had the highest GUR, but the site of maximum GUR and lactate did not always coincide because of lactate accumulation in ventricles and in cystic and necrotic areas.[283,286] Below-median GURs were measured in gliomas when lactate was not present.[286] In some tumors, higher-than-normal GURs have also been measured when lactate was absent, but GURs were significantly higher in solid anaplastic tumors compared with low-grade tumors.[283] The relationship between lactate measured by ^{1}H MRS and tumor metabolism is clearly not a simple one, but the techniques of ^{1}H MRSI and PET are complementary for studying glycolysis and lactate deposition.[286] In MRSI, high tCho levels are usually seen in the solid tumor mass and may be indicative of proliferating tissue.[43,283] Normalized tCho could not be used to discriminate grade, because the average tCho level in high-grade tumors is reduced by regions of necrosis (which are frequently visible by MRI).[283] Correlation of 3-D MRSI with histology of resected tumors also showed that the trend for elevated tCho in high-grade tumors is offset by increased micronecrotic regions (which are below MR visibility) in the highest-grade cancers.[285] Hydrogen-1 spectroscopy of aqueous and organic phases of homogenized tumor biopsies (meningiomas and oligodendrogliomas) demonstrate that the in vivo tCho signal comes from water-soluble choline compounds in highly cellular regions.[284] Both in vivo MRSI and in vitro MRS showed tCho to be absent, but there were high lactate concentrations in necrotic and cystic tissue.

Although the therapeutic strategies for brain tumors are limited, several studies have demonstrated ^{1}H MRS changes after treatment. Effective therapeutic embolization of meningiomas led to an acute increase in lactate and reduction in tCho.[287] In another study, 4 days after embolization of a meningioma, the high lipid content and lack of other metabolites suggested that tumor necrosis was complete and that ^{1}H MRS could be used for optimizing the timing of surgery.[288] Following radiotherapy of inoperable gliomas, tCho signals were reduced and the lactate signal, initially present in high grades, disappeared.[289] Abnormal metabolite levels (elevated tCho and lipids, reduced NAA and tCr) in a cerebral lymphoma returned to normal as treatment with radiotherapy progressed.[290] Hydrogen-1 MRS has shown the effect of therapeutic radiation on normal brain tissue to be a reduction in NAA concentration[291] or increased tCho/NAA,[292] indicating neuronal loss or demyelination. The ability of ^{1}H MRS to monitor the metabolic response of tumors to therapy may make it more sensitive to the early response to treatment than MRI or CT, but more studies are still needed to establish this.

Initial attempts at tumor grading using in vivo ^{1}H MRS data were disappointing. In two large studies, no correlation between lactate level and glioma grade was observed,[265] and lipid levels in astrocytomas did not distinguish low- from high-grade tumors.[276] A successful approach has been to use techniques that allow a statistical comparison of all peaks in the spectrum. Grading of gliomas using single-voxel ^{1}H MRS data[293] and differentiation of tumor type and grade using ^{1}H MRSI data[294] has been achieved. Use of statistical pattern recognition analyses to determine tumor type and grade from high-resolution ^{1}H spectra of biopsy samples and in vivo spectra is discussed in the Pattern Recognition section under Advanced Techniques.

Fluorine-19 Pharmacokinetics

Fluorine-19 MRS may be used to monitor the uptake and metabolism of the anticancer agent 5FU.[295] The kinetics of 5FU uptake, and its main catabolite FBAL, have been measured in the livers of tumor patients undergoing chemotherapy.[26,27] Modulation of 5FU by interferon-α has recently been observed on patients with colorectal cancer.[28] When interferon-α was given, those patients that responded to treatment showed an increase of 5FU and of cytotoxic anabolites in metastases in the liver. In patients with extensive liver metastases of colorectal carcinoma, responders to intravenous 5FU had enhanced 5FU levels compared with nonresponders.[296] In this study, the 5FU levels also correlated with the volume of the metastases. Cytotoxicity has been shown to correlate with the half-life of 5FU clearance in tumors, which was greater than 20 min in all patients who responded to treatment.[297] A recent quantitative study of 5FU catabolism measured 1 mM FBAL (20% of the injected dose) in liver at 60 min after bolus injection.[298] The metabolism of 5FU is very patient-dependent, and the use of ^{19}F MRS to monitor 5FU uptake and kinetics on an individual-patient basis may identify those most likely to respond to 5FU and also aid optimization of dose regimens and biochemical modulation in adjuvant chemotherapy.[299]

ADVANCED TECHNIQUES

In vivo MRS is still an expanding field, both in the diverse application of current methods and the development of new techniques. For example, new designs of RF pulses, such as those that provide uniform excitation with a surface coil,[300] can be used in ^{31}P CSI studies.[77] As the technology used in clinical MR systems advances, in the area of gradient design[301] and RF coils,[102] for example, experimental techniques that were originally the province of high-resolution NMR spectrometers or small-bore animal systems can be applied to human studies.

Diffusion-Weighted Spectroscopy

Analogous to diffusion-weighted imaging (DWI), diffusion-weighted spectroscopy (DWS) is used to measure the apparent diffusion coefficient (ADC) of metabolites.[302] To measure metabolite ADCs in human brain tissue, careful sequence design and cardiac gating are required so as to minimize the effects of bulk tissue motion.[303] Apparent diffusion coefficient values of between 0.1 and 0.2 10^{-3} mm^2/s have been obtained for NAA, tCr, and tCho.[303,304] These are much lower than water ADCs (typically 0.9 10^{-3} mm^2/s), probably reflecting the larger molecular size of metabolites and their restriction to intracellular compartments that contain large macromolecules. Anisotropic metabolite ADCs have been reported in human white matter.[304] Metabolite ADC is sensitive to the intracellular milieu, and, although technically difficult, may provide information on cellular damage in conditions such as ischemia[302] or even response to therapy prior to tumor regression as already seen in animal studies.[305]

Functional Spectroscopy

Functional MRI (fMRI), by which dynamic imaging of the human brain can associate a task with localized brain function, now has its correlate in functional MRS (fMRS). Hydrogen-1

MRS of the visual cortex during photic stimulation has shown a transient elevation of lactate, suggesting there is a brief period of anaerobic glycolysis before an increased blood flow can supply the extra demand for oxygen.[306] Other studies of photic stimulation have shown a reduction in glucose but no lactate accumulation,[307] an increase in glucose metabolism,[308] and a PCr/P_i decrease with an alkalotic pH shift.[309]

Hydrogen-1 Decoupling and Multinuclear Spectroscopy

The spectral resolution of coupled peaks in ^{13}C and ^{31}P spectra can be significantly improved using ^{1}H decoupling and the SNR improved by nuclear Overhauser enhancement (NOE) (Fig. 2–20). Issues of patient safety and RF power deposition have been addressed, and human in vivo [1]H-decoupling/NOE studies include [13]C[310,311] and [31]P[312,313] of normal volunteers and ^{31}P of patients with non-Hodgkin's lymphoma.[246]

    Hydrogen-1 and ^{31}P MRS provides complementary metabolic information; for example, in cerebral ischemia, elevated lactate can be measured by ^{1}H MRS and pH changes by ^{31}P MRS. Acquisition of both types of spectra is aided by optimized localization techniques to minimize set-up times.[314,315] Greater time saving is possible by interleaved acquisition[316] or even simultaneous acquisition[317] of MR signals from the two nuclei.

Data Analysis

A major problem with MRS, as opposed to MRI, is the length of time necessary to acquire spectra with adequate SNR. In ^{1}H MRS, reducing the echo time below its current typical value of 30 ms does not provide a major improvement in SNR of the dominant metabolites, although it may enable more accurate quantitation of metabolites with complex spin systems, such as Gln and Glu. The development of spectral analysis techniques that use the prior knowledge of chemical shifts and spin couplings can provide greater accuracy in the analysis of low SNR data, thereby keeping the necessary acquisition time to a minimum.[318] The use of mathematical models of peak patterns, derived from spectra acquired from separate chemical solutions, under the same acquisition parameters as the in vivo study, provides automated and unbiased estimation of metabolite concentrations.[66] The large data sets produced by 2-D and 3-D CSI

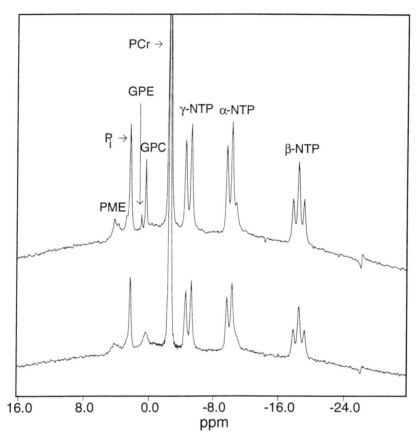

Figure 2–20. Phosphorus-31 spectra from the calf muscle of a normal volunteer demonstrating the effects of proton irradiation. ***Lower:*** Nondecoupled. ***Upper:*** With ¹H decoupling and NOE enhancement. The effect of ¹H decoupling is to resolve the broad PDE peak into two sharp peaks corresponding to glycerophosphoethanolamine (GPE) and glycerophosphocholine (GPC). Increases in peak intensities due to NOE are approximately 50% for NTP and P_i, 60% for PCr, and 80% for GPC. *(Reproduced, with permission, from Brown TR, Stoyanova R, Greenberg T, et al: NOE enhancements and T_1 relaxation times of phosphorylated metabolites in human calf muscle at 1.5 T. Magn Reson Med 1995;33:417–421.)* Abbreviations: NOE = nuclear Overhauser enhancement; PDE = phosphodiester; NTP = nucleoside triphosphate; P_i = inorganic phosphate; PCr = phosphocreatine.

techniques present a formidable task for manual spectrum analysis. The development of reliable automated processing routines to generate metabolite maps, from which individual spectra can be easily extracted, is thus necessary.[319–321]

Pattern Recognition

The human interpretation of spectral data is biased by two factors. First, the perceived prominence of individual peaks (eg, good enough resolution and high signal to noise) and, second, prevailing biochemical knowledge (ie, expectation of which metabolites may change with pathological processes) may skew data analysis toward a particular resonance (eg, does the lactate concentration correlate with the severity of cerebral ischemia?). Biochemical insights have indeed arisen from in vivo MRS data, but usually when there is a large change in a highly visible peak (eg, depletion of mI in hepatic encephalopathy). An advantage of MRS is that it is nonspecific, and although a spectrum contains signals from a plethora of mobile chemical species, many of these signals overlap in vivo while others only contribute to a broad background signal. The converse of this is for high-resolution in vitro data in which there may be too many well-resolved peaks to be individually analyzed. To take advantage of all the information in a spectrum, rather than selected peaks, statistical analysis techniques using artificial neural networks for pattern recognition are being developed.[322,323] Such techniques have been successfully applied in differentiating between tumors using ^{1}H spectra from extracts[324] and between animal tumors using in vivo ^{31}P spectra.[325] That such patterns exist in the metabolite profiles of in vivo human ^{1}H MRS data has now been demonstrated for distinguishing different types of brain tumor[293,294] and for characterizing different neurological diseases.[326] Figure 2–21 is an elegant demonstration of the different metabolite profiles (peaks from tCho, tCr, NAA, Ala, Lac, and lipids) from five tumor types and normal brain tissue as classified by linear discriminant analysis.[294] Magnetic resonance spectroscopic imaging data were acquired, and each spectrum is the average of several voxels within the tumor, thereby averaging the effects of tumor heterogeneity. The power of pattern recognition techniques can be simply appreciated by observing that within any class, even if the ratio of any two metabolites has a large variability, the overall patterns produced by all the peaks are remarkably similar.

A result from a "Principle Component Analysis"[323] of a database of ^{1}H spectra of tumor extracts is shown in Figure 2–22. The principle component vector corresponds to regions in the ^{1}H spectra that are correlated. Being able to associate a particular resonance or group of resonances with the disease or its

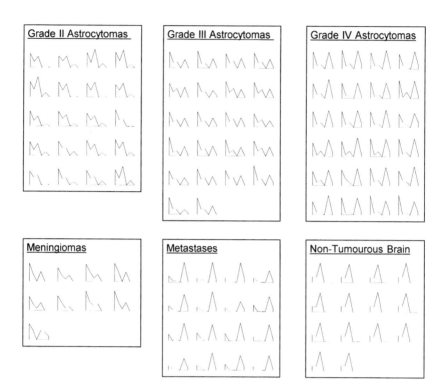

Figure 2–21. Profiles of metabolite peak intensities for ¹H MRSI data classified according to type of tissue. Within each group, the profiles are quite similar, and across the different tissue types, they are quite distinct. From the MRSI data set of each patient, a mean intensity for each metabolite was measured from an average of all the spectra from voxels entirely filled by tumor. Metabolite ratios were calculated relative to tCr in noninvolved brain tissue. For each profile, the six metabolite ratios are plotted in the order with which the metabolite would appear in the ¹H spectrum: From left to right, the peaks refer to the relative amount of tCho, tCr, NAA, Ala, Lac, and lipid. Not all metabolites are present in each tissue type; for example, Ala, Lac, and lipids do not appear in nontumorous brain tissue. Spectroscopy acquisition parameters: PRESS, *TE* = 272 ms, *TR* = 2000 ms, 32 × 32 phase encodes, 25-cm FOV, nominal voxel size 1 mL. *(Reproduced, with permission, from Preul MC, Caramanos Z, Collins DL, et al: Accurate, non-invasive diagnosis of human brain tumors by using proton magnetic resonance spectroscopy.* Nature Med *1996;2:323–325.)* Abbreviations: MRSI = magnetic resonance spectroscopic imaging; tCr = total creatine; tCho = total choline; NAA = *N*-acetyl aspartate; Ala = alanine; Lac = lactate; PRESS = point-resolved spectroscopy; FOV = field of view.

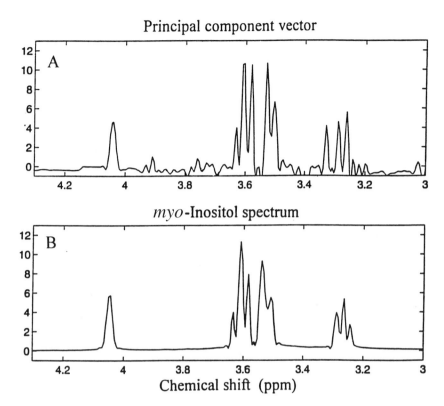

Figure 2–22. A. One of the principal component vectors obtained from a database of high-resolution ^{1}H spectra from different tumor biopsies. The amplitude at each point indicates how strongly regions of the spectrum are correlated between samples. **B.** A high-resolution ^{1}H spectrum (digitized to be directly comparable to the principal component in **A.** of a *myo*-Inositol solution. The similarity between the principal component in **A** and the spectrum in **B** suggests that *myo*-Inositol levels may be a factor in distinguishing tumor types. *(Unpublished data courtesy of R Mazucco, R Maxwell, and Dr C Arus.)*

successful treatment may provide information of the underlying biochemical processes involved. This has a potential role in the prediction of successful cancer therapy.[327] Multicenter trials and some standardization of MRS protocols will ultimately be desirable if a database of clinical MRS data is to be created for general use.[328]

CONCLUSIONS

Over the last 25 years, MRS techniques have developed that now allow the biochemical study of a wide variety of human (and animal) tissue in situ rather than from excised or perfused tissue. The majority of the current successes of MRS have been in the realm of basic science, in the study of animal and human biochemistry in both normal and diseased states. Although it is restricted (at present) to some 30 different chemical species, it is the only practical noninvasive technique for their assay and allows for repeated study of the same tissue under different physiological conditions and of pathological conditions to follow the effects of therapy. The sophistication of MR systems is such that, for ^{1}H MRS of the brain, automated data acquisition and processing is possible; the transfer of the MRS technique from a research to a routine clinical setting is, therefore, in progress. Several diseases exist for which it is already feasible to use MRS to provide a clinically useful diagnosis (eg, Alzheimer's disease, HE, and AIDS) and others for which it promises to affect patient treatment and therapy (eg, multiple sclerosis, stroke, and cancer).

ACKNOWLEDGMENTS

I thank Dr M Stubbs and Prof JR Griffiths for their helpful comments during the preparation of this manuscript and other colleagues at St. George's Hospital Medical School and elsewhere for permission to use their clinical MRS data and reprint their figures.

REFERENCES

1. Iles RA, Stevens AN, Griffiths JR: NMR studies of metabolites in living tissue. *Prog NMR Spectrosc* 1982;15:49–200.
2. Ackerman JJH, Grove TH, Wong GG, et al: Mapping of metabolites in whole animals by ^{31}P using surface coils. *Nature* 1980;283:167–170.
3. Griffiths JR, Cady E, Edwards RHT, et al: ^{31}P-NMR studies of a human tumour in situ. *Lancet* 1983;i:1435–1436.
4. Hands LJ, Bore PJ, Galloway G, et al: Muscle metabolism in patients with peripheral vascular disease investigated by ^{31}P nuclear magnetic resonance spectroscopy. *Clin Sci* 1986;71:283–290.
5. Cady EB, Costello Amde L, Dawson MJ, et al: Non-invasive investigation of cerebral metabolism in new born infants by phosphorus nuclear magnetic resonance spectroscopy. *Lancet* 1983;1:1059–1062.

6. Stubbs M, Bhujwalla ZM, Tozer GM, et al: An assessment of ^{31}P MRS as a method of measuring pH in rat tumours. *NMR Biomed* 1992;5:351–359.
7. Gadian DG, Bates TE, Williams SR, et al: Approaches to editing, assignment and interpretation of proton spectra. *NMR Biomed* 1991;4:85–89.
8. Michaelis T, Merboldt KD, Hänicke W, et al: On the identification of cerebral metabolites in localized ^{1}H NMR spectra of human brain in vivo. *NMR Biomed* 1991;4:90–98.
9. Miller BL: A review of chemical issues in ^{1}H NMR spectroscopy: N-acetyl-L-aspartate, creatine and choline. *NMR Biomed* 1991;4:47–52.
10. Kreis R, Farrow N, Ross BD: Localized ^{1}H NMR spectroscopy in patients with chronic hepatic encephalopathy: Analysis of changes in cerebral glutamine, choline and inositols. *NMR Biomed* 1991;4:109–116.
11. Bovee WMMJ: Quantification of glutamate, glutamine, and other metabolites in *in vivo* proton NMR spectroscopy. *NMR Biomed* 1991;4:81–84.
12. Michaelis T, Helms G, Merboldt K-D, et al: Identification of scyllo-Inositol in proton NMR spectra of human brain in vivo. *NMR Biomed* 1993;6:105–109.
13. Merboldt K-D, Bruhn H, Hänicke W, et al: Decrease of glucose in the human visual cortex during photic stimulation. *Magn Reson Med* 1992;25:187–194.
14. Gruetter R, Rothman DL, Novotny EJ, et al: Detection and assignment of the glucose signal in ^{1}H MR difference spectra of the human brain. *Magn Reson Med* 1992;27:183–188.
15. Gadian DG: *Nuclear Magnetic Resonance Spectroscopy and its Application to Living Systems.* 2nd ed. Oxford: Oxford University Press, 1996.
16. Taylor JS, Vigneron DB, Murphy-Boesch J, et al: Free magnesium levels in normal human brain and brain tumors: [31]P chemical-shift imaging measurements at 1.5 T. *Proc Natl Acad Sci USA* 1991;88:6810–6814.
17. Negendank W: Studies of human tumors by MRS: A review. *NMR Biomed* 1992;5:303–324.
18. Bottomley PA: Noninvasive study of high-energy phosphate metabolism in human heart by depth-resolved ^{31}P NMR spectroscopy. *Science* 1985;229:769–772.
19. Ross B, Michaelis T: Clinical applications of magnetic resonance spectroscopy. *Magn Reson Quart* 1994;4:191–247.
20. Gruetter R, Novotny EJ, Boulware SD, et al: Localised ^{13}C NMR in the human brain of amino acid labeling from D-[1-^{13}C] glucose. *J Neurochem* 1994;63:1377–1385.
21. Beckmann N: In vivo ^{13}C spectroscopy in humans. In Diehl P, Fluck E, Günther H, et al (eds): *NMR Basic Principles and Progress,* Vol. 28, Berlin: Springer-Verlag, 1992; pp. 73–100.
22. Jue T, Rothman DL, Tavitian BA, et al: Natural-abundance ^{13}C NMR study of glycogen repletion in human liver and muscle. *Proc Natl Acad Sci USA* 1989;86:1439–1442.
23. Heerschap A, Luyten PR, van der Heyden JI, et al: Broadband proton decoupled natural abundance ^{13}C NMR spectroscopy of humans at 1.5 T. *NMR Biomed* 1989;2:124–132.
24. Bachert P, Bellemann ME, Layer G, et al: *In vivo* [1]H,[31]P-{[1]H} and [13]C-{[1]H} magnetic resonance spectroscopy of malignant histiocytoma and skeletal muscle tissue in man. *NMR Biomed* 1992;5:161–170.
25. Prior MJW, Maxwell RJ, Griffiths JR: Fluorine-19 NMR spectroscopy and imaging in vivo. In Diehl P, Fluck E, Günther H, et al (eds): *NMR Basic Principles and Progress,* Vol. 28. Berlin: Springer-Verlag, 1992, pp. 101–130.

26. Semmler W, Bachert-Baumann P, Guckel F, et al: Real-time follow-up of 5-fluorouracil metabolism in the liver of tumor patients by means of ^{19}F MR spectroscopy. *Radiology* 1990;174:141–145.

27. Schlemmer H-P, Bachert P, Semmler W, et al: Drug monitoring of 5-fluorouracil: *In vivo* ^{19}F NMR study during 5-FU chemotherapy in patients with metastases of colorectal adenocarcinoma. *Magn Reson Imaging* 1994;12:497–511.

28. Findlay MPN, Leach MO, Cunningham D, et al: The non-invasive monitoring of low dose, infusional 5-fluorouracil and its modulation by interferon using *in vivo* ^{19}F magnetic resonance spectroscopy in patients with colorectal cancer: A pilot study. *Ann Oncol* 1993;4:597–602.

29. Frahm J, Merboldt KD, Hänicke W: Localised proton spectroscopy using stimulated echoes. *J Magn Reson* 1987;72:341–344.

30. Frahm J, Bruhn H, Gyngell ML, et al: Localized high-resolution proton NMR spectroscopy using stimulated echoes: Initial applications to human brain *in vivo*. *Magn Reson Med* 1989;9:79–93.

31. Bottomley P: Depth resolved surface coil spectroscopy (DRESS). *NMR Basic Princ Prog* 1992;26:67–102.

32. Ordidge RJ, Connelly A, Lohman JAB: Image-selected *in vivo* spectroscopy (ISIS): A new technique for spatially selective NMR spectroscopy. *J Magn Reson* 1986;66:283–294.

33. Ordidge RJ, Helpern JA: Image guided volume selective spectroscopy: A comparison of techniques for *in vivo* ^{31}P NMR spectroscopy of human brain. *NMR Basic Princ Prog* 1992;26:103–117.

34. Brown TR, Kincaid BM, Ugurbil K: NMR chemical shift imaging in three dimensions. *Proc Natl Acad Sci USA* 1982;79:3523–3526.

35. Brown TR: Practical applications of chemical shift imaging. *NMR Biomed* 1992;5:238–243.

36. Duyn JH, Gillen J, Sobering G, et al: Multisection proton MR spectroscopic imaging of the brain. *Radiology* 1993;188:277–282.

37. Posse S, DeCarli C, Le Bihan D: Three-dimensional echo-planar MR spectroscopic imaging at short echo times in human brain. *Radiology* 1994;192:733–738.

38. Sharp JC, Leach MO: Conformal NMR spectroscopy: Accurate localization to noncuboidal volumes with optimum SNR. *Magn Reson Med* 1989;11:376–388.

39. Connelly A, Counsell C, Lohman JAB, et al: Outer volume suppressed image related *in vivo* spectroscopy (OSIRIS), a high sensitivity localisation technique. *J Magn Reson* 1988;78:519–525.

40. Moonen CT, Von Kienlin M, van Zijl PC, et al: Comparison of single-shot localization methods (STEAM and PRESS) for *in vivo* proton NMR spectroscopy. *NMR Biomed* 1989;2:201–208.

41. Lim KO, Pauly J, Webb P, et al: Short TE phosphorus spectroscopy using a spin-echo pulse. *Magn Reson Med* 1994;32:98–103.

42. Granot J: Selected volume spectroscopy (SVS) and chemical shift imaging: A comparison. *J Magn Reson* 1986;66:197–200.

43. Luyten PR, Marien AJH, Heindel W, et al: Metabolic imaging of patients with intracranial tumors: ^{1}H MR spectroscopic imaging and PET. *Radiology* 1990;176:791–799.

44. den Hollander JA, Luyten PR, Marien AJH: ^{1}H NMR spectroscopy and spectroscopic imaging of the human brain. *NMR Basic Princ Prog* 1992;27:151–175.

45. Segebarth CM, Balériaux DF, Luyten PR, et al: Detection of metabolic heterogeneity of human intracranial tumors *in vivo* by ^{1}H NMR spectroscopic imaging. *Magn Reson Med* 1990;13:62–76.

46. Hugg JW, Matson GB, Twieg DB, et al: Phosphorus-31 MR spectroscopic imaging (MRSI) of normal and pathological human brain. *Magn Reson Imaging* 1992;10:227–243.

47. Haase A, Frahm J, Hänicke W, et al: ^{1}H NMR chemical shift selective (CHESS) imaging. *Phys Med Biol* 1985;30:341–344.

48. van Zijl PCM, Moonen CTW: Solvent suppression strategies for *in vivo* magnetic resonance spectroscopy. *NMR Basic Princ Prog* 1992;26:67–108.

49. Klose U: *In vivo* proton spectroscopy in presence of eddy currents. *Magn Reson Med* 1990;14:26–30.

50. Spielman D, Webb P, Macovski A: Water referencing for spectroscopic imaging. *Magn Reson Med* 1989;12:38–49.

51. Bottomley PA, Hardy CJ, Roemer PB, et al: Problems and expediencies in human ^{31}P spectroscopy. The definition of localised volumes, dealing with saturation and the technique-dependence of quantification. *NMR Biomed* 1989;2:284–289.

52. van Vaals JJ, Bergman AH, den Boef JH, et al: A single-shot method for water-suppressed localization and editing of spectra, images, and spectroscopic images. *Magn Reson Med* 1991;19:136–160.

53. SF Keevil, Barbirolli B, Collins DJ, et al: Quality assessment in *in vivo* NMR spectroscopy, IV. A multicentre trial of test objects and protocols for performance assessment in clinical NMR spectroscopy. *Magn Reson Imaging* 1995;13:139–157.

54. Shungu DC, Glickson JD: Sensitivity and localization enhancement in multinuclear *in vivo* NMR spectroscopy by outer volume presaturation. *Magn Reson Med* 1993;30:661–671.

55. Howe FA, Stubbs M, Rodrigues LM, et al: An assessment of artefacts in localised and nonlocalised ^{31}P MRS studies of phosphate metabolites and pH in rat tumours. *NMR Biomed* 1992;5:351–359.

56. Decorps M, Bourgeois D: Localised spectroscopy using static magnetic field gradients: Comparison of techniques. *NMR Basic Princ Prog* 1992;27:119–149.

57. Young IR, Cox IJ, Coutts GA, et al: Some considerations concerning susceptibility, longitudinal relaxation time constants and motion artifacts in *in vivo* human spectroscopy. *NMR Biomed* 1989;2:329–339.

58. Posse S, Schuknecht B, Smith ME, et al: Short echo time proton MR spectroscopic imaging. *J Comput Assist Tomogr* 1993;17:1–14.

59. Leach MO, Collins DJ, Keevil S, et al: Quality assessment in *in vivo* NMR spectroscopy, III. Clinical test objects: design, construction and solutions. *Magn Reson Imaging* 1995;13:131–138.

60. Kreis R, Ross BD, Farrow NA, et al: Metabolic disorders of the brain in chronic hepatic encephalopathy detected with ^{1}H MR spectroscopy [see comments]. *Radiology* 1992;182:19–27.

61. Cady EB: Determination of absolute concentrations of metabolites from NMR spectra. *NMR Basic Princ Prog* 1992;26:249–282.

62. Michaelis T, Merboldt K-D, Bruhn H, et al: Absolute concentrations of metabolites in the adult human brain *in vivo:* Quantification of localised proton MR spectra. *Radiology* 1993;187:219–227.

63. Barker PB, Soher BJ, Blackband SJ, et al: Quantitation of proton NMR spectra of the human brain using tissue water as an internal concentration reference. *NMR Biomed* 1993;6:89–94.

64. Christiansen P, Henriksen O, Stubgaard M, et al: *In vivo* quantification of brain metabolites by ¹H-MRS using water as an internal standard. *Magn Reson Imaging* 1993;11:107–118.

65. Cady EB, Azzopardi D: Absolute quantitation of neonatal brain spectra acquired with surface coil localization. *NMR Biomed* 1989;2:305–311.

66. Provencher SW: Estimation of metabolite concentrations from localized *in vivo* proton NMR spectra. *Magn Reson Med* 1993;30:672–679.

67. van der Veen JWC, De Beer R, Luyten PR, et al: Accurate quantification of *in vivo* ³¹P NMR signals using the variable projection method and prior knowledge. *Magn Reson Med* 1988;6:92–98.

68. De Beer R, van Ormondt D: Analysis of NMR data using time domain fitting procedures. *NMR Basic Princ Prog* 1992;26:201–248.

69. Soher BJ, van Zijl PCM, Duyn JH, Bartzer PB: Quantitative proton MR spectroscopic imaging of the human brain. *Magn Reson Med* 1996;3S:356–363.

70. Kreis R, Ernst T, Ross BD: Development of the human brain: *In vivo* quantification of metabolite and water content with proton magnetic resonance spectroscopy. *Magn Reson Med* 1993;30:424–437.

71. Sappey-Marinier D: High-resolution NMR spectroscopy of cerebral white matter in multiple sclerosis. *Magn Reson Med* 1990;15:229–239.

72. Bruhn H, Frahm J, Gyngell ML, et al: Cerebral metabolism in man after acute stroke: New observations using localized proton NMR spectroscopy. *Magn Reson Med* 1989;9:126–131.

73. Moats RA, Ernst T, Shonk TK, et al: Abnormal cerebral metabolite concentrations in patients with probable Alzheimer disease. *Magn Reson Med* 1994; 32:110–115.

74. Kreis R, Ernst T, Ross BD: Absolute quantification of water and metabolites in the human brain, II. Metabolite concentrations. *J Magn Reson* 1993;102:9–19.

75. Boska MD, Hubesch B, Meyerhoff DJ, et al: Comparison of ³¹P and ¹H MRI at 1.5 and 2.0 T. *Magn Reson Med* 1990;13:228–238.

76. Buchthal SD, Thoma WJ, Taylor JS, et al: *In vivo* T1 values of phosphorus metabolites in human liver and muscle determined at 1.5 T by chemical shift imaging. *NMR Biomed* 1989;2:298–304.

77. Sakuma H, Nelson SJ, Vigneron DB, et al: Measurement of T1 relaxation times of cardiac phosphate metabolites using BIR-4 adiabatic RF pulses and a variable nutation method. *Magn Reson Med* 1993;29:688–691.

78. Meyerhoff DJ, Karczmar GS, Matson GB, et al: Non-invasive quantitation of human metabolites using image-guided ³¹P magnetic resonance spectroscopy. *NMR Biomed* 1990;3:17–22.

79. Buchli R, Meier D, Martin E, et al: Assessment of absolute metabolite concentrations in human tissue by ³¹P MRS *in vivo,* II. Muscle, liver, kidney. *Magn Reson Med* 1994;32:453–458.

80. Webb PG, Sailasuta N, Kohler SJ, et al: Automated single voxel proton MRS: Technical development and multisite verification. *Magn Reson Med* 1994;31:365–373.

81. Chance B, Leigh JS, Clark BJ, et al: Control of oxidative metabolism and oxygen delivery in human skeletal muscle: A steady-state analysis of the work/energy cost transfer function. *Proc Natl Acad Sci USA* 1985;82:8384–8388.

82. Laurent D, Authier B, Lebas JF, et al: Effect of prior exercise in P_i/PC ratio and intracellular pH during a standardized exercise: A study on human muscle using [^{31}P] NMR. *Acta Physiol Scand* 1992;144:31–38.

83. Barbirolli B: ^{31}P MRS of human skeletal muscle. In de Certaines JD, Boveé WMMJ, Podo F (eds): *Magnetic Resonance Spectroscopy in Biology and Medicine.* Oxford: Pergamon Press, 1992, pp. 369–386.

84. Kemp GJ, Radda GK: Quantitative interpretation of bioenergetic data from ^{31}P and ^{1}H magnetic resonance spectroscopic studies of skeletal muscle: An analytical review. *Magn Reson Q* 1994;10:43–63.

85. Kemp GJ, Thompson CH, Barnes PR, et al: Comparisons of ATP turnover in human skeletal muscle during ischemic and aerobic exercise using ^{31}P magnetic resonance spectroscopy. *Magn Reson Med* 1994a;31:248–258.

86. Ross BD, Radda GK, Gadian DG, et al: Examination of a case of suspected McArdle's syndrome by ^{31}P nuclear magnetic resonance. *N Engl J Med* 1981; 304:1338–1342.

87. Kemp GJ, Taylor DJ, Dunn DF, et al: Cellular energetics of dystrophic muscle. *J Neurol Sci* 1993;116:201–206.

88. Arnold DL, Taylor DJ, Radda GK: Investigations of human mitochondrial myopathies by phosphorus magnetic resonance spectroscopy. *Ann Neurol* 1985; 18:189–196.

89. Taylor DJ, Krige D, Barnes PR, et al: A ^{31}P magnetic resonance spectroscopy study of mitochondrial function in skeletal muscle of patients with Parkinson's disease. *J Neurol Sci* 1994;125:77–81.

90. Chance B, Bank W: Genetic disease of mitochondrial function evaluated by NMR and NIR spectroscopy of skeletal tissue. *Biochim Biophys Acta* 1995;1271:7–14.

91. Nelson SJ, Taylor JS, Vigneron DB, et al: Metabolite images of the human arm: Changes in spatial and temporal distribution of high energy phosphates during exercise. *NMR Biomed* 1991;4:268–273.

92. Hetherington HP, Hamm JR, Pan JW, et al: A fully localised ^{1}H homonuclear editing sequence to observe lactate in human skeletal muscle after exercise. *J Magn Reson* 1989;82:86–96.

93. Bruhn H, Frahm J, Gyngell ML, et al: Localised proton NMR spectroscopy using stimulated echoes: Applications to human skeletal muscle *in vivo. Magn Reson Med* 1991;17:82–94.

94. Kreis R, Boesch C: Liquid-crystal-like structures of human muscle demonstrated by *in vivo* observation of direct dipolar coupling in localised proton magnetic resonance spectroscopy. *J Magn Reson* 1994;B104:189–192.

95. Schick F, Eismann B, Jung W-I, et al: Comparison of localised proton NMR signals of skeletal muscle and fat tissue *in vivo:* Two lipid compartments in muscle tissue. *Magn Reson Med* 1993;29:158–167.

96. Boesch C, Slotboom H, Puntschart A, et al: Measurement of intramyocellular lipid-signals in ^{1}H MR spectra of human muscle in vivo (abstr). *Book of Abstracts: Society of Magnetic Resonance,* Berkely, CA: Society of Magnetic Resonance 1995, p. 426.

97. Taylor R, Price TB, Katz LD, et al: Direct measurement of change in muscle glycogen concentration after a mixed meal in normal subjects. *Am J Physiol* 1993;265:E224–E229.

98. Beckmann N, Seelig J, Wick H: Analysis of glycogen storage disease by in vivo ^{13}C NMR: Comparison of normal volunteers with a patient. *Magn Reson Med* 1990;16:150–160.

99. Weiss RG, Bottomley PA, Harvey CJ, et al: Regional myocardial metabolism of high-energy phosphates during isometric exercise in patients with coronary artery disease. *N Engl J Med* 1990;323:1593–1600.

100. Blackledge MJ, Rajagopalan B, Oberhaensli RD, et al: Quantitative studies of human cardiac metabolism by ^{31}P rotating-frame NMR. *Proc Natl Acad Sci USA* 1987;84:4283–4287.

101. Menon RS, Hendrich K, Hu X, et al: ^{31}P NMR spectroscopy of the human heart at 4 T: Detection of substantially uncontaminated cardiac spectra and differentiation of subepicardium and subendocardium. *Magn Reson Med* 1992;26:368–376.

102. Hardy CJ, Bottomley PA, Rohling KW, et al: An NMR phased array for human cardiac ^{31}P spectroscopy. *Magn Reson Med* 1992;28:54–64.

103. Bottomley PA: MR spectroscopy of the human heart: The status and the challenges. *Radiology* 1994;191:593–612.

104. van Doddenburgh JO, Lekkerkerk C, van Echteld CJA: Saturation correction in human cardiac ^{31}P MR spectroscopy at 1.5 T. *NMR Biomed* 1994;7:218–224.

105. Yabe T, Mitsunami K, Okada M, et al: Detection of myocardial ischemia by ^{31}P magnetic resonance spectroscopy during handgrip exercise. *Circulation* 1994; 89:1709–1716.

106. Cox J, Menon DK, Sargentoni J, et al: Phosphorus-31 magnetic resonance spectroscopy of the human liver using chemical shift imaging techniques. *Hepatology* 1992;14:265–275.

107. Cox IJ, Coutts GA, Gadian DG, et al: Saturation effects in phosphorus-31 magnetic resonance spectra of the human liver. *Magn Reson Med* 1992;17:53–61.

108. Iles RA, Cox IJ, Bell JD, et al: [31]P magnetic resonance spectroscopy of the human paediatric liver. *NMR Biomed* 1990;3:90–94.

109. Oberhaensli R, Rajagopalan B, Galloway GJ, et al: Study of human liver disease with ^{31}P magnetic resonance spectroscopy. *Gut* 1990;31:463–467.

110. Angus PW, Dixon RM, Rajagopalan B, et al: A study of patients with alcoholic liver disease by ^{31}P nuclear magnetic resonance spectroscopy. *Clin Sci* 1990; 78:33–38.

111. Munakata T, Griffiths RD, Martin PA, et al: An *in vivo* ^{31}P MRS study of patients with liver cirrhosis: Progress towards a non-invasive assessment of disease severity. *NMR Biomed* 1993;6:168–172.

112. Menon DK, Harris M, Sargentoni J, et al: In vivo hepatic ^{31}P magnetic resonance spectroscopy in chronic alcohol abusers. *Gastroenterology* 1995;108:776–778.

113. Dagnelie PC, Menon DK, Cox IJ, et al: Effect of L-alanine infusion on ^{31}P nuclear magnetic resonance spectra of normal human liver: Towards biochemical pathology *in vivo*. *Clinical Science* 1992;83:183–190.

114. Rothman DL, Magnusson I, Katz LD, et al: Quantitation of hepatic glycogenolysis and gluconeogenesis in fasting humans with ^{13}C NMR. *Science* 1991; 254:573–576.

115. Taylor R, Magnusson I, Rothman DL, et al: Direct assessment of liver glycogen storage by ^{13}C nuclear magnetic resonance spectroscopy and regulation of glucose homeostasis after a mixed meal in normal subjects. *J Clin Invest* 1996;97: 126–132.

116. Hwang J-H, Perseghin G, Rothman DL, et al: Impaired net hepatic glycogen synthesis insulin-dependent diabetic subjects during mixed-meal ingestion. *J Clin Invest* 1995;95:783–787.

117. Dixon RM, Frahm J: Localised proton MR spectroscopy of the human kidney in vivo by means of short echo time STEAM sequences. *Magn Reson Med* 1994; 31:482–487.

118. Tweig DB, Meyerhoff DJ, Hubesch B, et al: Phosphorus-31 magnetic resonance spectroscopy in humans by spectroscopic imaging: Localised spectroscopy and metabolite imaging. *Magn Reson Med* 1989;12:291–305.

119. Passe TJ, Charles HC, Rajagopalan P, et al: Nuclear magnetic resonance spectroscopy: A review of neuropsychiatric applications. *Prog Neuropsychopharm Biol Psychiatry* 1995;19:541–563.

120. Moats R, Watson L, Shonk T, et al: Added value of automated clinical proton MR spectroscopy of the brain. *J Comp Assist Tomogr* 1995;19:480–491.

121. Frahm J, Bruhn H, Gyngell ML, et al: Localised proton NMR spectroscopy in different regions of the human brain in vivo: Relaxation times and concentrations of cerebral metabolites. *Magn Reson Med* 1989;11:47–63.

122. Saunders DE, Howe FA, van den Boogaart A, et al: Aging of the human adult brain: In vivo quantitation of metabolite content with proton magnetic resonance spectroscopy (abstr). *Book of Abstracts: Society of Magnetic Resonance.* Berkely, CA: Society of Magnetic Resonance, 1995, p. 1840.

123. Christiansen P, Toft P, Larsson HBW, et al: The concentration of *N*-acetyl aspartate, creatine plus phosphocreatine, and choline in different parts of the brain in adulthood and senium. *Magn Reson Imag* 1993;11:799–806.

124. Vigneron DB, Nelson SJ, Murphy-Boesch J, et al: Chemical shift imaging of human brain: Axial, sagittal and coronal ^{31}P metabolite images. *Radiology* 1990; 177:643–649.

125. Hugg JW, Matson GB, Tweig DB, et al: Phosphorus-31 MR spectroscopic imaging (MRSI) of normal and pathological human brains. *Magn Reson Imag* 1992;10:227–243.

126. Lara RS, Matson GB, Hugg JW, et al: Quantitation of in vivo phosphorus metabolites in human brain with magnetic resonance spectroscopic imaging (MRSI). *Magn Reson Imaging* 1993;11:273–278.

127. McNamara R, Arias-Mendoza F, Brown TR: Investigation of broad resonances in ^{31}P NMR spectra of the human brain *in vivo*. *NMR Biomed* 1994;7:237–242.

128. Moseley ME, Butts K, Yenari MA, et al: Clinical aspects of DWI. *NMR Biomed* 1995;8:387–396.

129. Symon L, Pasztor E, Branston NM: The distribution and density of reduced cerebral blood flow following acute middle cerebral artery occlusion: An experimental study by the technique of hydrogen clearance in baboons. *Stroke* 1974; 5:355–364.

130. Prichard JW: The ischemic penumbra in stroke: Prospects for analysis by nuclear magnetic resonance spectroscopy. In Waxman SG (ed): *Molecular and Cellular Approaches to the Treatment of Neurological Disease.* New York: Raven Press, 1993, pp. 153–174.

131. Richards TL, Keniry MA, Weinstein PR, et al: Measurement of lactate accumulation by *in vivo* proton NMR spectroscopy during global ischemia in rats. *Magn Reson Med* 1987;5:353–357.

132. van der Toorn A, Verheul HB, van der Sprenkel JWB, et al: Focal ischemia in cat brain assessed with localized proton MR spectroscopy. *Magn Reson Med* 1994;32:685–691.

133. Duijn JH, Matson GB, Maudsley AA, et al: Human brain infarction: Proton MR spectroscopy. *Radiology* 1992;183:711–718.

134. Graham GD, Blamire AM, Howseman AM, et al: Proton magnetic resonance spectroscopy of cerebral lactate and other metabolites in stroke patients. *Stroke* 1992;23:333–340.

135. Saunders DE, Howe FA, van den Boogaart A, et al: Continuing ischemic damage after acute middle cerebral artery infarction in humans demonstrated by short-echo proton spectroscopy. *Stroke* 1995;26:1007–1013.

136. Mathews VP, Barker PB, Blackband SJ, et al: Cerebral metabolites in patients with acute and sub-acute strokes: Concentrations determined by quantitative proton MR spectroscopy. *Am J Roent* 1995;165:633–638.

137. Barker PB, Gillard JH, van Zijl PC, et al: Acute stroke: Evaluation with serial proton spectroscopic imaging. *Radiology* 1994;192:723–732.

138. van der Grond J, Balm R, Kappelle LJ, et al: Cerebral metabolism of patients with stenosis or occlusion of the internal carotid artery: A ^{1}H-MR spectroscopic imaging study. *Stroke* 1995;26:822–828.

139. Hetherington HP, Pan JW, Mason GF, et al: 2-D ^{1}H spectroscopic imaging of the human brain at 4.1 T. *Magn Reson Med* 1994;32:530–534.

140. Graham GD, Blamire AM, Rothman DL, et al: Early temporal variation of cerebral metabolites after human stroke: A proton magnetic resonance imaging study. *Stroke* 1993;24:1891–1896.

141. Lanferman H, Kugel H, Heindel W, et al: Metabolic changes in acute and subacute cerebral infarctions: Findings at proton spectroscopic imaging. *Radiology* 1995;196:203–210.

142. Behar KL, Rothman DL, Spencer DD, et al: Analysis of macromolecule resonances in ^{1}H NMR spectra of human brain. *Magn Reson Med* 1994;32:294–302.

143. Hwang J-H, Graham GD, Behar KL, et al: Short echo proton magnetic resonance spectroscopic imaging of macromolecules and metabolite signal intensities in the human brain. *Magn Reson Med* 1996;35:633–639.

144. Saunders DE, Howe FA, van den Boogaart A: Discrimination of metabolite from lipid and macromolecule resonances in cerebral infarction in humans using short echo proton spectroscopy. *J Magn-Reson Image* 1997; in press.

145. Gideon P, Henriksen O: In vivo relaxation of *N*-acetyl aspartate, creatine plus phosphocreatine, and choline containing compounds during the course of brain infarction: A proton MRS study. *Magn Reson Imaging* 1992;10:983–988.

146. Blamire AM, Graham GD, Rothman DL, et al: Proton spectroscopy of human stroke: Assessment of transverse relaxation times and partial volume effects in single volume STEAM MRS. *Magn Reson Imaging* 1994;12:1227–1235.

147. Levine SR, Helpern JA, Welch KM, et al: Human focal cerebral ischemia: Evaluation of brain pH and energy metabolism with ^{31}P NMR spectroscopy. *Radiology* 1992;185:537–544.

148. Helpern JA, Vande Linde AM, Welch KM, et al: Acute elevation and recovery of intracellular [Mg^{2+}] following cerebral ischemia. *Neurology* 1993;43:1577–1581.

149. Gyulai L, Schnall M, McLaughlin AC, et al: Simultaneous ^{31}P- and ^{1}H-nuclear magnetic resonance studies of hypoxia and ischemia in the cat brain. *J Cereb Blood Flow Metab* 1987;7:543–551.

150. Bottomley PA, Drayer BP, Smith LS: Chronic adult cerebral infarction studied by phosphorus NMR spectroscopy. *Radiology* 1986;160:763–766.

151. Hugg JW, Duijn JH, Matson GB, et al: Elevated lactate and alkalosis in chronic human brain infarction observed by ^{1}H and ^{31}P MR spectroscopic imaging. *J Cereb Blood Flow Metab* 1992;12:734–744.

152. Rothman DL, Howseman AM, Graham DG, et al: Localised proton NMR observation of [3-^{13}C]lactate in stroke after [1-^{13}C]glucose infusion. *Magn Reson Med* 1991;21:302–307.

153. Hope PL, Costello AM, Cady EB, et al: Cerebral energy metabolism studied with phosphorus NMR spectroscopy in normal and birth-asphyxiated infants. *Lancet* 1984;2(8399):366–270.

154. Azzopardi D, Wyatt JS, Cady EB, et al: Prognosis of new-born infants with hypoxic-ischemic brain injury assessed by phosphorus magnetic resonance spectroscopy. *Pediatric Res* 1989;25:445–451.

155. Cady EB, Lorek A, Penrice J, et al: ^{1}H magnetic resonance spectroscopy of the brains of normal infants and after perinatal hypoxia-ischemia. *Magnetic Resonance Materials in Physics, Biology and Medicine* 1994;2:353–355.

156. de Stefano N, Matthews PM, Arnold DL: Reversible decreases in *N*-acetylaspartate after acute brain injury. *Magn Reson Med* 1995;34:721–727.

157. Bottomley PA, Hardy CJ, Cousins JP, et al: AIDS dementia complex: Brain high-energy phosphate metabolite deficits. *Radiology* 1990;176:407–411.

158. Menon DK, Baudouin CJ, Tomlinson D, et al: Proton MR spectroscopy and imaging of the brain in AIDS: Evidence of neuronal loss in regions that appear normal with imaging. *J Comp Assist Tomogr* 1990;14:882–885.

159. Barker PB, Lee RR, McArthur JC: AIDS dementia complex: Evaluation with proton MR spectroscopic imaging. *Radiology* 1995;195:58–64.

160. Chong WK, Paley M, Wilkinson ID, et al: Localized cerebral proton MR spectroscopy in HIV infection and AIDS. *Am J Neurorad* 1994;15:21–25.

161. McConnell JR, Swindells S, Ong CS, et al: Prospective utility of cerebral proton magnetic resonance spectroscopy in monitoring HIV infection and its associated neurological impairment. *AIDS Res Hum Retroviruses* 1994;10:977–982.

162. Vion-Dury J, Confort-Gouny S, Nicoli F, et al: Localized brain proton MRS metabolic patterns in HIV-related encephalopathies. *Compt Rend Acad Sci - Serie Iii* 1994;317:833–840.

163. Wilkinson ID, Paley M, Chong WK, et al: Proton spectroscopy in HIV infection: Relaxation times of cerebral metabolites. *Magn Reson Imaging* 1994;12:951–957.

164. Lopez-Villegas D, Lenkinski RE, Frank I: Biochemical changes in the frontal lobe of HIV infected individuals without AIDS dementia complex detected by magnetic resonance spectroscopy (abstr). *Book of Abstracts: International Society of Magnetic Resonance in Medicine 1996.* Berkely, CA: International Society of Magnetic Resonance in Medicine, 1996, p. 309.

165. Chang L, Miller BL, McBride D, et al: Brain lesions in patients with AIDS: ^{1}H MR spectroscopy. *Radiology* 1995;195:525–531.

166. Taylor-Robinson SD, Sargentoni J, Mallalieu RJ, et al: Cerebral phosphorus-31 magnetic resonance spectroscopy in patients with chronic hepatic encephalopathy. *Hepatology* 1994;20:1173–1178.

167. Kreis R, Farrow N, Ross BD: Localised ^{1}H NMRS spectroscopy in patients with chronic hepatic encephalopathy: Analysis of changes in cerebral glutamine, choline and inositols. *NMR Biomed* 1991;4:109–116.

168. Ross BD, Jacobson S, Villamil F, et al: Subclinical hepatic encephalopathy: Proton MR spectroscopic abnormalities. *Radiology* 1994;193:457–463.

169. Danielsen ER, Ernst T, Geissler A, et al: Is encephalopathy a disturbance of cerebral osmolytes? (abstr). *Book of Abstracts: Society of Magnetic Resonance.* Berkely, CA: Society of Magnetic Resonance, 1995, p. 1839.

170. Häussinger D, Laubenberger J, vom Dahl S, et al: Proton magnetic resonance spectroscopy studies on human brain *myo*-inositol in hypo-osmolarity and hepatic encephalopathy. *Gastroenterology* 1994;107:1475–1480.

171. Arnold DL, Matthews PM, Francis G, et al: Proton magnetic resonance spectroscopy of human brain in vivo in the evaluation of multiple sclerosis: Assessment of the load of the disease. *Magn Reson Med* 1990;14:154–159.

172. Miller DH, Austin SJ, Connelly A, et al: Proton magnetic resonance spectroscopy of an acute and chronic lesion in multiple sclerosis. *Lancet* 1991; 337:58–59.

173. Bruhn H, Frahm J, Merboldt K-D, et al: Multiple sclerosis in children: Cerebral metabolic alterations monitored by localised proton magnetic resonance spectroscopy in vivo. *Ann Neurol* 1992;32:140–150.

174. Davie CA, Hawkins CP, Barker GJ, et al: Serial proton magnetic resonance spectroscopy in acute multiple sclerosis lesions. *Brain* 1994;117:49–58.

175. Husted CA, Goodin DS, Hugg JW, et al: Biochemical alterations in multiple sclerosis lesions and normal appearing white matter detected by in vivo ^{31}P and ^{1}H spectroscopic imaging. *Ann Neurol* 1994;36:157–165.

176. Roser W, Hagberg G, Mader I, et al: Proton MRS of gadolinium-enhancing MS plaques and metabolic changes in normal-appearing white matter. *Magn Reson Med* 1995;33:811–817.

177. Davie CA, Barker GJ, Webb S, et al: Persistent functional deficit in multiple sclerosis and autosomnal dominant cerebellar ataxia is associated with axon loss. *Brain* 1995;118:1583–1592.

178. Koopmans RA, Li DKB, Zhu G, et al: Magnetic resonance spectroscopy of multiple sclerosis: In vivo detection of myelin breakdown products. *Lancet* 1993; 341:631–632.

179. Husted CA, Matson GB, Adams DA, et al: In vivo detection of myelin phospholipids in multiple sclerosis with phosphorus magnetic resonance spectroscopic imaging. *Ann Neurol* 1994;36:239–241.

180. SE Davies, Newcombe J, Williams SR, et al: High resolution proton NMR spectroscopy of multiple sclerosis lesions. *J Neurochem* 1995;64:742–748.

181. Meyerhoff DJ, MacKay S, Constans JM, et al: Axonal injury and membrane alterations in Alzheimer's disease suggested by in vivo proton spectroscopic imaging. *Ann Neurol* 1994;36:40–47.

182. McClure RJ, Kanfer JN, Panchalingam K, et al: Magnetic resonance spectroscopy and its application to aging and Alzheimer's disease. *Neuroimaging Clin North Am* 1995;5:69–86. Review.

183. Miller BL, Moats R, Shonk T, et al: Alzheimer disease: Depiction of increased cerebral *myo*-Inositol with proton MR spectroscopy. *Radiology* 1993;187:433–437.

184. Shonk TK, Moats RA, Gifford P, et al: Probable Alzheimer disease: Diagnosis with proton MR spectroscopy. *Radiology* 1995;195:65–72.

185. Pettegrew JW, Panchalingam K, Klunk WE, et al: Alterations of cerebral metabolism in probable Alzheimer's disease a preliminary study. *Neurobiol Aging* 1994;15:117–132.

186. Murphy DG, Bottomley PA, Salerno JA, et al: An in vivo study of phosphorus and glucose metabolism in Alzheimer's disease using magnetic resonance spectroscopy and PET. *Arch Gen Psychiatry* 1993;50:341–349.

187. Cuenod CA, Kaplan DB, Michot JL, et al: Phospholipid abnormalities in early Alzheimer's disease: In vivo phosphorus-31 magnetic resonance spectroscopy. *Arch Neurol* 1995;52:89–94.

188. Hwang C, Haseler L, Tolaney S: Clinical impact of magnetic resonance spectroscopy on probable Alzheimer's disease and other common dementias (abstr). *Book of Abstracts: International Society of Magnetic Resonance in Medicine 1996.* Berkely, CA: International Society of Magnetic Resonance in Medicine, 1996, p. 930.

189. Breiter SN, Arroyo S, Mathews VP, et al: Proton MR spectroscopy in patients with seizure disorders. *Am J Neuroradiol* 1994;15:373–384.

190. Connelly A, Jackson GD, Duncan JS, et al: Magnetic resonance spectroscopy in temporal lobe epilepsy. *Neurology* 1994;44:1411–1417.

191. Cendes F, Andermann F, Dubeau F, et al: Proton magnetic resonance spectroscopic images and MRI volumetric studies for the lateralization of temporal lobe epilepsy. *Magn Reson Imaging* 1995;13:1187–1191.

192. Garcia PA, Laxer KD, Ng T: Application of spectroscopic imaging in epilepsy. *Magn Reson Imaging* 1995;13:1181–1185.

193. Petroff OA, Rothman DL, Behar KL, et al: Initial observations on effect of vigabatrin on in vivo ^{1}H spectroscopic measurements of gamma-aminobutyric acid, glutamate and glutamine in human brain. *Epilepsia* 1995;36:457–464.

194. Deicken RF, Calabrese G, Merrin EL, et al: Basal ganglia phosphorous metabolism in chronic schizophrenia. *Am J Psychiatry* 1995;152:126–129.

195. Pettegrew JW, Keshavan MS, Panchalingam K, et al: Alterations in brain high-energy phosphate and membrane phospholipid metabolism in first episode, drug-naive schizophrenics: A pilot study of the dorsal prefrontal cortex by in vivo phosphorus-31 nuclear magnetic resonance spectroscopy [see comments]. *Arch Gen Psychiatry* 1991;48:563–568.

196. Stanley JA, Williamson PC, Drost DJ, et al: An in vivo study of the prefrontal cortex of schizophrenic patients at different stages of illness via phosphorus magnetic resonance spectroscopy. *Arch Gen Psychiatry* 1995;52;399–406.

197. Calabrese G, Deicken RF, Fein G, et al: ^{31}Phosphorus magnetic resonance spectroscopy of the temporal lobes in schizophrenia. *Biol Psych* 1992;32:26–32.

198. Buckley PF, Moore C, Long H, et al: ^{1}H-magnetic resonance spectroscopy of the left temporal and frontal lobes in schizophrenia: Clinical, neurodevelopmental, and cognitive correlates. *Biol Psychiatry* 1994;36:792–800.

199. Nasrallah HA, Skinner TE, Schmalbrook P, et al: Proton magnetic resonance spectroscopy (^{1}H MRS) of the hippocampal formation in schizophrenia: A pilot study. *Br J Psychiatry* 1994;165:481–485.

200. Pettegrew JW, Keshavan MS, Minshew NJ: ^{31}P nuclear magnetic resonance spectroscopy: Neurodevelopment and schizophrenia. *Schizophr Bull* 1993;19:35–53.

201. Sibbit Jr WL, Haseler LJ, Griffey RH, et al: Analysis of cerebral structural changes in systemic lupus erythematosus by proton MR spectroscopy. *Am J Neuroradiol* 1994;15:923–928.

202. Brooks WM, Sibbit WL, Sabet A, et al: Spectroscopic imaging in neuropsychiatric systemic lupus erythmatosis (abstr). *Book of Abstracts: Society of Magnetic Resonance in Medicine 1995.* Berkely, CA: Society of Magnetic Resonance in Medicine, 1995, p. 58.

203. Kruse B, Barker PB, van Zijl PCM, et al: Multislice proton magnetic resonance spectroscopic imaging in X-linked adrenoleukodystrophy. *Ann Neurol* 1994;36: 596–608.

204. Bruhn H, Weber T, Thorwirth V, et al: In vivo monitoring of neuronal loss in Creutzfeld-Jacob disease by proton magnetic resonance spectroscopy. *Lancet* 1991;337:1610–1611.

205. Kreis R, Pietz J, Penzien J, et al: Identification and quantitation of phenylalanine in the brain of patients with phenylketonuria by means of localized in vivo ^{1}H magnetic-resonance spectroscopy. *J Magn Reson* 1995;B107:242–251.

206. Heindel W, Kugel H, Roth B: Non-invasive detection of increased glycine content by proton MR spectroscopy in the brains of two infants with nonketotic hyperglycinaemia. *Am J Neuroradiol* 1993;14:629–635.

207. Marks HG, Caro PA, Wang Z, et al: Use of computed tomography, magnetic resonance imaging, and localized ^{1}H magnetic resonance spectroscopy in Canavan's disease: A case report. *Ann Neurol* 1991;30:106–110.

208. Austin SJ, Connelly A, Gadian DG, et al: Localized ^{1}H NMRS spectroscopy in Canavan's disease: A report of two cases. *Magn Reson Med* 1991;19:439–445.

209. Denenkamp J: The choice of experimental models in cancer research: The key to ultimate success of failure? *NMR Biomed* 1992;5:234–237.

210. Robinson SJ, McCoy CL, Griffiths JR: Spectroscopic studies of animal tumor models. In DM Grant, RK Harris (eds): *An Encyclopedia of Nuclear Magnetic Resonance,* Vol. II, Chichester, England: J Wiley & Sons, 1996, pp. 828–833.

211. Daly PF, Cohen JS: Magnetic resonance spectroscopy of tumors and potential *in vivo* clinical applications: A review. *Canc Res* 1989;49:770–779.

212. Oberhaensli RD, Bore PJ, Rampling RP, et al: Biochemical investigations of human tumours in vivo with phosphorus-31 magnetic resonance spectroscopy. *Lancet* 1986;2(8497):8–11.

213. Glickson JD: Clinical NMR spectroscopy of tumors: Current status and future directions. *Invest Radiol* 1989;24:1011–1016.

214. Stubbs M (ed): Tumour assessment and response to therapy studied by magnetic resonance spectroscopy. Proceedings of the 17th L.H. Gray conference, Canterbury, England, 13–16 April 1992. *NMR Biomed* 1992; pp. 215–328.

215. Leach MO: Magnetic resonance spectroscopy applied to clinical oncology. *Technol Healthcare* 1994;2:235–246.

216. Leach M, le Moyec L, Podo F: MRS of tumours: Basic principles. In de Certaines JD, Bovee WMMJ, Podo F (eds): *Magnetic Resonance Spectroscopy in Biology and Medicine.* Oxford, England: Pergamon Press, 1992, pp. 295–344.

217. Warburg O: *The Metabolism of Tumours.* London, Arnold Constable, 1930.

218. Griffiths JR: Are cancer cells acidic? *Br J Cancer* 1991;64:425–427. Review.

219. Gillies RJ, Liu Z, Bhujwalla Z: [31]P—MRS measurements of extracellular pH of tumors using 3-aminopropylphosphonate. *Am J Physiol Cell* 1994;36:c195–c203.

220. Stubbs M, Rodrigues L, Howe FA, et al: Metabolic consequences of a reversed pH gradient in rat tumors. *Cancer Res* 1994;54:4011–4016.

221. Sostman HD, Charles HC, Rockwell S, et al: Soft-tissue sarcomas: Detection of metabolic heterogeneity with ^{31}P MR spectroscopy. *Radiology* 1990;176:837–843.

222. Brinkmann G, Melchert UH, Emde L, et al: In vivo ^{31}P MR-spectroscopy of focal hepatic lesions: Effectiveness of tumor detection in clinical practice and experimental studies of surface coil characteristics and localisation technique. *Invest Radiol* 1995;30:56–63.

223. Koutcher JA, Ballon D, Graham M, et al: ^{31}P NMR spectra of extremity sarcomas: Diversity of metabolic profiles and changes in response to chemotherapy. *Magn Reson Med* 1990;16:19–34.

224. Bryant DJ, Bydder GM, Case HA, et al: Use of phosphorus-31 MR spectroscopy to monitor response to chemotherapy in non-Hodgkin lymphoma. *J Comput Assist Tomog* 1988;12:770–774.

225. Smith SR, Martin PA, Davies JM, et al: The assessment of treatment response in non-Hodgkin's lymphoma by image guided ^{31}P magnetic resonance spectroscopy. *Br J Cancer* 1990;61:485–490.

226. Redmond OM, Stack JP, O'Connor NG, et al: ^{31}P MRS as an early prognostic indicator of patient response to chemotherapy. *Magn Reson Med* 1992;25:30–44.

227. Redmond OM, Bell E, Stack JP, et al: Tissue characterisation and assessment of preoperative chemotherapeutic response in musculoskeletal tumors by in vivo ^{31}P magnetic resonance spectroscopy. *Magn Reson Med* 1992;27:226–237.

228. Sijens PE, Wijrdeman HK, Moerland MA, et al: Human breast cancer in vivo: [1]H and ^{31}P MR spectroscopy at 1.5 T. *Radiology* 1988;169:615–620.

229. Twelves CJ, Porter DA, Lowry M, et al: Phosphorus-31 metabolism of post menopausal breast cancer studied *in vivo* by magnetic resonance spectroscopy. *Br J Cancer* 1994;69:1151–1156.

230. Glaholm J, Leach MO, Collins DJ, et al: *In vivo* [31]P magnetic resonance spectroscopy for monitoring treatment response in breast cancer. *Lancet* 1989;1: 1326–1327.

231. Kalra R, Wade KE, Hands L, et al: Phosphomonoester is associated with proliferation in human breast cancer: A ^{31}P MRS study. *Br J Cancer* 1993;67:1145–1153.

232. Smith TAD, Bush C, Jameson C, et al: Phospholipid metabolites, prognosis and proliferation in human breast carcinoma. *NMR Biomed* 1993;6:318–323.

233. Merchant TE, Meneses P, Gierke LW, et al: [31]P Magnetic resonance phospholipid profiles of neoplastic human breast tissues. *Br J Cancer* 1991;63: 693–698.

234. Lowry M, Porter DA, Twelves CJ, et al: Visibility of phospholipids in ^{31}P NMR spectra of human breast tumors *in vivo*. *NMR Biomed* 1992;5:37–42.

235. Twelves CJ, Lowry M, Porter DA, et al: Phosphorus-31 metabolism of human breast: An in vivo magnetic resonance spectroscopic study at 1.5 Tesla. *Br J Radiol* 1994;67:36–45.

236. Gogas H, Mansi J, Stubbs M, et al: [31]P spectroscopy of human breast tumors: A 3D chemical shift imaging study (abstr). Proceedings 87th Annual Meeting of AACR 1996;37:311. Abstract No. 1445.

237. Cox IJ, Sargentoni J, Calam J, et al: Four-dimensional phosphorus-31 chemical shift imaging of carcinoid metastases in the liver. *NMR Biomed* 1988;1:56–60.

238. Glazer GM, Smith SR, Chenevert TL, et al: Image localized ^{31}P magnetic resonance spectroscopy of the human liver. *NMR Biomed* 1989;1:184–189.

239. Francis IR, Chenevert TL, Gubin B, et al: Malignant hepatic tumors: [31]P MR spectroscopy with one-dimensional chemical shift imaging. *Radiology* 1991;180: 341–344.

240. Bell JD, Cox IJ, Sargentoni J, et al: A ^{31}P and ^{1}H NMRS investigation in vitro of normal and abnormal human liver. *Biochim Biophys Acta* 1993;1225:71–77.

241. Schilling A, Geweise B, Berger G, et al: Liver tumors: Follow-up with ^{31}P MR spectroscopy after local chemotherapy and chemoembolization. *Radiology* 1992;182:887–890.

242. Meyerhoff DJ, Karczmar GS, Valone F, et al: Hepatic cancers and their response to chemoembolization therapy: Quantitative image-guided ^{31}P magnetic resonance spectroscopy. *Invest Radiol* 1992;27:456–464.

243. Sostman HD, Prescott DM, Dewhirst MW, et al: MR imaging and spectroscopy for prognostic evaluation in soft-tissue sarcomas. *Radiology* 1994;190:269–275.

244. Dewhirst MW, Sostman HD, Leopold KA, et al: Soft-tissue sarcomas: MR imaging and MR spectroscopy for prognosis and therapy monitoring. *Radiology* 1990;174:847–853.

245. Prescott DM, Charles HC, Sostman HD, et al: Therapy monitoring in human and canine soft tissue sarcomas using magnetic resonance imaging and spectroscopy. *Int J Radiat Oncol Biol Phys* 1994;28:415–423.

246. Negendank WG, Padavic-Shaller KA, Li C-W, et al: Metabolic characterisation of non-Hodgkin's lymphomas *in vivo* with the use of proton-decoupled phosphorus magnetic resonance spectroscopy. *Cancer Res* 1995;55:3286–3294.

247. Ballinger JR, Scott KN, Scarborough M: [1]H spectroscopy of musculoskeletal tumors in humans (abstr). *Book of Abstracts: Society of Magnetic Resonance* 1995. Berkely, CA: Society of Magnetic Resonance, 1995, p. 1714.

248. Thomas MA, Narayan P, Kurhanewicz J, et al: [1]H MR spectroscopy of normal and malignant human prostates *in vivo*. *J Magn Reson* 1990;87:610–619.

249. Liney GP, Lowry M, Turnbull LW, et al: Metabolic mapping of the prostate using ^{1}H MR spectroscopy and imaging (abstr). *Book of Abstracts: Society of Magnetic Resonance 1995*. Berkely, CA: Society of Magnetic Resonance, 1995, p. 1987.

250. Kurhanewicz J, Nelson S, Moyher S, et al: High resolution mapping of choline and citrate in the normal and pathologic human prostate (abstr). *Book of Abstracts: Society of Magnetic Resonance 1995*. Berkely, CA: Society of Magnetic Resonance, 1995, p. 543.

251. Narayan P, Kurhanewicz J: Magnetic resonance spectroscopy in prostate diseases: Diagnostic possibilities and future development. *Prostate* 1992;4(suppl):43–50.

252. Heindel W, Bunke J, Glathe S, et al: Combined [1]H-MR imaging and localized ^{31}P-spectroscopy of intracranial tumors in 43 patients. *J Comput Assist Tomog* 1988;12:907–916.

253. Arnold DL, Shoubridge EA, Villemure J-G, et al: Proton and phosphorus magnetic resonance spectroscopy of human astrocytomas *in vivo:* Preliminary observations on tumor grading. *NMR Biomed* 1990;3:184–189.

254. Tweig DB, Meyerhoff DJ, Hubesch, et al: Phosphorus-31 magnetic resonance spectroscopy in humans by spectroscopic imaging: Localized spectroscopy and metabolite imaging. *Magn Reson Med* 1989;12:291–305.

255. Hubesch B, Sappey-Marinier D, Roth K, et al: [31]P MR spectroscopy of normal human brain and brain tumors. *Radiology* 1990;174:401–409.

256. Hugg JW, Matson GB, Tweig DB, et al: Phosphorus-31 MR spectroscopic imaging (MRSI) of normal and pathological human brains. *Magn Reson Imaging* 1992;10:227–243.

257. Segebarth CM, Baleriaux DF, de Beer R, et al: [1]H image-guided localized ^{31}P MRS spectroscopy of human brain: Quantitative analysis of ^{31}P MR spectra measured on volunteers and on intracranial tumor patients. *Magn Reson Med* 1989;11:349–366.

258. Taylor JS, Vigneron DB, Murphy-Boesch J, et al: Free magnesium levels in normal human brain and brain tumors: [31]P chemical-shift imaging measurements at 1.5 T. *Proc Natl Acad Sci USA* 1991;88:6810–6814.

259. Ross BD, Tropp J, Derby KA, et al: Metabolic response of glioblastoma to adoptive immunotherapy: Detection by phosphorus MR spectroscopy. *J Comput Assist Tomogr* 1989;13:189–193.

260. Segebarth CM, Balériaux DF, Arnold DL, et al: MR image-guided ^{31}P MR spectroscopy in the evaluation of brain tumor treatment. *Radiology* 1987;165:215–219.

261. Arnold DL, Shoubridge EA, Emrich J, et al: Early metabolic changes following chemotherapy of human gliomas in vivo demonstrated by phosphorus magnetic resonance spectroscopy. *Invest Radiol* 1989;24:958–961.

262. Demaerel P, Johannik K, van Hecke P, et al: Localized ^{1}H NMR spectroscopy in fifty cases of newly diagnosed intracranial tumors. *Comput Assist Tomogr* 1991;15: 67–76.

263. Bruhn H, Michaelis T, Merboldt KD, et al: On the interpretation of proton NMR spectra from brain tumours *in vivo* and *in vitro*. *NMR Biomed* 1992;5:253–258.

264. Frahm J, Bruhn H, Hänicke W, et al: Localised proton NMR spectroscopy of brain tumors using short echo time STEAM sequences. *J Comput Assist Tomogr* 1991;15: 915–922.

265. Kugel H, Heindel W, Ernestus R-I, et al: Human brain tumors: Spectral patterns detected with localized ^{1}H MR spectroscopy. *Radiology* 1992;183:701–709.

266. Bruhn H, Frahm J, Gyngell ML, et al: Non-invasive differentiation of tumors with use of localized ^{1}H MR spectroscopy in vivo: Initial experience in patients with cerebral tumors. *Radiology* 1989;172:541–548.

267. Manton DJ, Lowry M, Blackband SJ, et al: Determination of proton metabolite concentrations and relaxation parameters in normal human brain and intracranial tumours. *NMR Biomed* 1995;8:104–112.

268. Howe FA, McLean MA, Saunders DE, et al: Metabolite nulling in short echo time *in vivo* ^{1}H MRS of brain tumors (abstr). *Book of Abstracts: Society of Magnetic Resonance 1995*. Berkely, CA: Society of Magnetic Resonance, 1995, p. 1705.

269. Sijens PE, Knopp MV, Brunetti A, et al: ^{1}H MRS spectroscopy in patients with metastatic brain tumors: A multicentre study. *Magn Reson Med* 1995;33:818–826.

270. Gill SS, Thomas GTT, van Bruggen N, et al: Proton spectroscopy of intracranial tumours: In vivo and in vitro studies. *J Comput Assist Tomogr* 1990;14:497–504.

271. Peeling J, Sutherland G: High-resolution ^{1}H NMR spectroscopy studies of extracts of human cerebral neoplasms. *Magn Reson Med* 1992;24:123–136.

272. Kinoshita Y, Kajiwara H, Yokota A, et al: Proton magnetic resonance spectroscopy of brain tumors: An in vitro study. *Neurosurgery* 1994;35:606–614.

273. Florian CL, Preece NE, Bhakoo KK, et al: Characteristic metabolic profiles revealed by ^{1}H NMR spectroscopy for three types of human brain and nervous system tumours. *NMR Biomed* 1995;8:253–264.

274. Florian CL, Preece NE, Bhakoo KK, et al: Cell type-specific fingerprinting of meningioma and meningeal cells by proton nuclear magnetic resonance spectroscopy. *Cancer Res* 1995;55:420–427.

275. Usenius JP, Vainio P, Hernesniemi J, et al: Choline-containing compounds in human astrocytomas studied by ^{1}H NMR spectroscopy in vivo and in vitro. *J Neurochem* 1994;63:1538–1543.

276. Ott D, Hennig J, Ernst T: Human brain tumors: Assessment with in vivo proton MR spectroscopy. *Radiology* 1993;186:745–752.

277. Kuesel AC, Sutherland GR, Halliday W, et al: ^{1}H MRS of high grade astrocytomas: Mobile lipid accumulation in necrotic tissue. *NMR Biomed* 1994;7: 149–155.

278. Martínez-Pérez I, Moreno A, Barba I, et al: Large lipid droplets observed by electron microscopy in six human brain tumors with lipid ^{1}H MRS *in vivo* pattern (abstr). *Book of Abstracts: International Society of Magnetic Resonance 1996*. Berkely, CA: International Society of Magnetic Resonance, 1996, p. 976.

279. Rémy C, Grand S, Laï ES, et al: ^{1}H MRS of human brain abscesses *in vivo* and *in vitro*. *Magn Reson Med* 1995;34:508–514.

280. Usenius JPR, Kauppinen RA, Vainio PA, et al: *J Comput Assist Tomogr* 1994;18:705–713.
281. López-Villegas D, Lenkinski RE, Werhli SL, et al: Lactate production by human monocytes/macrophages determined by proton MR spectroscopy. *Magn Reson Med* 1995;34:32–38.
282. Alger JR, Frank JA, Bizzi A, et al: Metabolism of human gliomas: Assessment with ^{1}H MR spectroscopy and ^{18}F fluorodeoxyglucose PET. *Radiology* 1990;177:633–641.
283. Fulham MJ, Bizzi A, Dietz MJ, et al: Mapping of brain tumor metabolites with proton spectroscopic imaging: Clinical relevance. *Radiology* 1992;185:675–686.
284. Chang L, Buchtal SD, Miller BL, et al: *In vivo* ^{1}H MRS and *in vitro* biochemical correlation of heterogeneous brain tumors (abstr). *Book of Abstracts: Society of Magnetic Resonance 1994.* Berkely, CA: Society of Magnetic Resonance, 1994, p. 1295.
285. Vigneron DB, Wald LL, Day M, et al: 3D ^{1}H MR spectroscopic imaging of brain tumors: Correlations with histology (abstr). *Book of Abstracts: International Society of Magnetic Resonance 1996.* Berkely, CA: International Society of Magnetic Resonance, 1996, p. 975.
286. Herholz K, Heindel W, Luyten PR, et al: In vivo imaging of glucose consumption and lactate concentration in human gliomas. *Ann Neurol* 1992;32:319–327.
287. Houkin K, Kamada K, Sawamura Y, et al: Proton magnetic resonance spectroscopy (^{1}H-MRS) for the evaluation of treatment of brain tumours. *Neuroradiology* 1995;37:99–103.
288. Jungling FD, Wakhloo AK, Hennig J: In vivo proton spectroscopy of meningioma after preoperative embolization (published erratum appears in *Magn Reson Med* 1993;30:649). *Magn Reson Med* 1993;30:155–160.
289. Heesters MA, Kamman RL, Mooyaart El, et al: Localised proton spectroscopy of inoperable brain gliomas: Response to radiation therapy. *J Neurooncol* 1993;17:27–35.
290. Bizzi A, Movsas B, Tedeschi G, et al: Response of non-Hodgkin lymphoma to radiation therapy: Early and long term assessment with ^{1}H MR spectroscopic imaging. *Radiology* 1995;194:271–276.
291. Usenius T, Usenius JP, Tenhunen M, et al: Radiation-induced changes in human brain metabolites as studied by ^{1}H nuclear magnetic resonance spectroscopy in vivo. *Int J Radiat Oncol Biol Phys* 1995;33:719–724.
292. Szigety SK, Allen PS, Huyser-Wierenga D, et al: The effect of radiation on normal human CNS as detected by NMR spectroscopy. *Int J Radiat Oncol Biol Phys* 1993;25:695–701.
293. Hagberg G, Burlina AP, Mader I, et al: *In vivo* proton MR spectroscopy of human gliomas: Definition of metabolic coordinates for multidimensional classification. *Magn Reson Med* 1995;34:242–252.
294. Preul MC, Caramanos Z, Collins DL, et al: Accurate, non-invasive diagnosis of human brain tumors by using proton magnetic resonance spectroscopy. *Nature Med* 1996;2:323–325.
295. Findlay MP, Leach MO: In vivo monitoring of fluoropyrimidine metabolites: Magnetic resonance spectroscopy in the evaluation of 5-fluorouracil. *Anticancer Drugs* 1994;5:260–280. Review.
296. Schlemmer HP, Bachert P, Semmler W, et al: Drug monitoring of 5-fluorouracil: In vivo ^{19}F NMR study during 5-FU chemotherapy in patients with metastases of colorectal adenocarcinoma. *Magn Reson Imaging* 1994;12:497–511.

297. Presant CA, Wolf W, Waluch V, et al: Association of intratumoral pharmacokinetics of fluorouracil with clinical response. *Lancet* 1994;343:1184–1187.
298. Li C-W, Negendank WG, Padavic-Shaller KA, et al: Quantitation of 5-fluorouracil catabolism in human liver in vivo by three dimensional localized ^{19}F magnetic resonance spectroscopy. *Clin Cancer Res* 1996;2:339–345.
299. Price P, Griffiths J: Tumor pharmacokinetics?—We do need to know. *Lancet* 1994;343:1174–1175.
300. Garwood M, Ke Y: Symmetric pulses to induce arbitrary flip angles with compensation for RF inhomogeneity and resonance offsets. *J Magn Reson* 1991; 511–525.
301. Majors A, Xue M, Ng TC, et al: Short echo time proton spectroscopy of human brain using a gradient head coil. *Magn Reson Imaging* 1992;10:649–654.
302. Nicolay K, van der Toorn A, Dijkhuizen RM: In vivo diffusion spectroscopy: An overview. *NMR Biomed* 1995;8:365–374.
303. Posse S, Cuenod CA, le Bihan D: Human brain: Proton diffusion MR spectroscopy. *Radiology* 1993;188:719–725.
304. Henriksen O, Karnick ES, Rosenbaum S: Apparent diffusion on metabolites in the human brain: A proton-MRS study (abstr). *Book of Abstracts: Society of Magnetic Resonance 1995.* Berkely, CA: Society of Magnetic Resonance, 1995, p. 1855.
305. Zhao M, Pipe JG, Bonnet J, et al: Early detection of treatment response by diffusion-weighted ^{1}H-NMR spectroscopy in a murine tumour *in vivo. Br J Cancer* 1996;73:61–64.
306. Prichard J, Rothman D, Novotny E, et al: Lactate rise detected by ^{1}H NMR in human visual cortex during physiologic stimulation. *Proc Natl Acad Sci USA* 1991;88:5829–5831.
307. Merboldt KD, Bruhn H, Hänicke W, et al: Decrease of glucose in the human visual cortex during photic stimulation. *Magn Reson Med* 1992;25:187–194.
308. Chen W, Novotny EJ, Zhu XH, et al: Localized ^{1}H NMR measurements of glucose consumption in the human brain during visual stimulation. *Proc Natl Acad Sci USA* 1993;90:9896–9900.
309. Sappey-Marinier D, Calabrese G, Fein G, et al: Effect of photic stimulation on human visual cortex lactate and phosphates using ^{1}H and ^{31}P magnetic resonance spectroscopy. *J Cereb Blood Flow Metab* 1992;12:584–592.
310. Bottomley PA, Hardy CJ, Roemer PB, et al: Proton-decoupled, Overhauser-enhanced, spatially localized carbon-13 spectroscopy in humans. *Magn Reson Med* 1989;12:348–363.
311. Heerschap A, Luyten PR, van der Heyden JI, et al: Broadband proton decoupled natural abundance ^{13}C NMR spectroscopy of humans at 1.5 T. *NMR Biomed* 1989;2:124–132.
312. Luyten PR, Bruntik G, Sloff FM, et al: Broadband proton decoupling in human ^{31}P NMR spectroscopy. *NMR Biomed* 1989;4:177–183.
313. Brown TR, Stoyanova R, Greenberg T, et al: NOE enhancements and T_1 relaxation times of phosphorylated metabolites in human calf muscle at 1.5 Tesla. *Magn Reson Med* 1995;33:417–421.
314. Cady EB: Quantitative combined phosphorus and proton PRESS of the brains of newborn human infants. *Magn Reson Med* 1995;33:557–563.
315. Yongbi NM, Payne GS, Leach MO: A gradient scheme suitable for localized shimming and *in vivo* ^{1}H/^{31}P STEAM and ISIS NMR spectroscopy. *Magn Res Med* 1994;32:768–772.

316. Gonen O, Hu J, Murphy-Boesch J, et al: Dual interleaved ^{1}H and proton-decoupled [31]P *in vivo* chemical shift imaging of human brain. *Magn Reson Med* 1994;32:104–109.

317. van Sluis R, Yongbi NM, Payne GS, et al: Simultaneous localized ^{1}H STEAM/^{31}P ISIS spectroscopy *in vivo*. *Magn Reson Med* 1996;35:465–470.

318. van den Boogaart A, Howe FA, Rodrigues LM, et al: *In vivo* ^{31}P MRS: Absolute concentrations, signal-to-noise and prior knowledge. *NMR Biomed* 1993;8: 87–93.

319. Maudsley AA, Lin E, Weiner MW: Spectroscopic imaging and display and analysis. *Magn Reson Imaging* 1992;10:471–485.

320. de Beer R, van den Boogaart A, van Ormondt D, et al: Application of time-domain fitting in the quantification of in vivo ^{1}H spectroscopic imaging data sets. *NMR Biomed* 1992;5:171–178.

321. Doyle TJ, Pathak R, Wolinsky JS, et al: Automated proton spectroscopic image processing. *J Magn Reson* 1995;B106:58–63.

322. Maxwell RJ, Howells SL, Peet AC, et al: Tumour classification using ^{1}H nuclear magnetic resonance spectroscopy, principle component analysis and a neural network. In Taylor M, Lisboa P (eds): *Techniques and Application of Neural Networks,* Ellis Horwood, 1993, pp. 64–75.

323. Capuani G, Miccheli A, Conti F: Principle component analysis as applied to NMR data. *Q Magn Res Biol Med* 1994;2:19–33.

324. Howells SL, Maxwell RJ, Griffiths JR: Classification of tumour ^{1}H NMR spectra by pattern recognition. *NMR Biomed* 1992;5:59–64.

325. Howells SL, Maxwell RJ, Howe FA, et al: Pattern recognition of ^{31}P magnetic resonance spectroscopy tumour spectra obtained *in vivo*. *NMR Biomed* 1993; 6:237–241.

326. Confort-Gouny S, Vion-Dury J, Nicoli F, et al: A multiparametric data analysis showing the potential of localized proton MR spectroscopy of the brain in the metabolic characterisation of neurological diseases. *J Neurol Sci* 1993;118: 123–133.

327. Griffiths JR, Maxwell RJ, Howells SL, et al: MRS studies of cancer. *Magnetic Resonance Materials in Physics, Biology and Medicine* 1994;2:1–5.

328. Leach MO, Arnold D, Brown TR, et al: International workshop on standardisation in clinical MRS measurements: Proceedings and recommendations. *Technol Healthcare* 1994;2:217–234.

BIBLIOGRAPHY AND REVIEW ARTICLES

NMR Basic Principles and Progress, Volume 26. In vivo Magnetic Resonance Spectroscopy I. Probeheads and radiofrequency analysis, spectrum analysis. Edited by Diehl P, Fluck E, Günther H, Kosfeld R and Seelig J. Berlin: Springer-Verlag, 1992.

NMR Basic Principles and Progress, Volume 27. In vivo Magnetic Resonance Spectroscopy II. Localisation and spectral editing. Edited by Diehl P, Fluck E, Günther H, Kosfeld R and Seelig J. Berlin: Springer-Verlag, 1992.

NMR Basic Principles and Progress, Volume 28. In vivo Magnetic Resonance Spectroscopy III. Potential and limitations. Edited by Diehl P, Fluck E, Günther H, Kosfeld R and Seelig J. Berlin: Springer-Verlag, 1992.

Nuclear Magnetic Resonance and Its Applications to Living Systems (2nd Edition). Gadian DG. Oxford: Clarendon Press, 1996.

Magnetic Resonance Spectroscopy in Biology and Medicine: Functional and pathological tissue characterisation. Edited by de Certaines JD, Bovee WMMJ, Podo F. Oxford: Pergamon Press, 1992.

Clinical Magnetic Resonance Imaging. Andrew ER, Bydder G, Griffiths J, Iles R, Styles P. Chichester: John Wiley, 1990.

Modern NMR Spectroscopy: A guide for chemists. Sanders JKM and Hunter BK. Oxford: Oxford University Press, 1988.

Magnetic resonance spectroscopy by Meyerhoff DJ, MacKay S, Baker A, Schaefer S and Weiner MW in Magnetic Resonance Imaging of the Body, 2nd Ed. Edited by Higgins CB, Hricak M and Helms CA. New York: Raven Press, 1992; 287–312.

Spectroscopy by Matson GB and Weiner MW in Magnetic Resonance Imaging, Volume 1, 2nd Ed. St. Louis: Mosby-Year Book, 1992; 438–478.

Human in vivo NMR spectroscopy in diagnostic medicine: Clinical tool or research probe? Bottomley, PA: *Radiology* 1989;170:1–15.

Proton spectroscopy in vivo: Howe FA, Maxwell RJ, Saunders DE, Brown MM and Griffiths JR. *Magn Reson Q* 1993; 9:31–59.

Localised NMR spectroscopy in vivo: Problems, strategies and application. Proceedings of the workshop held at the Max Planck Institut für Biophysikalische Chemie in Göttingen, 29–30th June, 1989. Guest editor, J. Frahm. NMR in Biomedicine 1989; Vol. 2, No. 5/6.

Proton spectroscopy in clinical medicine. Proceedings of the mini-categorical course from the 9th annual scientific meeting of the Society of Magnetic Resonance in Medicine in New York, 18–24th August, 1990. Guest editor, BD Ross. NMR in Biomedicine Vol. 4, No. 2.

CHAPTER THREE

IMAGE ARTIFACTS

Joseph P. Whalen and John A. Markisz

The word artifact first appeared in the 1821 edition of the Merriam-Webster Dictionary. The most often used definition refers to something created by humans, usually for use or an activity. The second, less common meaning is a product of an artificial activity. Image artifacts are associated with every radiologic imaging modality. Motion blurring on plain films, metallic star artifacts or detector-imbalance ring artifacts on CT scans, and refraction image distortion on ultrasound studies are but a few well-documented examples in radiology. In terms of the magnetic resonance (MR) image, an artifact is an abnormal area of signal within the image that does not normally arise from patient anatomy or pathology. It is important to recognize artifacts for two important reasons: to eliminate diagnostic error, so that the artifact does not hide a pathologic condition, or is not mistaken for one; and because recognition of certain artifacts can indicate particular problems within the system itself so that proper service or repair can be started before major problems occur.

In general, all artifacts fall into four categories: (1) those associated with the patient; (2) those associated with physiology; (3) those inherent in the principles of magentic resonance imaging (MRI); and (4) those associated with the hardware and software of the imaging system. As newer pulse sequences continue to be developed, new artifacts can be produced, and known artifacts can result from multiple causes, making the precise classification of these eccentricities more difficult.

Artifacts associated with the patient are normally due to random movement or metallic objects (either external or internal) that distort the image, and physiological artifacts are produced by breathing, cardiac or peristaltic motion, and blood flow. The imaging system produces artifacts that result either from the basic physical principles of MRI (chemical shift and flow) or from instrumental factors (radio frequency [RF], gradients, shims, or computer hardware). Although the most obvious artifacts can often be attributed to the patient, some suggestion of instrumental artifacts is present in almost all imaging situations (depending upon the pulse sequences and stability of the hardware). Most such artifacts manifest themselves in the direction of the phase-encoding gradients by combinations of rings, streaks, and ghosting that could either be patient or instrument based. Table 3–1 at the end of this chapter lists the various types of artifacts observed, the methods of determining the type of artifact encountered, and ways of eliminating artifacts. The development of a practical quality-assurance program for monitoring system performance and for efficiently using the manufacturer's field service and engineering staff is strongly dependent on the recognition and characterization of the image artifacts listed in this table.

TYPES OF ARTIFACTS

Artifacts Resulting From the Patient

Patient-related artifacts are almost always caused either by something the patient is doing (usually moving) or by something out of the ordinary that the patient has inside or outside of the body. The most common patient-caused artifact is motion during data acquisition. Motion artifacts are always propagated in the phase-encoding direction. Random patient motion appears as a blurring of the image (Fig. 3–1).

Random patient movements can be minimized by either sedation or patient education and cooperation. Patients who are unable to cooperate by lying still during the examination require sedation. These patients include those suffering from dementia, motion disorders, or extreme claustrophobia. Explaining the procedure to the patient and emphasizing the necessity to lie still is usually sufficient to ensure cooperation. Children or nervous patients may require additional reassurance by having someone in the room with them during the examination. If motion persists, taping or using Velcro straps to hold the body part secure partially immobilizes the area of interest and serves as a reminder to the patient to remain still.

Nonbiologic materials in or on the patient cause different types of artifacts, depending upon the composition of the specific object. These items can be classified as either metallic or nonmetallic. Some nonmetallic materials have mobile hydrogen atoms associated with them, others do not. If they do not have mobile hydrogen atoms, the objects will simply produce a signal void (no signal). Should there be a large difference in magnetic susceptibilities, such as with air and water, a susceptibility artifact will be produced. This will appear as a rim of high signal around the edge of the region of signal void (Fig. 3–2). If the material does have mobile protons, it will produce the appropriate signal for the type of material that it is.

Metallic objects can be categorized as nonmagnetic, slightly magnetic (or magnetizable), or highly magnetic. Nonmagnetic objects carried or worn outside of the body will not affect the scan. Nonmagnetic objects inside the body (prostheses, surgical clips, sutures, valves, plates, etc) will simply produce a region devoid of signal corresponding to the object, but they will not distort the image outside this region.

Objects that are slightly magnetic or magnetizable will cause a small region of magnetic distortion around the device. Note that patients can be scanned even if known magnetic implants are present, since valuable diagnostic information can often be obtained in regions not obscured by the foreign body. Such implants often produce a region of greatly enhanced signal around the periphery of the object. Since the most intense pixel in an image is part of the algorithm for allocating the gray scale, the effect of having a metallic object that produces an increase in regional signal intensity (often by a factor of 10 or more) is to severely limit the available gray scale for the rest of the image, producing a so-called washed-out image. Most implanted devices will experience minimal interactions with the magnetic field. We have not found any RF, gradient, or any other potential side effect to be at all significant with any prosthetic device. Because of possible effects of the magnetic fields on physiologic pacing devices or cerebral aneurysm clips, however, patients who have these devices are not scanned.

In those situations where the metallic object is highly magnetic, there will be significant distortion of the images, sometimes sufficient to render the study completely nondiagnostic

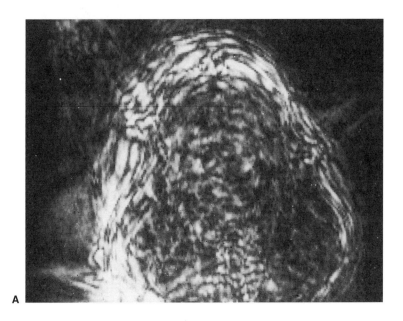

A

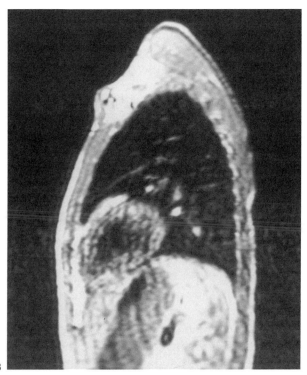

B

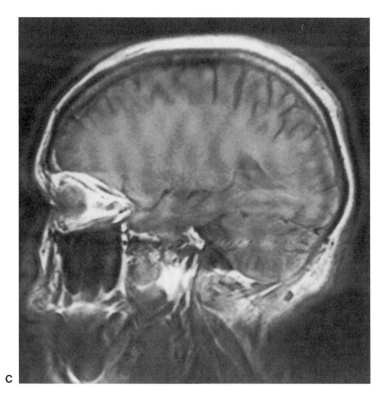

C

Figure 3–1. Various degrees of motion will produce different grades of artifact: **A.** Inability of patient to cooperate at all leads to a completely uninterpretable axial image of the head. **B.** Slight motion during the scan significantly decreases the resolution of this sagittal image of the chest. **C.** This patient having a head scan was sneezing during the sagittal acquisition.

(Fig. 3–3). More often, however, much useful information can be obtained even though part of the anatomy cannot be evaluated because of the metallic artifact.

Personal articles such as dentures, keys, jewelry, hair pins, snaps, and belt buckles will produce artifacts that may either cause local signal enhancement at the periphery of the object or effectively (if magnetic) distort part or all of the image (Fig. 3–4). Careful attention by the interviewing staff, patient education through appropriate interviews and questionnaires, and alert technologists can minimize these artifacts.

Of considerable interest and of increasing importance is the fact that new types of highly colored makeup (especially certain types of mascara containing ferromagnetic compounds) will cause magnetic artifacts (Fig. 3–5). Tattoos contain dyes that

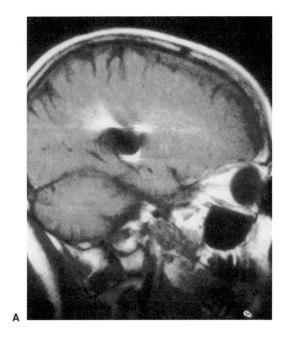

A

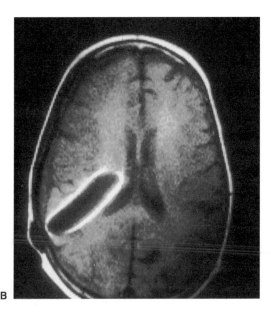

B

Figure 3–2. **A.** Sagittal and **B.** axial images through the head of a patient with a ventricular shunt. Note the high-intensity signal artifact at the edges of the shunt due to susceptibility effects.

have magnetic materials in them. The artifacts that they produce will be relatively small and on the surface of the skin. Technologists observing that a patient has a tattoo should make a note of it so that the radiologist will be aware of the source of the abnormality. More serious than the artifact problem is the fact that, especially with the new fast-scan techniques, tattooed regions may heat up because of excessive RF deposition in the metals and cause discomfort to the patient. Patients should be made aware of this fact, and sufficient time should be allowed for energy radiation between scans. In other words, these patients should be scanned more slowly than normal to ensure that no heating occurs. Artifacts must always be considered as a possible explanation when image abnormalities are observed.

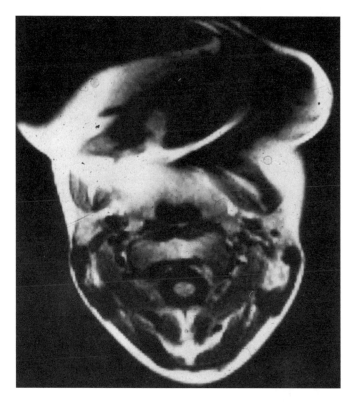

Figure 3–3. The anterior portion of inferior head is obscured by severe magnetic distortion from a nonremovable dental bridge. Note that the posterior portion, including the spinal cord, is well visualized.

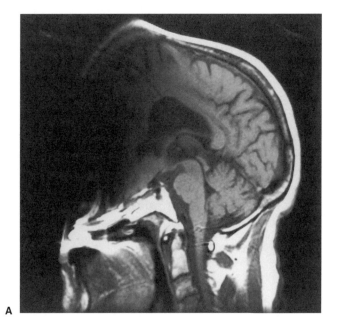

A

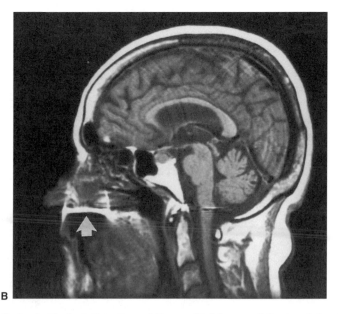

B

Figure 3–4. **A.** Marked distortion of the sagittal image of the head due to the patient's failure to remove a hair pin. **B.** Image after the hair pin was removed. Note that the metallic artifact due to a dental prosthesis (arrow) is still present.

Physiology-Related Artifacts

Physiologic motions are generally a more common source of artifacts than are voluntary movements. Physiologic motions are observed more in the body than in the head, since the only physiologic motions to produce artifacts in the head are blood flow and CSF pulsation. Artifacts due to a continuous or periodic motion, as occurs with respiration, cardiac pulsation, or blood flow, can be recognized as image blurring with ringed structures around and through the image in the direction of the phase-encoding gradient direction (Fig. 3–6). These ringed signals appear in "space," the empty area in the bore of the magnet where there is no tissue, as if they were ghosts; this type of artifact is referred to as **ghosting.**

Respiratory motion blurs image details and produces displaced signal artifacts in images of the chest, the abdomen, and sometimes the pelvis as well. These artifacts will be projected in

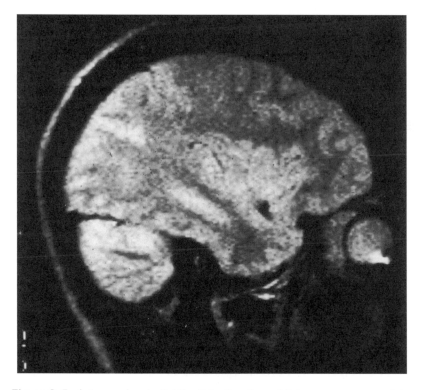

Figure 3–5. Intense signal slightly distorting the orbit from mascara containing ferromagnetic compounds.

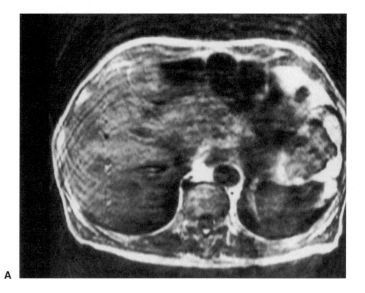

A

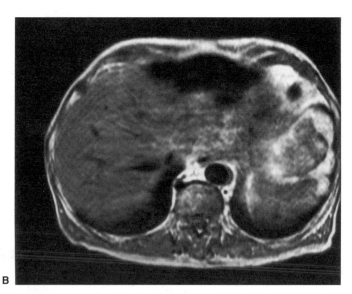

B

Figure 3–6. *A.* Proton-density axial image through the abdomen, demonstrating a ghosting artifact ringing through and above the image, with significant loss of motion and uninterpretable T_2-weighted image. ***B.*** Same section as in **A** except that respiratory compensation was applied, allowing multiple lesions to be observed in the liver on the T_2-weighted image *(C).*

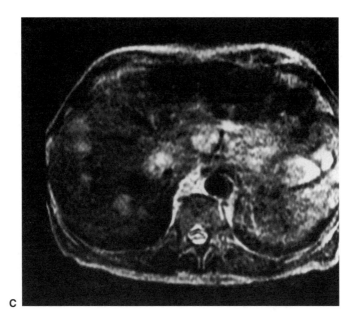

c

the direction of the phase-encoding direction, and usually, as long as they are recognized, will not interfere with image interpretation. On occasion, there will be a problem, which can usually be solved by repeating the sequence after switching the phase-encoding direction. More subtle motion effects are produced by the peristaltic activity of the bowel. Peristalsis is rarely sufficient to produce ghosting, so only a subtle blurring in the region of the bowel is observed, without effect on other structures. Administration of glucagon has been utilized to stop peristalsis with questionable success; however, fast-scanning techniques are now capable of greatly reducing bowel-motion effects.

Cardiac motion blurs image details in the neighborhood of the heart and produces a characteristic column of displaced signal equal to the width of the heart, observed in the phase-encoding direction. ECG-gating techniques usually improve images of the heart quite satisfactorily, and new fast-scanning techniques capture cardiac images so rapidly that they are not degraded by motion (Fig. 3–7).

The production of artifacts in an image due to flow is a complex subject, since many different factors can contribute to the appearance of flowing blood. It is impossible to eliminate most of these artifacts, so recognition of them is essential in order to make a proper diagnosis. The most usual appearance of flowing blood—no signal at all—can technically be considered

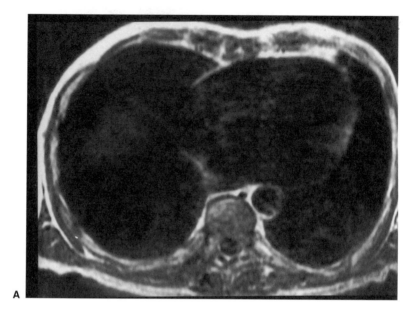

A

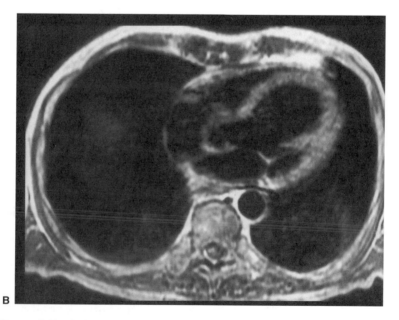

B

Figure 3–7. A. Nongated image of the chest shows blurring of the cardiac chambers. **B.** ECG-gated image through the same section improves resolution notably.

an artifact, since there is blood there, but it is not producing a signal (Fig. 3–8). As previously discussed, although the volume of blood within the section being imaged receives the initial 90° pulse, it has left the imaging plane before it can experience the refocusing pulse. Thus, under "normal" conditions flowing blood produces no signal, referred to as a "flow void." If, however, the blood is moving slowly enough, some of it may still be within the imaging region when the refocusing pulse is applied, and this blood may produce a signal. This type of artifact is appropriately called a "slow flow" artifact, or paradoxical enhancement. In tortuous vessels, or areas near a constriction, blood flow may not be uniform, but it can be turbulent (Fig.

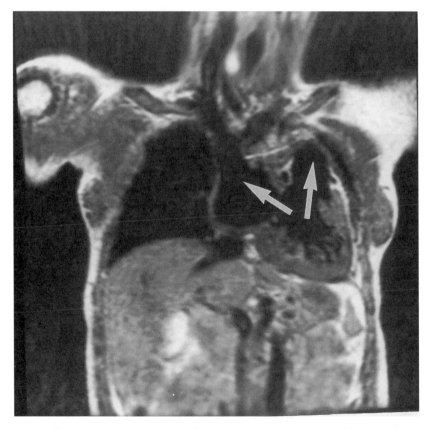

Figure 3–8. Normal blood flow (arrows) leaves a signal void as it flows through the aorta and pulmonary artery from a common ventricle, in this congenital heart variation.

3–9). In turbulent flow, the blood swirls around and back, eventually moving forward. Areas of turbulence will produce patchy and irregular signal within the lumen of the blood vessel. If the scan is repeated, the pattern will change, indicating that it is an artifact and not thrombus or plaque within the vessel; if a multi-echo sequence is used, the pattern will not remain constant, since the refocusing pulse for the second echo occurs after the blood has continued moving or swirling.

When blood remains in the imaging plane long enough to receive the refocusing pulse, another type of enhancement can occur for sections imaged during diastole in an ECG-gated study. Since blood flow is pulsatile, more so in arteries than in veins, during diastole, blood will be relatively stationary and will emit a signal (Fig. 3–10). The signal will be stronger at shorter repetition times. If the vessel is not perpendicular to the imaging plane (oblique sectioning of vessels), increased signal on the downstream edge of the oblique section is obtained, which can easily be confused with plaque or thrombus. In such cases, a magnetic resonance angiography (MRA) or confirmation by observation in another imaging plane should be obtained. During a multi-echo acquisition in a spin echo sequence, if echoes are obtained as

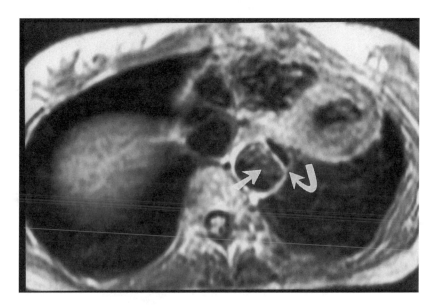

Figure 3–9. Turbulent flow (arrow) is observed in the lumen of this descending aorta. The intimal flap (curved arrow), which separates the true lumen from the false lumen in this descending dissection, is well seen.

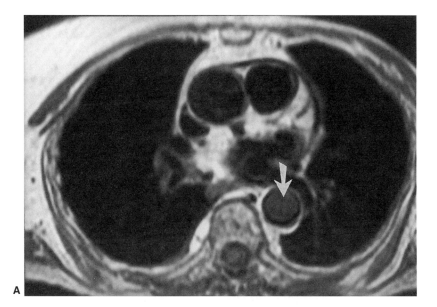

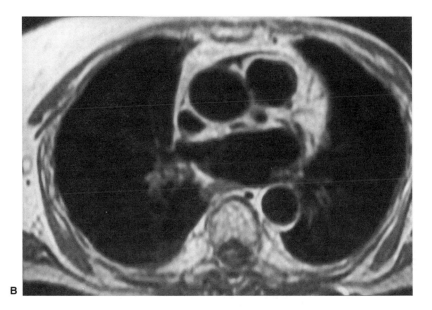

Figure 3–10. *A.* Signal is observed in the descending aorta (arrow) in this section obtained during late diastole, whereas in the adjacent slice *(B),* obtained during early diastole, the aorta is free of signal.

multiples of the echo time (30 ms, 60 ms, 90 ms, etc) nuclei that are out of phase (no signal) during acquisition of the first echo (30 ms) will be in phase (positive signal) 30 ms later, at 60 ms, when the second echo is acquired. This is easily recognized, since blood exhibits a normal flow void on odd-numbered echoes and produces a signal on even-numbered echoes.

Artifacts Caused by Instrumental Effects

A problem with any one of the many components of an MRI system can cause a problem with the final image; it is therefore easy to see that a great many types of image artifacts are caused by instrumentation. These artifacts can be created during data acquisition, data processing, image display, or filming. The two most easily corrected artifacts are those arising from display and filming, since these processes can be repeated very easily by redisplaying or refilming.

Most instrumental artifacts arise during data acquisition. The high-powered analog circuits necessary for data acquisition are much less reliable than the low-powered digital circuits used for data processing. These artifacts usually cannot be eliminated, and a new data set must be obtained after repairs have been effected. Changes in magnetic fields can present problems: Resistive magnets can have power-supply problems; permanent magnets can have thermal problems; and superconductive magnets can decay slowly or quench rapidly.

Most commonly, however, magnetic field artifacts result from problems with shims. The shims control multiple independent coils, and only one of these channels will fail at any given time. Depending upon which channel fails, the resulting spatial distortion in the image may be obvious or quite subtle; it may be more obvious in one imaging plane than another. These types of artifacts will usually be more evident in the body coil because of the larger field of view. They will appear as either a geometric distortion, usually due to a failure of the shim power supply, or fine ghosting due to shim–gradient interactions (Fig. 3–11). The problem can usually be corrected by checking the shim power supply, the shim settings, or the isolation circuits.

Gradient instabilities will produce blurring and loss of resolution, which may be subtle at times (Fig. 3–12). These instabilities can result from thermal overloads (which occur easily if the air conditioning isn't functioning properly). The shim–gradient

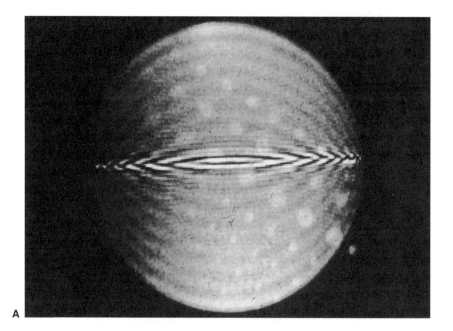

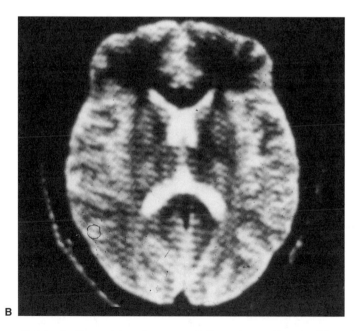

Figure 3–11. **A.** Geometric misrepresentation of a uniformly filled circular phantom due to gradient overheating. **B.** Gradient overheating causing motion-like artifact; however, the clarity of cerebral structures in this case should be contrasted with the general blurring observed when patient motion is present.

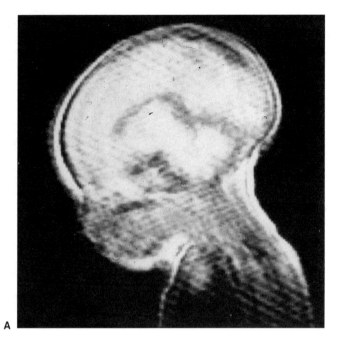

A

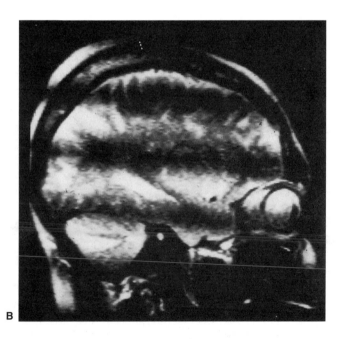

B

Figure 3–12. **_A._** Fine ghosting produced by gradient overheating. **_B._** Image banding caused in part by eddy current–gradient interaction. **_C._** Herringbone pattern throughout the image and background. **_D._** Complete gradient failure.

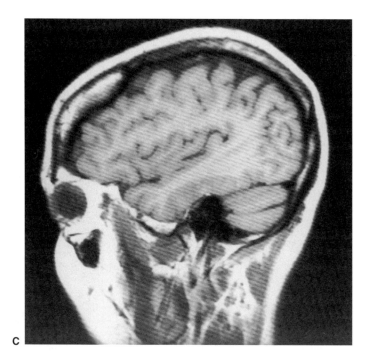

C

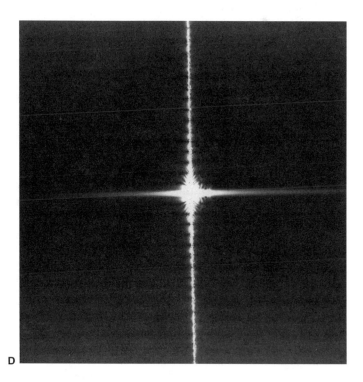

D

interactions that are produced by failures in the shim isolation circuits can progress to "singing" oscillations (oscillations in the audible range), which can be heard. Image banding can occur with a coupling of eddy currents to the gradient and RF body coil, especially in multi-echo sequences. This artifact is difficult to correct completely, but it may be remedied by checking and retuning the eddy current circuits. Truncation and aliasing can be corrected by using more phase-encoding steps.

Radio frequency problems can also occur. Discrete lines or streaks through the image are signs of an RF-shielding leak, or possibly an RF source coming from within the magnet room. Fluorescent light bulbs that are just about to burn out are a notorious cause of RF interference; as a result, most scanning rooms no longer utilize fluorescent lighting (Fig. 3–13). Instabilities in the RF transmitter produce ghosting patterns, or a "zipper" artifact.

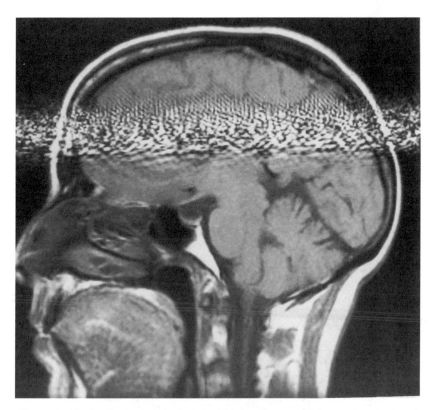

Figure 3–13. Radio frequency leak inside the magnet room produced a band of RF artifact through the affected frequency range in the frequency-encoding direction.

Decreased signal or increased noise can result from RF amplifier failure, improper tip angles, or incorrect matching of the impedance of coils to preamps. Highly nonuniform images are produced by RF coil inhomogeneities and by inclusion or reconstruction artifacts. Unless properly tuned, surface coils can receive so much signal from subcutaneous fat that the rest of the image may be compressed into the gray scale near the noise level. This can be corrected by adjusting the field of view to eliminate the subcutaneous tissue or by renormalizing the image.

After the analog signal has been converted to a digital format, the digitized image data is processed. This opens up a whole new category of artifacts: those produced during data processing (Fig. 3–14). All of these artifacts can be eliminated by

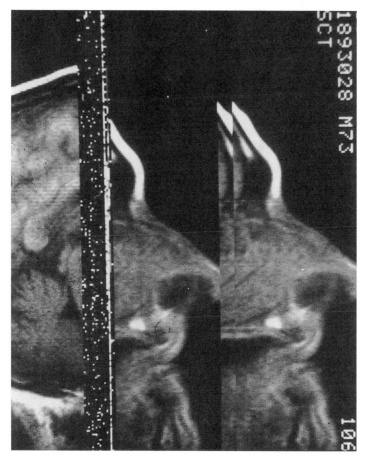

Figure 3–14. Reconstruction artifacts producing improper superimposition of several parts of an image.

reprocessing the image data, *if* it has not yet been deleted from the disk. Errors can be caused by a bit-drop, which can produce a herringbone effect, or if more severe, reduce the entire image to a geometric banding, or cause moiré patterns or variable patterns (Fig. 3–15). As data are transferred from one part of the computer to another, data transfer artifacts will be produced. Array processor errors may affect only one image in a series, or may corrupt an entire series, distorting them or turning them into geometric patterns (Fig. 3–16).

Artifacts Inherent in the Imaging Process

Several different types of artifacts can occur because of the very nature of the MRI procedure. The most important of these is

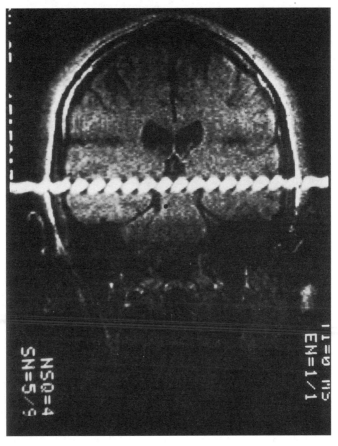

Figure 3–15. A bit-drop artifact produced an unusual addition to a coronal view of the head.

Figure 3–16. Array processor malfunction in an axial image of the chest.

called **aliasing,** or wraparound. This refers to a situation in which the edge of the left side of the object is superimposed on the right side of the image, and vice versa. If the part of the body being imaged extends outside of the field of view, a signal from these "excluded" tissues still will be produced. This can occur in both the frequency-encoding direction and the phase-encoding direction. Digital RF filters can eliminate the wraparound effect in the frequency-encoding direction by providing a sharp cutoff of signal frequency at the edges of the field of view in the directions of the frequency-encoding gradient. In the phase-encoding direction, however, no such filter exists. If part of the anatomy extends outside of the field of view in the phase-encoding direction, it experiences a phase shift that is similar to a point on the opposite side of the anatomy. It will emit a signal, then, that is identical to signal from the other side (Fig. 3–17). In order to avoid this, the number of phase-encoding steps is increased, but only the area of interest is reconstructed. This is called **oversampling.** The field of view (FOV) is increased and the pixel size is kept the same so as not to diminish resolution in the image. This requires the number of phase-encoding steps to be increased. Only the central pixels are reconstructed, and, although aliasing will still occur, it will

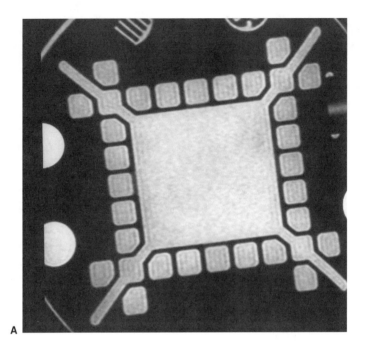

A

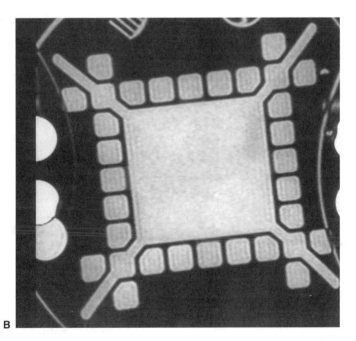

B

Figure 3–17. *A.* This is an example of a proper image of a phantom at a small FOV using an oversampling technique. *B.* If the oversampling correction is not employed, aliasing is observed in the phase-encoding direction.

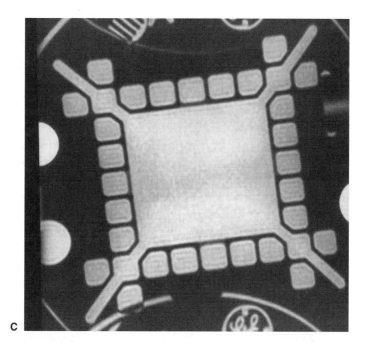

C

phase-encoding direction

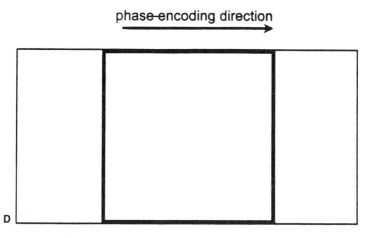

D

Figure 3–17. *(cont.) C.* By reversing the phase and frequency directions, the aliasing artifact is switched, always remaining in the direction of the phase-encoding gradient. *D.* A 256 × 256 matrix has been prescribed, with the no phase wrap, or oversampling option. The area of interest is contained in the central square (heavy lined box) but the area being scanned is outlined by the thinner lines. This additional area extends outward in the phase-encoding direction. Any aliasing artifact will appear in these outer boxes, but since only the central area is reconstructed there will not be an aliasing artifact in the image.

produce an artifact in a region that is not going to be recon-structed and thus will not appear in the image (Figure 3–17D). This is an option called "no phase wrap." It increases the area being imaged and also increases the imaging time or reduces the number of slices available for imaging. Since it does limit several options, it should be used only if anatomy extends be-yond the field of view in the phase-encoding direction.

During an MRI examination, we are imaging mobile pro-tons in the body. Essentially, there are two different types: pro-tons associated with water (essentially in soft tissue) and protons associated with fat. Although their signals are very close to each other, they are not identical. There is a difference in frequency (frequency shift) due to the differences in chemi-cal nature of the two types of protons. The fat signal appears at 3.7 ppm downfield (at the lower end) from the soft tissue signal. At 1.5 T, this amounts to a difference of about 240 Hz.

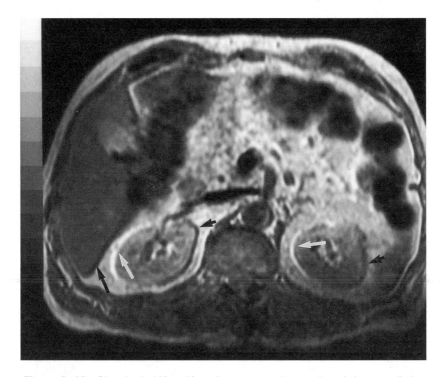

Figure 3–18. Chemical shift artifact demonstrated as a rim of decreased sig-nal at the fat–soft-tissue interfaces on the right sides of both kidneys and the liver (black arrows), and as a rim of increased signal on the left sides of both kidneys (white arrows).

This variance is small when considering that we are imaging at approximately 63 MHz, but it can have noticeable effects. The difference at 0.3 T would be 48 Hz, so the chemical shift effects are much more pronounced at higher field strengths. The effect is noticeable only at a boundary between soft tissue and fat (Fig. 3–18). The fat that we observe in an image is actually produced 3.7 ppm upfield (the signal is shifted 3.7 ppm downfield).

When fat is surrounded by soft tissues, a dark band appears at the upfield interface and a bright band appears at the downfield interface of the fatty region. The dark band results from the fat signal being shifted downfield and leaving behind

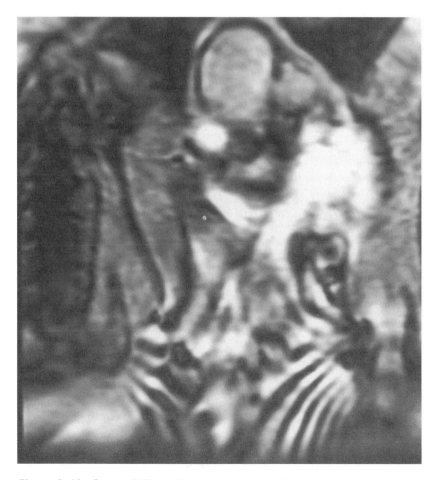

Figure 3–19. Susceptibility artifact due to surgical clips completely obscures this gradient echo image of the abdomen.

a signal void. The bright band results from the fat signal being shifted downfield and adding to the soft tissue signal already present.

When soft tissues are surrounded by fat, a bright band appears at the upfield interface and a dark band appears at the downfield interface of the soft tissue region. The bright band results from the fat signal being shifted downfield and re-enforcing the soft tissue signal already present. The dark band downfield results from the fat signal being shifted downfield and leaving behind a signal void.

Magnetic susceptibility is the ability of a material to become magnetized when placed in a magnetic field. This may cause a distortion in the local magnetic field and may also cause artifacts. Local variations in susceptibility, T_2^* effects, will cause regions of signal void with an intensely bright signal at the region of the interface. T_2^* effects are usually caused by a metallic foreign body, but iron from a hemorrhage can cause a similar effect. Gradient echo images are very sensitive to changes in susceptibility, and T_2^* effects can be magnified on these images (Fig. 3–19).

Chemical shift and T_2^* susceptibility artifacts are proof that the difference between an artifact and a diagnostic sign can fool

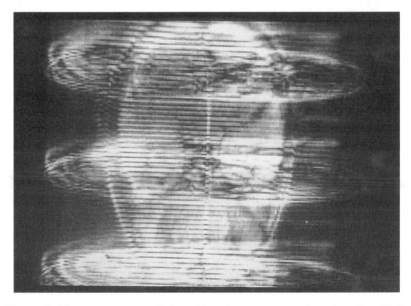

Figure 3–20. Strange yet artistic artifact from as-yet-undetermined multiple causes.

even the most experienced eye, if the existing artifacts are not kept in mind. There have been efforts both to suppress and to exploit both of these effects.

Some of the many different causes of image artifacts can be avoided by proper screening of patients, making sure that they do not have removable metal objects with them. Note should be made of any surgical appliances within the body, so they can be taken into account when interpreting the scan. Instrumental artifacts can be recognized and corrected or, with proper quality assurance, can be anticipated and avoided. Recognizing and understanding artifacts is important to the production and interpretation of images, and eventually to patient welfare (Fig. 3–20).

TABLE 3–1. CLASSIFICATION, SOURCES, AND CORRECTION OF ARTIFACTS.

Source	Artifact	Remedy	Comments
Patient-Related Artifacts			
Uncontrolled/random movement	Image blurring with displaced signal	Patient education/cooperation Small children and some adults may need sedation.	Certain conditions preclude patients from having MRIs (tremors, dementia, severe claustrophobia).
Foreign materials in or on body			
No mobile protons (nonmetallic)	Lack of signal in the area—no signal distortion	No correction necessary—recognition important.	Patient images not affected.
Sudden changes in magnetic susceptibility	Significantly increased rim of intensity around substance	Remove object if possible.	Recognition important.
Metallic objects (surgical implants)	Image will be distorted around the object, with the degree of distortion dependent upon the magnetic properties of the metal	Recognize as artifact.	Valuable diagnostic information can be obtained even from distorted images; renormalization of gray scale may be necessary for intensely bright metallic artifacts; patients with pacemakers and cerebral aneurysm clips not scanned.
Metallic objects (personal)	Metallic distortion, as above	Removal eliminates artifact.	Coins, keys, jewelry, clips, buckles, etc, not a problem if patient asked to remove them, or if patient is gowned. Hair pins always potential problem because of reluctance to remove them. Dentures should be removed for head and neck scans, if possible.

Artifact	Appearance	Remedy	Comments
Cosmetics	Ferromagnetic-based (usually highly colored), will produce local distortions	Caution patients in advance not to wear makeup.	Mascara most common offender.
Tattoos and permanently applied eyeliner	Local distortion	Notation should be made to help interpretation.	Heating effects may occur which will be uncomfortable and patients should be warned in advance.
Physiologic Artifacts			
Respiration	Image blurring; ghosting, displaced signal around and through image along the phase-encoding direction	Respiratory gating or compensation usually effective in reducing (not eliminating) effect; fast-scan techniques with breath holding very useful; anterior saturation pulses also helpful.	Compensation will reduce ghosting but less effective with image blurring.
Cardiac motion	Ghosting observed over width of heart in and out of the chest in the direction of the phase-encoding gradient; loss of resolution of cardiac and other mediastinal structures	ECG gating reduces ghosting and image blurring; scanning time reduced.	T_1 contrast modulated by heart rate.
Peristalsis	Blurring of bowel and surrounding structures; most conspicuous in anterior abdomen	Glucagon has been suggested but is of questionable practical value; fast-scanning techniques are promising.	
Flow	Absent signal	Elimination of these artifacts is usually not possible so recognition is key to the proper interpretive response.	
Rapid flow			
Decreased flow rate	Increased signal possible		
Even echo enhancement	Increased signal on even-numbered echoes		

(continued)

TABLE 3–1. (*continued*)

Source	Artifact	Remedy	Comments
Diastolic pseudogating	Increased signal on slices obtained during diastole		Caused by ECG gating.
Turbulence	Both increased and decreased signals observed	Pattern not consistent if scan repeated.	Pattern not consistent if multiple echoes obtained.
Oblique sectioning of vessels	Increased signal on downstream side of vessel		Easily confused with plaque or thrombus; confirmation in additional plane necessary.
Diffusion	Odd/even echo alternations		
Artifacts Inherent in the Imaging Process			
Chemical shift	Inclusion of fat signal in soft tissue pixels at fat/soft tissue interface on downfield side of frequency-encoded direction produces rim of increased signal; decreased signal on upfield side	Recognition key.	Artifact due to fat proton signal being 3 ppm lower than water proton signal.
T_2^* effects	Increased sensitivity to local variations in susceptibility	Eliminated by 180° pulse or by reversing gradient.	Effect permits hemorrhage to be observed earlier at lower magnetic field strengths.
System-Caused Artifacts			
Gradients	Periodic blurring in phase-encoding direction	Overheating (problem with air conditioning or water-cooling circuit); replace transistors in gradient drivers.	Easily confused with patient motion; can be checked on imaging phantom.
	Fine ghosting	Rigid securing of RF coil will minimize motion.	Due to slight motion of RF coil due to gradient drive.

Category	Observation	Action	Comments
	Truncation and aliasing	Use more phase-encoding gradient steps.	Different reconstruction methods may also be helpful.
	Banding	Retune or check eddy current circuits.	Caused by a coupling of eddy currents to gradient and RF body coils in multi-echo sequences; difficult to completely correct.
Shims	Geometric distortion	Check shim power supply.	Usually due to shim power-supply failure or incorrect shim settings.
	Ghosting from shim–gradient interactions	Check isolation circuits.	
RF effects	Discrete lines or streaks	Check RF shielding or possible RF sources in magnet room.	Local RF transmission; RF-shielding leak; local RF pickup may also occur via table/magnet coupling.
	Decreased signal, increased noise	Check amplifier gain, diodes, or tip angles (perform manual tune).	RF-amplifier failure; isolation diode failure; incorrect tip angles; incorrect impedance matching of coils to preamps.
	Inhomogeneities in image	Check tip angles; retune compensating gradients.	Coil or shim problems are also possible error sources.
	Image contrast changes	Check tip angles and pulse shapes.	Incorrect tip angles, pulse shapes, or compensating gradients.
Computer hardware	Moiré patterns; geometrical banding; highly variable distortions	Replace appropriate computer boards.	Bit-drop in data transfer.
	Miscellaneous patterns; incomplete or repetitive reconstructive patterns	Acquisition, transfer or storage errors will mean rescanning the patient; reconstruction or display errors can be corrected by software techniques.	Failures may occur during data acquisition, transfer, storage, reconstruction, or display.

CHAPTER FOUR

QUALITY ASSURANCE FOR MRI

Thomas Vullo, R. James R. Knowles, and Patrick T. Cahill

Quality assurance (QA) and cost containment (CC) for high-technology radiological imaging modalities are becoming increasingly important. Continued advancements in hardware and software, maximizing patient throughput while maintaining service and medical care, increased competition, and decreased insurance reimbursement have created the need to improve efficiency. Unfortunately, most aspects of QA and CC are neither required of nor performed by most imaging centers. Currently, the Food and Drug Administration only requires QA for mammography, and most state and certain local governments only require regular inspections of imaging modalities using ionizing radiation.

The American College of Radiology (ACR) has initiated a voluntary program for magnetic resonance imaging (MRI), ultrasound (US), US-guided biopsies, nuclear medicine, and radiation therapy. The ACR's program for each imaging modality follows the basic format of submitting to the ACR both phantom images and images of representative clinical studies of specific anatomical regions. Some issues involved in these voluntary accreditation programs are how to establish compliance, who pays for the costs, does this approach provide the needed credentialing of staff, and is the methodology complete for an effective QA–CC program. In the case of US, there are currently three groups that provide accreditation, which introduces the issue of how does a US practice decide on which accreditation program to pursue.

Unfortunately, the patient usually does not know the differences and implications of appropriate QA and CC of radiology centers. Specifically for MRI, controls have been enforced by selected labor unions in California, where reimbursement is denied for mobile MRI systems. There are other examples where insurance companies have set minimum standards for high-technology radiological modalities in order to approve reimbursement. The insurance company U.S. Healthcare (Aetna) requires that US-imaging sites meet the guidelines of the American Institute of Ultrasound in Medicine (AIUM) and of the ACR. In this regard, a 1992 study showed that 38% of 89 US facilities failed their first evaluation.[1]

The QA and CC goals clearly are focused on performing any examination correctly the first time, with the premise that a "lack of quality is more expensive than quality." Issues involving lack of QA directly affect the technical aspects and completeness of an MRI study. Poor system performance and incomplete studies in regard to the scope of the examination account for poor diagnoses, which reduce quality of health care, and increased costs due to the need for repeated studies. For example, small low-contrast lesions such as multiple sclerosis plaques in the brain and spine, metastatic and pituitary lesions, knee ligament and meniscus tears, and focal pathologies and blood vessels in the liver may be missed. The impact of CC becomes significant for unsatisfactory performance levels of 10 and 20% of studies for the high-technology radiology areas such as MRI, computed tomography (CT), and US. Table 4–1 contains estimates for the state of New Jersey. Here it was assumed that 4000 MRI studies per system per year are performed at an average reimbursement of $675 each; 5000 CT studies per year at $320 per examination; and 2000 US studies at $288 per examination. At the conservative estimate of 10% of studies producing unsatisfactory technical results, incomplete examinations, and/or inadequate reports, the cost would be $54, $48, and $28 million per year for MRI, CT, and US, respectively. At the more realistic 20% level, the costs for inadequate studies would be more than $260 million per year.

QA and CC with an audit trail also include the establishment of functional guidelines for imaging protocols, use of contrast agents, correct coding for billing and reimbursement, and ensuring that patients are obtaining the optimum radiologic

TABLE 4–1. ESTIMATED YEARLY COSTS IN MILLIONS OF DOLLARS PER MODALITY FOR THE 10 AND 20% UNSATISFACTORY STUDY LEVELS FOR THE STATE OF NEW JERSEY.

Modality	Total Number Devices	Yearly Income/ Device	Yearly Income All Devices	Costs for Unsatisfactory Performance	
				10%	20%
MRI	200	2.7	540	54	108
CT	300	1.6	480	48	96
US	500	.576	288	28	56

workup. For health maintenance organizations and other health care providers, functional QA and CC programs become cost effective by minimizing the number of radiologic exams performed, avoiding incorrect diagnoses, minimizing potential legal malpractice cases, and providing an essential marketing tool to the radiologist and patient.

Satisfactory QA and CC programs must include all of the following aspects:

1. Technical performance
2. Appropriate reason for the study
3. Completeness of the examination
4. Accuracy of the report
5. Appropriate billing procedures
6. Site credentials

To date, there have been few studies reported in the literature addressing QA and CC issues. In a study of 33 MRI centers,[2] where MRI examinations of the brain, spine, and extremities were independently reviewed by radiologists, only 90% were found to be technically adequate, 23% failed criteria for completeness of study, and 42% were unsatisfactory in the appropriateness of the report (22% affected treatment and 20% did not affect treatment). The technical factors considered were tissue contrast, presence of artifacts, and signal-to-noise ratio (SNR). Completeness of the examination involved the number and type of imaging planes and pulse sequences used and lack of or unnecessary use of contrast agents. Unsatisfactory reports were judged by either over or missed diagnoses and incorrect findings that did or did not affect future treatment.

In another report that involved a drug evaluation trial using MRI,[3] corrective measures by field service personnel had to be taken at 19 out of 35 MRI facilities. Technical problems involved gradients, shim calibrations and radio frequency (RF) coils, besides spatial distortions, low SNR, poor image quality, and presence of excessive artifacts.

Technological development of MRI hardware and software has made rapid advances in recent years. Stability of individual hardware components has improved, and the use of hardware self-diagnostics and other algorithms such as auto-shimming and RF coil tuning has expanded. The increased number of components and their complexity, available pulse sequences (which currently total over 100), and applications including echo-planar imaging, MR diffusion, and MR angiography have further necessitated the need for QA programs. Quality assurance includes not only hardware testing, but also involves patient preparation; maintenance of peripheral hardware such as cameras, film processors, and viewboxes; and maximizing the expertise of technologists and radiologists including continuing medical education (CME). Maintaining a broad range of system performance criteria ensures maximized patient throughput, diagnostic accuracy, and cost efficiency.

At installation time and following major upgrades, acceptance or performance testing are performed by the field service engineer. Here, the primary concerns are with system calibrations and in meeting the particular vendor's specifications. Preventative maintenance, which is of limited scope, is also performed by service engineers, generally once a month. On the other hand, QA focuses on the day-to-day maintenance of system performance criteria and must be done by the site personnel. Certain measurements should be performed every day, whereas others can be done weekly or monthly. Quality assurance tests should be designed to quickly and simply check major system components so that either images of consistently high quality can be acquired or appropriate vendor servicing can be scheduled.[4-6] However, because of time constraints and the need to maximize patient throughput, routine QA is more often than not neglected.

FACILITIES

A properly equipped MRI facility contains numerous features that contribute to comfort of patients and staff, safety, and image quality. A well-lighted, attractive, and comfortable waiting area with receptive and gracious staff members does much to alleviate the stress placed on patients who are concerned about their medical condition and often fear the worst in regard to their MRI test results. Courteous staff members are even more critical in a hospital-based facility, where many inpatients are bound to a wheelchair or stretcher and often have more severe medical conditions than those seen in private facilities.

Current magnet installations incorporate an RF-screened room, which minimizes RF noise that would otherwise degrade image quality. MRI-compatible monitoring and life-support equipment—such as electrocardiographs, pulse oximeters, and respiratory ventilators—are critical in preventing unwanted RF noise and guaranteeing their functionality and safety around strong magnetic fields.

Locked emergency crash carts must be situated in a convenient location and contain necessary emergency supplies and pharmaceuticals in the unlikely event that they may be required. Inventory should be checked periodically, as should the expiration dates of applicable items. Syringes, needles, angiocatheters, and the like must be maintained in a locked cabinet to prevent unauthorized use. Other standard medical supplies—such as gauze, bandaids, and alcohol wipes—need not be so secured. Fresh linens should be available for each patient. Staff use of protective gloves is essential when administering intravenous agents such as contrast media or intravenous fluids. All site personnel should be fully trained as to the safe handling of patients with readily transmissible medical conditions such as respiratory ailments and blood-borne pathogens. They should not hesitate to use face masks, eye shields, and disposable gowns when appropriate. Staff members must also be properly trained as to the hazards of working around magnetic fields. Careful screening of all items entering the magnet room is essential to prevent the introduction of magnetic objects, which can become dangerous projectiles if strongly attracted to the static magnetic field. Little data are available as to the effects of magnetic fields on the developing fetus. As a precaution, pregnant staff members should minimize their time spent in the magnet room. Pregnant patients who need MRI for a diagnosis should sign special consent forms.

SITE CREDENTIALS

A properly staffed MRI facility will include board-certified radiologists who have completed a residency or other training in MRI; technologists who are certified by the American Registry of Radiologic Technologists (ARRT) and have specific training in MRI and in allied health and patient care; a nurse or other appropriate staff member for administration of contrast agents and to tend to other patient care requirements as the situation dictates; and a board-certified physicist or MR scientist either on staff or by a consulting agreement.

MRI is a rapidly evolving area of radiology, and CME is critical to maintain competence in this area. The appropriate CME in MRI should be a normal procedure for radiologists, technologists, and physicists. Successful completion of the ACR voluntary MRI accreditation program demonstrates the highest level of credentials that is currently available. This program will be discussed in detail later.

PATIENT PREPARATION

In everyday practice, few simple measures contribute as much to good image quality and patient safety as proper patient preparation. Standard patient screening should include evaluation of risk factors such as metallic implants.[7,8] Cardiac pacemakers can be triggered by gradient and RF pulses,[9] and nonremovable magnetizable objects such as aneurysm clips, surgical staples, and residual shrapnel can be displaced by the static magnetic field, causing potentially hazardous tissue damage. Most surgical implants such as Harrington rods and similar devices are minimally magnetic and well anchored, and will not be displaced by the magnetic field; however, electric conduction is often induced by the gradient and RF fields, potentially causing electric shocks and heating as well as eddy current effects.[10] In the case of most surgical implants, scans may be performed even though some internal heat loading occurs from the currents circulating in the conductor.[7,8] A signal void will occur in the area of the implant and some small distortions often happen around it, causing image quality degradations. Note that MRI can be done for hip and shoulder implants, cardiac valves, and nonelectrical prostheses. However, a large fraction of bullets have magnetic properties, and a screening x-ray should be initially taken to determine whether the bullet is in a critical anatomical location should displacement in the static magnetic field occur.

External magnetizable and nonmagnetizable metallic materials such as hair pins, jewelry, watches, or assorted pocket items (pens, coins) may be unconsciously overlooked. At the least, their presence will necessitate the repeat of an imaging protocol, and in the worst-case scenario, they can become an injury-threatening projectile. Use of gowns for body studies is normally recommended to minimize risks. Dentures can in the extreme case lock shut if magnetized by the static magnetic field, rendering them useless and possibly incurring a legal suit. In addition, some cosmetics contain iron oxides,[11] which induce magnetic field distortions and image artifacts. External electronic monitoring equipment such as electrocardiographs not specially designed to be MRI compatible may be damaged and the patient shocked or burned.

Attention must also be paid to the patient's comfort and psychology. Anxious and uncomfortable patients produce imaging delays and motion artifacts. An advantage of MRI compared to CT is that friends and relatives of the patient can be present in the scanning room. Simple measures such as a cushion placed under the knees to relieve low-back stress while the patient is lying flat can return large dividends in terms of image quality. Similarly, attention to proper temperature and ventilation can reduce claustrophobic reactions in tight magnet tunnels, as can periodic verbal inquiries and reassurances. Extreme claustrophobia cannot be addressed without sedation; however, moving a patient out of the magnet between imaging sequences will help, as does the use of open-air magnets. MRI-compatible stereo systems usually help and may even reduce the effects of gradient noise. Earplugs should always be offered to the patient.

Certain considerations must be taken when handling "precaution" patients, such as those with contagious respiratory ailments like tuberculosis or blood-borne infectious agents such as human immunodeficiency virus (HIV). Severe respiratory conditions should be handled with the proper face mask, gloves, and disposable gown. Many institutions, when possible, schedule respiratory precaution patients as their last study of the day, so as not to expose another patient to the same pathogens. Patients with open cuts or sores should always be handled with gloves to prevent the potential transmission of HIV or other viral agents. This is true regardless of whether the patient is considered HIV positive or not. Accident victims with major lacerations entering hospital emergency rooms and scheduled for MRI should be treated with the utmost care.

Following MRI of special precaution patients, linens that cover the MRI patient's bed must always be removed and handled in the proper manner to prevent spread of contamination. Injection of contrast agents or introduction of any other vascular component such as an angiocatheter for administration of intravenous fluids must always be performed with gloved hands regardless of the medical status of the patient.

Yearly, thousands of cases of needle pricks to hospital staff members occur following intravenous injections. Common-sense precautions must always be taken to avoid this risk. Many institutions also recommend that staff use face masks, gowns, and goggles when performing injections on known HIV-positive patients in the unlikely event that blood splattering may result.

CONTRAST AGENTS

Contrast agents have improved the diagnostic accuracy of various pathologies using both MRI and CT. The use of contrast agents in head and spine studies, and more recently in body cases, has increased greatly. The decision to administer contrast agents, however, should not be based on the possibility that increased reimbursement from insurance companies will result in additional site income. Ideally, a radiologist should determine the need for contrast agent administration based upon the appearance of pre-injection images and reason for study.

Although uncommon, there are known risks to the patient associated with contrast administration. Most often reported are headache, nausea, and vomiting. Slow injection, at a rate no greater than recommended by the contrast agent manufacturer, will reduce the frequency of these side effects. In rare situations, patients will exhibit severe allergic reactions to the contrast agent, and staff members must be aware of this possibility and trained as to how to handle it medically if it occurs.

QUALITY ASSURANCE OF MRI HARDWARE

There are a limited number of reports as to the need for QA of MRI hardware.[1-3] Although local and federal governments require the measurement of patient exposure for modalities utilizing ionizing radiation, standards for image quality do not exist. The first attempt to set minimum standards for MRI was introduced by the ACR.[12] The ACR recently instituted a voluntary MRI accreditation program (MAP) similar to that available for mammography.[13] The development of the MAP by the ACR was in response to three factors: the success of the mammography accreditation program; the conclusion of the 1992 Radiology Summit Meeting that the ACR should develop programs for other modalities including MRI[12]; and general concern about the imaging and diagnostic quality of hospital-based and private MRI centers. Additional considerations include the expanding need to patrol radiology centers that increasingly tend to maximize patient throughput and profits at the expense of exam completeness and patient care.

ACR ACCREDITATION

The ACR accreditation program aims to set minimum standards for MRI system performance. Currently, the program is purely voluntary, and it is debatable as to how many MRI facilities will invest the required time and costs. One feeling is that once a few sites become accredited, display their certificate announcing such, and most likely use it as a marketing tool, other sites will follow in order to remain competitive. An additional issue is whether insurance companies will require accreditation for reimbursement.[2] This latter issue is becoming increasingly important as both insurance companies and the Medicare program strive to cut costs while furthering the quality of health care.

The ACR accreditation program consists of several aspects. An entry application to the ACR requests system information and serves to evaluate credentials of physicians, MR scientists, and technologists. Upon approval of the entry application, phantom images are acquired using the designated ACR phantom and in turn forwarded to the ACR with typical clinical images consisting of routine brain, cervical and lumbar spine, and knee images. The images and required information tabulated by the site physicist or MR scientist are evaluated by the ACR, which then makes its decision as to whether to grant accreditation. On-site review and random film checks may be performed for validation purposes at the discretion of ACR officials.

ACR Phantom

The ACR test phantom, which was designed strictly for use in the RF head coil, must be purchased by each site following acceptance of the entry application. It is cylindrical in nature and contains numerous internal features to allow evaluation of different MRI hardware and software parameters. Its accurate positioning in the magnetic and gradient field centers is critical for the acquisition of properly prescribed transaxial slices. Phantom positioning is determined using standard laser alignment lights built into most MRI systems, a simple leveling device, and acquisition of a sagittal localizer. The internal geometry of the phantom contains structures that test for high-contrast spatial resolution, slice thickness and geometric accuracy, signal uniformity, T_1 ghosting, and low-contrast detectability.

ACR Imaging Protocols

The ACR accreditation program requires only three imaging sequences: a sagittal localizer for proper positioning of the phantom and prescription of transaxial slices and conventional spin echo T_1-weighted and dual-echo T_2-weighted protocols. Acquisition of these sequences and interpretation of quantitative image data should be performed by an independent board-certified physicist or MR scientist to maintain proper integrity. In order to reduce costs of the MAP, the tendency would be to have technologists or vendor service engineers acquire this information rather than pay for services of a consulting physicist.

The T_1 and dual-echo T_2 spin echo sequences must be acquired using the identical spatial imaging parameters: at least 11 slices having a 0.5-cm thickness and 0.5-cm interslice gap, 25-cm field of view, and 256×256 imaging matrix. Other recommended parameters are for the T_1-weighted sequence $TR/TE = 500/20$, one signal average and bandwidth equal to that used for standard brain studies; and for the T_2-weighted sequence $TR/TE = 2000/20,80$ with one signal average. Clinical images submitted to the ACR must have imaging parameters consistent with those used for the phantom images.

Limitations

The ACR MAP is deficient in several aspects:

1. The high costs associated with ACR accreditation will hinder most sites from voluntarily entering the program. Currently, the cost of the designated phantom, which each site must purchase, is approximately $500. The high ACR survey and evaluation fee is $1500 for the first general-purpose magnet and $1400 for each additional general-purpose magnet operated by the site. A board-certified physicist or MR scientist performing the required measurements will typically charge upwards of $1000 for his or her services.
2. Routine QA is recommended but not mandated by the program. Hardware instabilities can occur at any time, and image quality and diagnostic integrity will suffer. The ACR requires a reevaluation only after major system upgrades.
3. Only T_1 and dual-echo T_2-weighted imaging sequences are evaluated (Fig. 4–1). The vast majority of centers also employ numerous other protocols including but not limited to gradient-recalled echo (GRE), fast-spin echo (FSE), and echo planar (EP) (Fig. 4–2). Due to the nature of gradient modulation of these latter sequences, artifacts are often seen that can negatively affect the image quality and diagnosis (Fig. 4–3). Note that conventional multi-echo T_2-weighted sequences have been replaced by FSE in many cases to save time and increase patient throughput.
4. The ACR phantom is designed only for use in the RF head coil. The performance of other commonly used RF coils—including body, knee, and those for various levels of the spine—is not tested. Artifacts from static and gradient magnetic field nonlinearities in larger fields of view, sometimes seen using fields of view greater than 25 cm as is typical with use of the body coil, are not determined (Fig. 4–4).
5. No considerations are made for the evaluation of magnetic resonance angiography (MRA).[14-16] Use of MRA has become widespread and little or no QA is performed to guarantee the

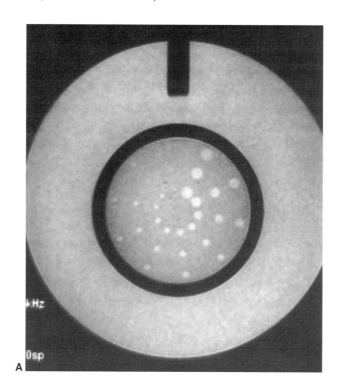

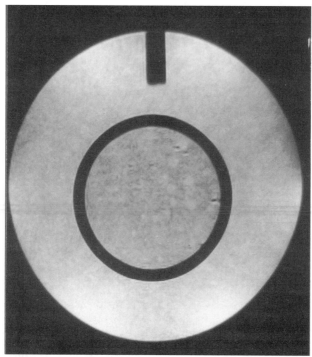

accuracy of angiographic flow rate or vessel lumen diameter determinations. Since MRAs are usually reimbursed at the same value as MRI exams, QA and CC programs need to be established with the same standards as MRI.

6. The ACR does not sufficiently consider other factors such as patient preparation issues including risk factors (pacemakers, aneurysm clips, reactions to contrast), performance of unnecessary patient exams solely for the purpose of increased insurance reimbursement (multiple exams, added MRA, unnecessary use of contrast), and expediency of production of reports.

ROUTINE QA MEASUREMENTS

Quality assurance measurements should be scheduled on the basis of two primary considerations. The first concern is the importance of various parameters to image quality; the second is the proven stability of a particular hardware parameter. Parameters critical to image quality or most likely to fluctuate need to be tested most frequently. With the expanding need to maximize patient throughput and profits, some consideration must be given to the difficulty and time required for an array of measurements. An efficient daily QA program can be performed within a 15-minute time frame. Early detection of hardware instabilities ultimately reduces system downtime and increases efficiency, patient throughput, and diagnostic accuracy.

All QA results should be permanently recorded in a format that allows easy comparisons between values from different dates. Tabulations and bar or line graphs are suitable in this aspect. A month's worth of daily QA measurements can easily be presented in such fashion. The real significance of any particular result may only become apparent as part of a larger pattern or trend of information. Thus, one should always strive to make the perception of trends as easy and natural as possible.

Figure 4–1. An image acquired on an optimum tuned MR should show 3 rings, each ring containing 10 circles of different diameters. **A.** All 30 circles are seen. **B.** The same pulse technique was used, but the machine was from a different vendor.

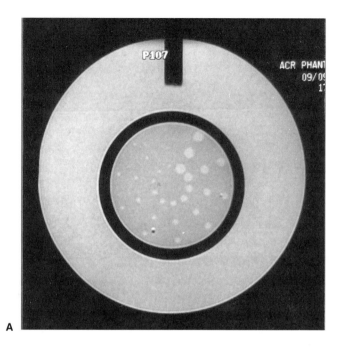

A

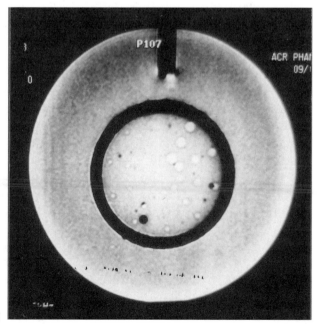

B

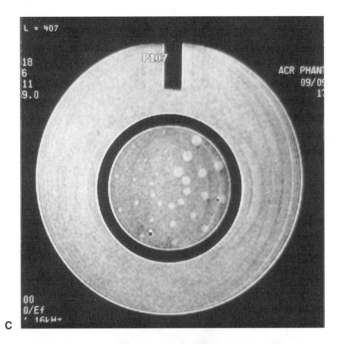

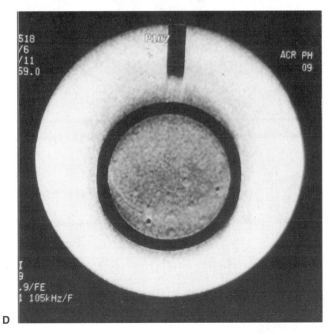

Figure 4–2. This is a set of four images taken with different pulse sequences. *A.* Spin echo. *B.* Gradient echo. *C.* Fast-spin echo. *D.* Echo planar. How many of the 30 circles can you count in each case?

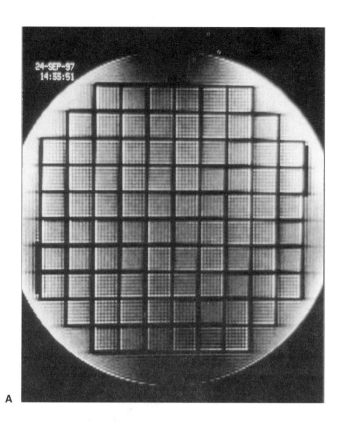

A

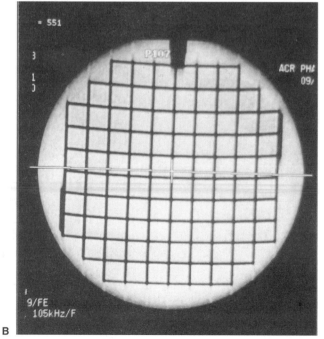

B

DAILY MEASUREMENTS

Numerous daily QA procedures should be performed and a record of results maintained for comparison to ensure continued high-quality system performance. Ideally, all commonly used RF coils should be evaluated, but time constraints may prevent this. At the minimum, QA measurements should be performed using the RF head coil, because brain imaging studies account for the majority of cases at most sites. An appropriate phantom should be selected so that it fills at least 80% of the cross-sectional area of the RF coil in all three orthogonal planes. Quality assurance imaging parameters should be consistent with those used in normal clinical practice and should include the use of spin echo, GRE, FSE, and EP. The same static phantom should be used and placed in the identical position inside the magnet to eliminate measurement variables. Some of the suggestions listed in the next sections will not apply to all sites due to their specific hardware configurations and inability to access such information. This inaccessibility is vendor and model specific. A QA protocol must thus be designed to fit the needs of each specific MRI system and must fit within the time constraints of patient scheduling.

Film Processor QA

As in all other subdivisions of radiology, daily cleaning of crossovers and rollers, routine sensitometry and densitometry, as well as measuring developer temperature should be done first thing in the morning. Such procedures should become second nature to anyone involved in film processing and have pre-

---

Figure 4–3. Artifacts, distortions, and signal loss were observed at various MR sites. In these images, a grid is displayed where artifacts are observed by the induced lines between the grids. This is particularly important when MR studies of the spine are performed, where ringing artifacts can significantly reduce the radiologist's ability to interpret the images. In *A,* there is loss of signal intensity on top and bottom of the image and aliasing is seen inside the grid. In *B,* the center white line is the true horizontal, and, in this case, significant geometrical distortions have occurred, which again could produce incorrect interpretations of mass effects in MR.

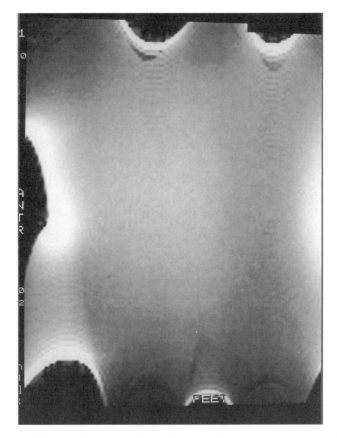

Figure 4–4. This is an image of a large uniform phantom typical for evaluation of body imaging, such as chest, abdomen, and pelvis. Note that there are significant signal voids at either end and in the middle, where geometrical distortions are also present. These artifacts are due to magnetic field inhomogeneities which could be corrected by proper shimming.

viously been clearly detailed in many good references.[17–19] Filmless sites, which have installed a picture archival and communications system (PACS)[20] or similar hardware, will of course bypass this procedure.

RF Transmission

Optimization of the RF transmission is basic to any pre-scan protocol. The RF is readily available on most systems and is vendor specific. In general, this frequency is very stable and unlikely to have a standard deviation of more than one part in a million. If larger changes do suddenly occur or a regular shift from day to day is seen, something may be seriously wrong with the magnet or magnetic shims.

All magnets are sensitive to changes in the peripheral location of magnetic materials. These changes can usually be corrected by active shim coils. Although permanent magnets are sensitive to temperature, shifts are easily correctable by adjusting the RF. On the other hand, electromagnets are dependent on the stability of the power supply, and superconductive magnets depend on the maintenance of a near-perfect vacuum, cryogen levels, and active shims. If deviations in RF frequency, beyond those dictated by vendor specifications, occur on systems containing these latter two types of magnets, their respective maintenance requirements need to be evaluated by a field service engineer.

Tip (Flip) Angles

Depending on the system manufacturer, tip angles refer either to RF transmission power levels or transmission attenuation values for the standard 90° and 180° pulses as well as receiver attenuation values for proper signal strength ranging. Some manufacturers do not use variable-tip angles but rather employ constant-output transmit coils for all applications and operate head, spine, or other dedicated coils in receive mode only. Where applicable, measurement of tip angles for a given phantom at a fixed location in a given coil provides a rough measure of RF stability and coil performance. In general, RF power or attenuation values vary far more than RF and yield standard deviations between 10 and 20%, depending on the method used to determine the tip angles. The only site servicing that can be performed here is to check the status of the RF coil connector.

Signal Strength

For a given receiver attenuation and phantom, the signal strength should also be constant. To quantitate this constancy, a phantom with a relatively large, uniform volume should be used. Such a phantom avoids edge effects while allowing field uniformity and overall distortion to be quickly gauged visually. Choice of solution within the phantom should be such that its

T_1 and T_2 relaxation times yield a signal similar to those encountered in most soft tissues, and the imaging sequence used should be typical of those employed in actual clinical practice (eg, a multislice spin echo sequence with at least two echoes). The signal from a small region of interest (ROI) in a central cross-section of the phantom should have a standard deviation of around 5% or a little more for the early echo and about twice that for a second echo with an echo time twice the first or more. Measuring at least two echoes also documents the T_2 constant, a crucial element in many diagnoses.

Signal-to-Noise Ratio

More precisely, the total signal strength measured in any given ROI consists of two contributions: true signal and noise (both stray RF and electronic). High levels of signal (short of electronic saturation) are desirable, but high levels of noise reduce low-contrast resolution, an important component of MR image quality and accurate diagnosis. These relationships are compactly expressed by the SNR, in which higher numbers imply better image quality. Measuring the true SNR can be technically demanding,[21,22] but figures of merit that vary in the same general manner as the SNR are easily available. The ratio of the average is one such figure. Another more common method of determining SNR is the signal minus the background divided by the square root of the background signal. If the signal strength itself has not dropped, declines in this ratio usually indicate increased noise from electronic- or room-shielding failures. Electronics have greatly improved; however, breakdown of individual components, such as capacitors or diodes, can produce noise artifacts in addition to a reduction in signal strength and resulting in a drop in SNR. Use of equipment within the magnet room that is not considered MRI compatible, or failure of RF screening, can also introduce RF noise and degrade the SNR.

Low-Contrast Resolution

Much of the diagnostic power of MRI derives from its ability to discriminate between various soft tissues. This ability, in turn, usually results from relaxation time effects, because there is little variation in spin density (8 to 10%) to distinguish most soft tissues. Thus, image contrast usually depends on relaxation time differences. Decreases in low-contrast resolution reduce one's ability to diagnose many subtle pathological changes.

Minimally, one should surround a uniform phantom with 5 to 10 small containers (but large enough to avoid edge effects) of different solutions spanning the most important ranges of relaxation times. The signals from these containers should be recorded and compared. Standard deviations increase with T_1 and decrease with T_2 but should generally vary between 5 and 10%.

Gross Distortion

One should quickly look through the entire sequence of multi-slice phantom images for gross distortions, phase ghosting, and other artifacts. The technologists should be able to identify the cause of these distortions. Likewise, the same considerations should be taken throughout the day when viewing clinical images. Lack of distortions and phase ghosting is a rough indication of proper shimming as well as of adequate gradient performance and stability. On occasion, metallic objects such as paperclips, bobby pins, or pens may find their way into the magnet, in which case their identification and elimination are simplistic.

Magnetic Field Shims

Magnetic field shims, which improve the homogeneity of the static magnetic field, are either passive or active (including superconductive) depending on the type of magnet. Auto-shimming of active shim coils is routine practice for certain manufacturers of high-field, superconductive systems. Minor variations in auto-shim values can result from susceptibility differences between one patient and another or slightly different positioning of a static phantom in the main magnetic field. Major differences can be the result of the introduction of small magnetic materials inside the magnet or larger magnetic objects around the periphery of the magnet (which can also cause image distortions) or failure or quenching of one or more superconductive shim coils. Care should be taken to avoid the introduction of any magnetic objects into the magnet room for safety and image quality concerns. Quenched superconductive shims will require a visit by the vendor service engineer and may create considerable system downtime.

MONTHLY MEASUREMENTS

Parameters tested in the recommended daily QA protocol are general and will only test for changes associated with the static or gradient magnetic field, tuning or other variations of the RF head coil, and changes in system electronics associated with signal gain and processing. A broader analysis should be performed, which is inclusive of all commonly used RF coils including head, body, knee, cervical, thoracic and lumbar spines, and any other coil available at the individual sites. These tests will evaluate the performance of all RF coils and the nature of other system hardware at a broader range of gradient strength, field of view, and other imaging parameters. Because of the time required for these measurements, testing of individual coils should be performed on different days. Alternately, an arrangement can be made with the site's MR scientist to perform the recommended monthly QA. In either case, a detailed audit analysis should be maintained.

Unlike the case in most of the other medical imaging modalities, MRI geometry is not ultimately defined by collimators, apertures, or physical movement. Instead, MRI geometry is determined by the dynamic interaction of radio waves with magnetic fields. Thus, image geometry can vary with the uniformity of the static magnetic field, as with the uniformity of both gradient and RF fields and the shape and timing of these gradient and RF pulses. In addition, slice profiles depend on the responses of relaxation times in the slice to both recovery and echo times.[23–25]

Because image geometry can vary as a function of position in any direction and can even vary as a function of image sequence or echo timing, many days of imaging time can be devoted to explore all the possible iterations. As a practical matter, however, this cannot be routinely done, but some control of these important variables must be implemented at periodic time intervals. What follows should be viewed as a minimal effort.

High-Contrast Resolution

In MRI, measurement of high-contrast resolution remains primarily a test for image geometry and is of lesser importance to image quality and edge detection of adjacent tissues than is low-contrast resolution. One of the simplest tests of image geometry is to measure the high-contrast resolution both centrally and peripherally in all three orthogonal directions. This is easily accomplished using a dedicated phantom containing central and peripheral line patterns, analogous to the phantoms once developed for use in CT. The ACR phantom also has characteristics for determining high-contrast resolution. Warping of these patterns or changes in resolution suggest shimming or gradient problems. Accuracy of image geometry is important for radiation treatment planning, performing biopsies, and volume analysis.

Slice Geometry and Spatial Resolution

Perhaps the most direct test of image geometry would be to measure a grid pattern in all three orthogonal directions. The ACR phantom provides such a grid pattern but only in the transaxial plane (Fig. 4–3). Physical rotation of the ACR phantom is thus necessary for evaluation in all three orthogonal directions. Other helical phantoms have been developed to locate slice centers and provide some estimate of slice thicknesses. Such measurements test field uniformity and gradient linearity. They also check on RF and gradient pulse timing specific to MRI, such as whether a given slice in a multislice multi-echo sequence has the same central location and average thickness for each of the various echoes and for different repetition times.

Details of internal slice geometry can best be examined by viewing individual slice projections while using the same gradient for reading the signal as was used for slice selection. These slice profiles allow one to quickly assess the effects of pulse timing, relaxation times, and slice spacing—all of which may alter the actual geometry. Access to such techniques is generally not available to the end-user and requires interaction with service personnel.

Evaluation of the accuracy of oblique angle selection is somewhat more complex. Grid-containing phantoms can also be used, but more complex measurements are required incorporating the trigonometric lengths of the grid components seen in the resulting evaluation images. Accuracy of the three perpendicular orthogonal planes should first be determined to validate system calibration before proceeding to oblique angle testing. If the orthogonal planes are accurate, then a cone-shaped phantom can also be used for oblique angle calibration.

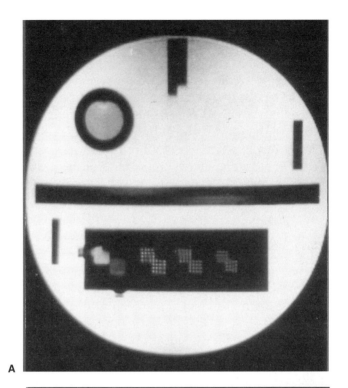

A

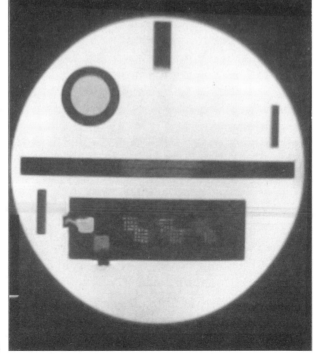

B

Evaluation of spatial resolution is critical in order to detect small lesions. Variations in spatial resolution for two different MRI systems are shown in Figure 4–5 in addition to variations seen using different pulse sequences performed on the same system in Figure 4–6.

Monitors, Cameras, and Viewboxes

MRI technologists need to be properly trained to recognize tissue abnormalities seen on MR images and photograph them at the proper window and level so that the radiologist can make the proper diagnosis. Ideally, the film on the viewbox should reproduce the signal and contrast characteristics of the image as seen on the monitor. Importantly, film quality in respect to contrast and textural noise should be better than that seen on the monitor. If not, service should be performed immediately. Even if one uses computer-generated corrections to allow for differences in the response curves of phosphor and film, there are still differences of tint and absolute luminance. Cathode ray tubes (CRTs) can degrade over time, and monitoring QA to measure the absolute luminance and its uniformity may be necessitated at regular intervals. Furthermore, film and phosphor interact differently with ambient light levels. Thus, one is usually limited to establishing an acceptable compromise and then checking to see that the elements of this particular compromise do not change with time.

Displaying and filming the Society of Motion Pictures and Television Engineering Society (SMPTE) video test pattern (Fig. 4–7) can help in this effort. In general, one must make certain that all the gray levels resolved on the monitor are also resolved on film, and vice versa. Particular attention should be paid to the 5% differences built into both ends of the SMPTE test pattern gray scale. The optical density of the 11 gray scales, ranging from 0 to 100% in 10% increments, should be measured. Spatial resolution at the four corners and center of the SMPTE pattern should be visually examined. Magnification and photographing the pattern on a 14 × 17-inch sheet of film will also test for

Figure 4–5. These images show the spatial resolution sensitivity for two different MR systems. In the black rectangular box, there are three sets of two matrices with different diameter rods: (left to right) 1.1, 1.0, and 0.9 mm. **A** demonstrates satisfactory resolution, compared to **B,** taken from a different site.

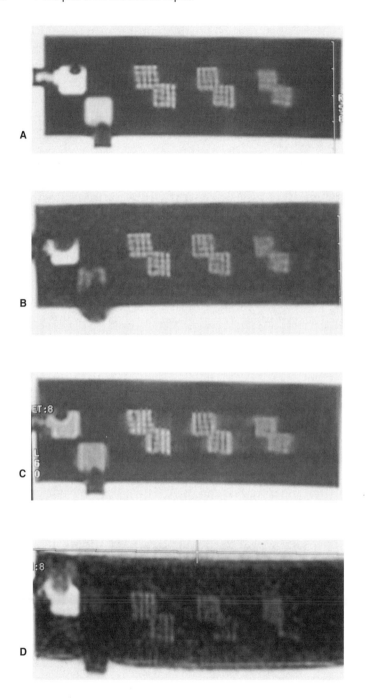

Figure 4–6. These are four images taken from the same MR system using four different pulse sequences. ***A.*** Spin echo. ***B.*** Gradient echo. ***C.*** Fast-spin echo. ***D.*** Echo planar. Note, spatial distortion is seen in ***D.***

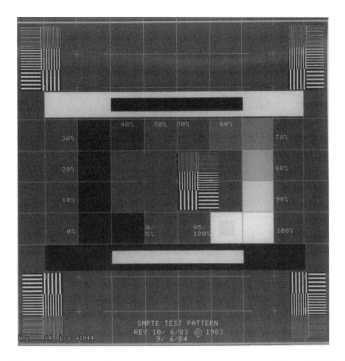

Figure 4–7. SMPTE test phantom for quality assurance testing of CRT, showing the 5% areas at 0% and 100% for contrast sensitivity and spatial resolution grids in the center and the four corners.

processor variables. In addition, the light output from the viewboxes must be checked, plus its overall uniformity. When either the uniformity or the absolute light output falls below some predetermined level, the plastic diffuser should be cleaned and any suboptimal tubes replaced.

Picture Archival and Communications Systems

The advent of telemedicine and PACS[20] is a critical factor in maximizing efficiency and productivity in today's emerging health care market. PACS has greatly eliminated the need for film and its associated costs, which has greatly cost justified the implementation of PACS in large private radiology groups and hospital-based radiology departments.

The need for QA for PACS is twofold: image archival and monitor viewstations. Image archival systems for image storage and retrieval are generally reliable, but redundancy is needed. Built-in hardware fault tolerance, however, should be incorporated into any PACS to eliminate the possibility of system down-time and loss of patient image data. If images are automatically transferred to a PACS, audit trail must be established to ensure that all the patient exams and images have been transmitted. The need to maintain the system viability during software up-grades is essential for access to radiology images and continued patient service. Monitors are the primary PACS hardware com-ponent. Variability of the monitor's CRT is well known, and CRT QA is crucial to maintain diagnostic integrity. Decreased ab-solute luminance and nonuniform luminance across the CRT field can cause image distortions and variability in the appear-ance of tissue contrast and spatial resolution. Quantitative mea-surements made with a photometer and an appropriate phan-tom image or the SMPTE video test pattern displayed on the monitor are more indicative of CRT degradation than visual as-sessment by a PACS engineer or radiologist.[26] A regular QA pro-gram for PACS CRTs should be implemented starting with initial tests at time of installation and followed by repeated measure-ments at regular intervals to verify stability. There are three levels of QA for CRTs that need to be performed at different intervals: (1) a daily test, where the radiologist evaluates a standardized test pattern such as a Briggs or SMPTE pattern upon sign-on; (2) a weekly test of luminance, spatial linearity, and contrast; and (3) a monthly evaluation of spectral quality, fo-cus, and detailed luminance versus digital signal input.

MAGNETIC RESONANCE ANGIOGRAPHY

MRA has evolved as a noninvasive tool for the evaluation of the medical status of various aspects of the arterial system.[14] It is most commonly performed for studying the carotid arteries and arter-ies of the brain. Most MRI centers use MRA as a screening tool for the diagnosis of gross arterial abnormalities and, if seen, refer pa-tients to undergo x-ray angiography. One important issue is whether many MRA protocols—which are added to standard neuroimaging exams, require approximately 5 minutes of imaging time, and are billed as separate studies—are necessary, or whether they are performed purely to increase insurance reimbursement. The second issue is the accuracy of MRA measurements.

Except for standard checks of MRI hardware, QA for MRA is not performed. Unfortunately, dynamic flow phantoms with realistic normal and pathologic arterial geometries are currently not available for this purpose. Some direct imaging comparisons have been made between MRA and x-ray angiography[15,16]; however, these comparisons do not guarantee the performance or stability of individual systems. MRA will continue to evolve, and, as it does, the need for QA will increase. It is expected that satisfactory dynamic flow phantoms will soon be developed that will help address this important issue.

OTHER MEASUREMENTS

There are at least two very useful sets of object parameters for which it is relatively easy to obtain reasonable qualitative results but for which it can be surprisingly difficult to obtain accurate quantitative information. These quantitative complications emerge from a complex interaction of various object and instrumental factors.

Relaxation Times

Relaxation times contribute most of the soft-tissue contrast that is so highly valued in MRI, and maintaining the constancy of this contrast is an important element of basic QA. On the other hand, it is a much more technically demanding task to attempt to obtain credible relaxation times even from relatively simple phantom images.[27] The first step is to calibrate each region of the image with a series of unknown relaxation times, because one cannot assume that the center yields the same values as those found at the periphery, and so on, because the numbers calculated are affected by magnetic field inhomogeneities and pulse imperfections.[28,29] In multi-echo sequences, complex echoes may build up,[30] whereas multislice sequences may create interslice excitation overlap problems.[31] Gradients plus diffusion, furthermore, create more traditional problems.[32] All of this, however, does not begin to address the more complex questions of how image noise propagates into relaxation time errors, because these errors also depend on the relationship between pulse times and relaxation times.[33] In biological systems, edge and partial volume effects can also occur as well as multiexponential relaxation behavior. Thus, the step from QA of image contrast to QA of accurate relaxation times is a big one and demands far more effort than most are willing to invest.

Flow and Diffusion

Flow and diffusion effects present a challenge similar to that provided by relaxation times. Numerous hospital-based facilities are employing diffusion-weighted imaging for the evaluation of various pathologies. It is one thing to run a fluid of known relaxation times in three orthogonal directions to check the effects of gradient moment nulling on the image,[34-36] but quite another to calibrate an imaging unit so that flow or diffusion can be quantitatively measured.[37-39] Unfortunately, there is no currently available standardized method to calibrate or quantitatively measure the effects of diffusion and perfusion on standard imaging protocols or dedicated diffusion-weighted sequences. Phantoms containing porous materials are a first attempt at this. The utility of using such phantoms for quantitations of diffusion effects has yet to be established.

CONCLUSION

Traditional radiographic images encode essentially only one variable: attenuation. Even modern ultrasonic images encode only two: attenuation and velocity. MR images, on the other hand, encode at least four variables: spin density, two relaxation times, and velocity. Additional variables, such as the kinetic rates of saturation transfers, may, with equal justice, also be included. Rapid advances in many MRI applications, including MRA, diffusion imaging echo planner, and clinical magnetic resonance spectroscopy, have necessitated an increased need for QA. It is therefore not accidental that MRI QA should present more challenges and demand more effort than other medical imaging modalities. This becomes increasingly important as MRI continues to evolve at a much greater rate than other imaging modalities. It is difficult to do justice to the technology involved in the small amount of time customarily allotted to QA, and any help must be welcomed. Hence, one must especially encourage current attempts to integrate QA with preventive maintenance in ways that use QA results and methods to make servicing MRI equipment more efficient.

    The ACR accreditation program is the first attempt to standardize QA for MRI. This program is still in its infancy, and it is hoped that it will be expanded and that MRI QA and CC will become a requirement by insurance companies and government agencies alike. Only this will help ensure technical system performance and optimization of health care trends in respect to quality assurance and cost containment.

REFERENCES

1. Clair MR, Kessler HP, Pasto M, et al: US Healthcare (HMO PA/NJ) obstetrical US quality assurance program. Radiology 1992;185P, p. 143.
2. Friedman DP, Rosetti GF, Flanders AE, et al: MR imaging: Quality assessment method and ratings at 33 centers. *Radiology* 1995;196:219–226.
3. Felmlee JP, Lanners DM, Rettman DW, et al: MR imaging quality control measurements taken as part of a multicenter trial: Initial results. Radiology 1997; 204P, p. 619.
4. Knowles RJR, Markisz JA: *Quality Assurance and Image Artifacts in Magnetic Resonance Imaging.* Boston: Little, Brown and Company, 1988.
5. Dixon RL (ed): *MRI Acceptance Testing and Quality Control: The Role of the Clinical Medical Physicist.* Madison, WI: Medical Physics Publishing Corporation, 1988.
6. American Institute of Physics: *Acceptance Testing of Magnetic Resonance Imaging Systems.* AAPM report no. 34. New York: American Institute of Physics, 1992.
7. Shellock FG: MR imaging of metallic implants and materials: A compilation of the literature. *AJR* 1988;151:811–814.
8. Shellock FG, Morisoli S, Kanal E: MR procedures and biomedical implants, materials, and devices: 1993 update. *Radiology* 1993;189:587–599.
9. Erlebacher JA, Cahill PT, Pannizzo R, et al: Effect of magnetic resonance imaging on DDD pacemakers. *Am J Cardiol* 1986;57:437–440.
10. Camach CR, Plewes DB, Henkelman RM: Nonsusceptibility artifacts due to metallic objects in MR imaging. *J Magn Reson Imaging* 1995;5:75–88.
11. Bellon EM, Haacke EM, Coleman PE, et al: MR artifacts: A review. *AJR* 1986;147:1271–1281.
12. Bradley WG: MR site accreditation. *J Magn Reson Imaging* 1993;3:808–810.
13. McLelland R, Hendrick RE, Zinninger MD, Wilcox PA: The American College of Radiology Mammography Accreditation Program. *AJR* 1991;157:473–479.
14. Brant-Zawadzki M, Boyko OB, Jensen MC, Gillan GD: *MR Angiography: A Teaching File.* New York: Raven Press, 1993.
15. Kido DK, Barsotti JB, Rice LZ, et al: Evaluation of the carotid artery bifurcation: Comparison of magnetic resonance angiography and digital arch aortography. *Neuroradiology* 1991;33:48–51.
16. Polak JF, Bajakian RL, O'Leary DH, et al: Detection of internal carotid artery stenosis: Comparison of MR angiography, color Doppler sonography, and arteriography. *Radiology* 1992;182:35–40.
17. McLemore JM: *Quality Assurance in Diagnostic Radiology.* Chicago: Year Book Publishers, 1981.
18. Gray JE, Winkler NT, Stears J, et al: *Quality Control in Diagnostic Imaging: A Quality Control Cookbook.* Baltimore: University Park Press, 1983.
19. Sweeney RJ: *Radiographic Artifacts: Their Cause and Control.* New York: Lippincott, 1983.

20. Cahill PT, Vullo T: Picture archiving and communications systems: Status, problems, and needs. *Information Display* 1996;12:36–40.

21. Edelstein WA, Bottemley PA, Pfeifer LM: A signal-to-noise calibration procedure for NMR imaging systems. *Med Phys* 1984;11:180–185.

22. Wagner RF, Brown DG: Unified SNR analysis of medical imaging systems. *Phys Med Biol* 1985;30:489–518.

23. Young IR, Bryant DF, Payne JA: Variation in slice shape and absorption as artifacts in the determination of tissue parameters in NMR imaging. *Magn Reson Med* 1985;2:355–389.

24. McRobbie DW, Lerski RA, Straughan K, et al: Investigation of slice characteristics in nuclear magnetic resonance imaging. *Phys Med Biol* 1986;31:613–626.

25. Robinson EM, Hickey DS, Aspden RM, et al: Computer simulation of the slice profile in magnetic-resonance imaging. *Phys Med Biol* 1987;32:1531–1544.

26. Parsons D, Kim Y, Haynor D: Quality control of cathode-ray tube monitors for medical imaging using a simple photometer. *J Digit Imaging* 1995;8:10–20.

27. Masterson ME, McGary R, Schmitt K, et al: Accuracy and reproducibility of image derived relaxation times on a clinical 1.5 T magnetic resonance scanner. *Med Phys* 1989;16:225–233.

28. Majumdar S, Orphanoudakis SC, Gmitro A, et al: Errors in the measurements of T_2 using multiple-echo MRI techniques, I. Effects of radiofrequency pulse imperfections. *Magn Reson Med* 1986;3:397–417.

29. Majundar S, Orphanoudakis SC, Gmitro A, et al: Errors in the measurements of T_2 using multiple-echo MRI techniques, II. Effects of static field homogeneity. *Magn Reson Med* 1986;3:562–574.

30. Crawley P, Henkelman RM: Errors in T_2 estimation using multislice multiple-echo imaging. *Magn Reson Med* 1987;4:34–47.

31. Kneeland JB, Shimakawa A, Wehrli FW: Effect of intersection spacing on MR imaging contrast and study time. *Radiology* 1986;158:819–822.

32. Carr HY, Purcell EM: Effects of diffusion on free precession in nuclear magnetic resonance experiments. *Phys Rev* 1954;94:630–638.

33. Kurland RJ: Strategies and tactics in NMR imaging relaxation time measurements, I. Minimizing relaxation time errors due to image noise: The ideal case. *Magn Reson Med* 1985;2:136–158.

34. Wehrli FW: *Fast-Scan Magnetic Resonance: Principles and Applications.* New York: Raven Press, 1991.

35. Wood ML, Zur Y, Neuringer LJ: Gradient moment nulling for steady-state precession MR imaging of cerebrospinal fluid. *Med Phys* 1991;18:1038–1044.

36. Hinks RS, Constable RT: Gradient moment nulling in fast spin echo. *Magn Reson Med* 1994;32:698–706.

37. Meier D, Meier S, Bosiger P: Quantitative flow measurements on phantoms and on blood vessels with MR. *Magn Reson Med* 1988;8:25–34.

38. Le Bihan D, Breton E, Lallemand D, et al: Separation of diffusion and perfusion in intravoxel incoherent motion MR imaging. *Radiology* 1988;168:497–505.

39. Lee H, Price RR: Diffusion imaging with the MP-RAGE sequence. *J Magn Reson Imaging* 1994;4:837–842.

CHAPTER FIVE

MRI MICROSCOPY

Zang Hee Cho, Soon-Chil Lee, Joon-Young Chung, and E. K. Wong

Visualizing small objects, profiles as well as internal structures, has been one of the important issues in physical sciences. Several types of microscopes, such as the scanning tunneling microscope,[1] have been developed in the past decades to satisfy this need. Scanning tunneling microscopes now boast subangstrom resolution, making it possible to visualize a single atom. Optical and electron microscopes have inherent limitations for the study of living objects in vivo, however. They observe only the surface of cells or damage living cells by energetic probing particles.

Recently, nuclear magnetic resonance (NMR) imaging techniques have been developed and have demonstrated diverse imaging capabilities for diagnostic purposes.[2-5] Nuclear magnetic resonance imaging (also known as magnetic resonance imaging [MRI]) has demonstrated superior performance in diagnostic imaging over many other existing imaging modalities such as x-ray computed tomography (CT). The major advantages of NMR imaging are, among others, its variety of imaging parameters (eg, spin density, spin–lattice and spin–spin relaxation times, chemical shift, flow velocity, diffusion coefficient, etc) and its nonionizing nature. The spectroscopic imaging capability of NMR can also be an important advantage; for example, phosphorous spectroscopy and imaging are now almost routinely used in humans. A most important characteristic of NMR imaging is its inherent high-contrast and high-resolution capability. Toward this end, much work has been carried out recently.

Nuclear magnetic resonance microscopy is one of the newly emerging tools for high-resolution, three-dimensional imaging of live animals and plants for biological and medical research.[6-10] More recent developments include engineering applications of NMR microscopy such as the imaging of porous materials and microflow, the study of which is essential for oil research.[11] One of the main attractions of NMR microscopy is its potential for truly noninvasive three-dimensional, high-resolution imaging with which micron resolution can be achieved.[12,13] Similar to other microscopes, spatial resolution is the most important requirement of the NMR microscope. From theoretical analysis and preliminary experiments, it was found that the most serious problems in micron-resolution microscopic imaging are the diffusion-related effects and the low signal-to-noise ratio (SNR) due to small voxel size.[14] Many investigators have reported that diffusion causes random phase dispersion of excited spins when spatial gradient fields are applied.[15,16] Random phase dispersion prevents an image from being reconstructed correctly in Fourier transform (FT) MRI. Also, the NMR signal decays faster due to random phase dispersion and thereby decreases SNR. As will be discussed, low SNR due to reduced voxel size appears to decide the fundamental resolution limit when the resolution approaches the micron level, rather than other effects such as diffusion. This fact can be demonstrated by the following example: A voxel size of conventional imaging (1 mm^3) reduced to that of microscopic imaging (1 μm^3) is $1:10^{-9}$. This means the expected SNR reduction will be a factor of 10^{-9}.

We present the theoretical limitations of micron-resolution NMR microscopy, which include bandwidth and diffusion-related resolution behaviors, relevant experimental imaging techniques, and problems associated with microscopic NMR imaging.

SNR, BANDWIDTH LIMITATION, AND DIFFUSION EFFECTS ON RESOLUTION

Signal-to-Noise Ratio

The fundamental resolution limit of NMR microscopy comes from the SNR.[6] The imaging voxel size that generates the signal of an image pixel decreases with increasing resolution. If the NMR signal from a voxel is not larger than noise even after a large number of signal averagings, then resolution cannot be improved further. The SNR is related to various factors, such as the main magnetic field strength, voxel size, radiofrequency (RF) coil sensitivity, data acquisition time, and imaging technique. It is known that the SNR of a voxel is proportional to[6]

$$\text{SNR} \propto \left[\frac{\omega_0^2 B_1}{R^{1/2} (BW)^{1/2}} \right] \left[A(D, G, T_{\text{acq}}) V \right] \qquad (1)$$

where

ω_0 is the resonance frequency ($\omega_0 = \gamma B_0$, B_0 being the static magnetic field),

B_1 is the RF field in the transverse plane produced by unit current,

R is the noise resistance due to coil and sample,

BW is the receiver bandwidth,

A is the attenuation factor due to diffusion,

V is the voxel volume,

D is the self-diffusion coefficient,

G is the gradient field strength, and

T_{acq} is the data acquisition time.

The terms in the first bracket in Equation 1 are the instrumental factors, including the main magnetic field (ω_0) and RF coil (B_1 and R), whereas the terms in the second bracket depend mainly on imaging conditions. For a given bandwidth or resolution, noise resistance, voxel volume, and magnetic field are most important factors affecting the SNR, which are discussed later in some detail.

Noise Resistance

The equivalent noise resistance R in Equation 1 can be broken down into coil resistance, R_c, and sample resistance, R_s. Since pick-up coils used in microscopic imaging are usually much smaller than those used in conventional imaging, a variety of coil types are used. Solenoidal coils are most effective as far as SNR is concerned. For a solenoidal coil whose ratio of diameter to height is 1, and with a sample of the same shape and size of the coil, the coil and sample noise resistances are given by [6]

$$R_c = \frac{3kn^2 \, \rho_c^{1/2} \, \mu_c^{1/2} \, \omega_0^{1/2}}{2^{3/2}} \qquad (2)$$

and

$$R_s = \frac{\pi \, \omega_0^2 \mu_0^2 n^2 d^3}{256 \rho_s} \tag{3}$$

where k is the proximity effect factor, n is the number of coil turns; ρ_c and ρ_s are the specific resistivities of the coil and sample, respectively; μ_0 and μ_c are the permeability of the free space and coil (copper), respectively; and d is the coil size. The coil noise resistance is independent of the coil size, whereas the sample noise resistance is proportional to the cube of the sample size, which is the same as the coil size in this case. In Figure 5–1, these two noise resistances are plotted as a function of the coil size at various resonance frequencies. Contrary to conventional imagings in which imaging object sizes are usually in the order of centimeters, the thermal noise in a coil is the dominant noise source in microscopy, where the sample size is usually less than 1 to 5 mm. The dominance of the coil thermal noise over the sample noise in microscopic imaging has important consequences in NMR microscopy since the SNR is critically dependent on voxel size and magnetic field.

Voxel Size
As mentioned earlier, coil thermal noise, which is dominant in microscopic imaging, is independent of sample size. The RF field, B_1, of a solenoidal coil is inversely proportional to the coil size, therefore, the SNR can be written from Equations 1 and 3 as

$$SNR \propto [VB_1] \propto d^2 \tag{4}$$

Equation 4 shows that the SNR of a voxel is proportional to the voxel volume and inversely proportional to the coil size, resulting in an SNR proportional to d^2. This result is interesting since intuitively the SNR is expected to be proportional to d^3. This theoretical estimation of the dependence of the SNR on voxel size matches well with experimental work.[6]

Magnetic Field
The frequency dependencies of the coil and sample noise are quite different as seen in Equations 2 and 3; that is, R_c is proportional to $\omega_0^{1/2}$ due to the skin depth effect, whereas R_s is proportional to ω_0^2. Since the signal amplitude is proportional to B_0^2 and

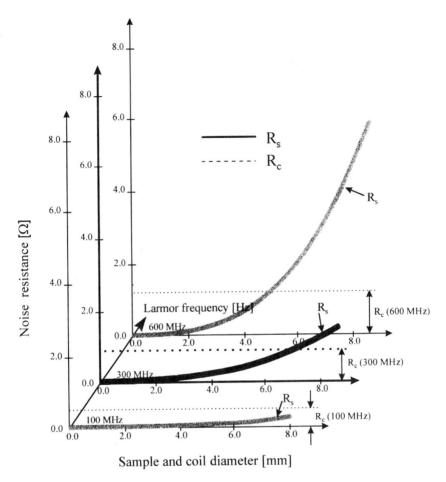

Figure 5–1. Plots of the equivalent noise resistances of the coil and sample as a function of coil and sample diameter at three different NMR operating frequencies: 100, 300, and 600 MHz.

inversely proportional to $R^{1/2}$ as seen in Equation 1, the resulting SNR is proportional to $B_0^{7/4}$ when the coil thermal noise is dominant. This result is different from the result previously known in conventional imaging in which SNR is proportional to B_0 when the sample noise is dominant. Therefore, in microscopic imaging where coil thermal noise is dominant, the $B_0^{7/4}$ rule is generally applicable. This implies that a large signal enhancement can be achieved by increasing the main magnetic field.

Finite Bandwidth

In this section, we derive the basic relationship between the desired spatial resolution and bandwidth, which is determined by the gradient amplitude and duration. Let us assume that the SNR is sufficiently high and the detection system is ideal; that is, there is no uncertainty in measurement. Since NMR imaging is a phase-encoding technique, it is natural to consider the relationship between spatial resolution and minimally detectable phase difference. The basic imaging equation given here provides some insight to the problem.

$$S(t) = M_0 \int d^3 \mathbf{r} \rho(\mathbf{r}) \exp\left(i\gamma\mathbf{r} \cdot \int_0^t \mathbf{G}(t')dt'\right) \tag{5}$$

where $S(t)$ is a spin signal, M_0 is the magnetization at thermal equilibrium, $\rho(\mathbf{r})$ is the spatially dependent spin density, γ is the gyromagnetic ratio, and $\mathbf{G}(t)$ is the gradient. Equation 5 predicts that the phase change, $\phi(\mathbf{r})$, during the data acquisition period of an object located at $\mathbf{r}$ is

$$\phi(\mathbf{r}) = \gamma\mathbf{r} \cdot \int_0^{T_{acq}} \mathbf{G}(t')dt' \tag{6}$$

where T_{acq} is data acquisition time. The difference between the phases of two objects located at $\mathbf{r}_1$ and $\mathbf{r}_2$ is, therefore, given by

$$\delta\phi = \gamma(\mathbf{r}_1 - \mathbf{r}_2) \cdot \int_0^{T_{acq}} \mathbf{G}(t')dt' = \gamma(\delta r)GT_{acq} \tag{7}$$

where the gradient amplitude G is assumed to be a constant. From Equation 7, the bandwidth-limited intrinsic resolution can be defined as

$$(\delta r)_B = \frac{\delta\phi_{min}}{(\gamma GT_{acq})} \tag{8}$$

The minimally detectable phase, $\delta\phi_{min}$, depends on the reconstruction algorithm. For example, it is π in the FT reconstruction of a half-echo data set. For a given minimally detectable phase, resolution can be improved by increasing either the gradient amplitude or data acquisition time. As can be seen in the following discussion, data acquisition time cannot be increased indefinitely because of T_2 decay and signal attenuation due to diffusion. Usually, strong gradient fields are therefore used in microscopic imaging. Gradient fields used in micron resolution imaging are usually three orders of magnitude stronger (100–1000 G/cm) than that used in conventional NMR whole-body imaging (0.1–0.5 G/cm). The gradient fields and data acquisition times required for given resolutions are shown graphically in Figure 5–2 in the case of FT NMR imaging.

Diffusion Effect

The effect of diffusion on the NMR signal in an inhomogeneous magnetic field has been studied for a long time, and Hahn's formula of echo height is most famous. The echo height decays as $\exp(-2\gamma^3G^2D\tau^3/3)$, where 2τ is the time of echo formation. This formula implies that echo height is extremely sensitive to the change of the diffusion coefficient as well as the field gradient.

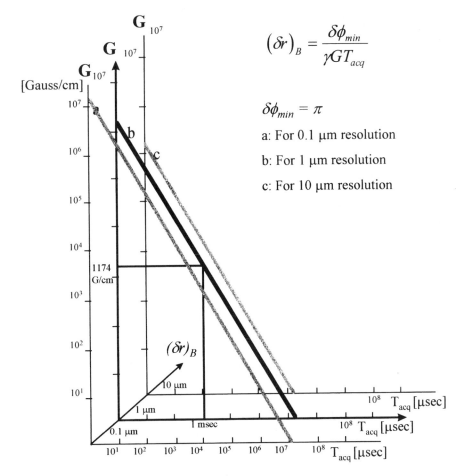

Figure 5–2. A plot of bandwidth-limited intrinsic resolution in the Fourier transform reconstruction NMR microscopy.

We therefore expect that diffusion has a great effect on NMR microscopic imaging where a very strong magnetic gradient field is used. Since the most important factor in microscopic imaging is resolution, the major emphasis of the present work focuses on the effect of diffusion on image resolution.

Diffusion generates a dispersion in spin phases of nuclei located at the same position. This is because the nuclei that gathered at the same position in the presence of a magnetic gradient field have different phases depending on each particle's (spin's) path history. The real position of a spin therefore becomes uncertain, and it is clear that we cannot increase resolution beyond this uncertainty. Dispersion in spin phase is also reflected as extra signal attenuation, which leads to line broadening, therefore, image resolution degradation (Lorentzian line broadening).

In many practical cases, however, such as biological sample imaging, the nuclei in a sample do not diffuse freely in infinite space. In general, the purpose of NMR imaging is to distinguish the domains in which imaging parameters, such as spin density and physical or chemical properties (T_1, T_2, χ), are different, provided that nuclei belonging to one domain barely move to neighboring domains, at least during data acquisition time. That is, impenetrable boundaries exist between the domains within an object. The general analysis based on free diffusion is therefore not suitable for NMR microscopy of small regions confined by boundaries, since, in this case, diffusion is no longer free. It is also important to note that in imaging, resolution matters only near the boundaries, since there is no need to distinguish two neighboring pixels inside a homogeneous domain far from the boundaries. Lauterbur and colleagues[14] and Pütz and co-workers[15] have reported how these impenetrable boundaries or walls can distort or even enhance images at the microscopic scale in MRI. Image intensity is enhanced near the boundaries when the diffusion coefficient is modest and increases or focuses around the center of the domain when the diffusion coefficient becomes large. Pütz and co-workers[15] derived an expression of the lineshape function for the case of bounded diffusion by solving the diffusive Bloch equation. Similar results were obtained by means of Monte Carlo simulation based on the random-walk molecular-diffusion process.[16] In the latter, although similar effects were observed, it was found that the results depended heavily on the pulse sequence employed.[16]

Edge Enhancement Effect of Bounded Spins Due to Motional Narrowing

To observe the diffusion-dependent edge enhancement effect, a series of Monte Carlo simulations are made. In Figure 5–3, the spatial spin distribution and the phase distribution of spins diffusing near an impenetrable wall in a linear gradient field obtained by the Monte Carlo simulation are plotted. The spins are distributed initially at position 0 over an infinitesimally thin slab. As can be seen, the profile of the spatial distribution of the spins that diffuse freely in an infinite space is very close to the normal gaussian distribution. In the case of bounded diffusion, however, the spin density near the wall is increased. Those spins that are supposed to be outside the wall are now symmetrically folded over toward the inside (see Fig. 5–3(a)). The important factor for imaging is not the position but the phase distribution of these spins. The linear gradient field added in MRI gives phase variation along the imaging direction; that is, the phase value increases linearly as the position moves either to the right or left in the absence of diffusion. As expected, the phase of diffusing spins is not linear with position. For free diffusion, the phase dispersion follows a gaussian curve as the position distribution (see Fig. 5–3(a)). In the case of bounded diffusion, however, the phase distribution differs from the position distribution as shown in Figure 5–3(b). This difference generates image distortion.

The effect of bounded diffusion in imaging is shown in Figure 5–4, in which the spin phase distributions of a one-dimensional rectangular spin distribution in a linear gradient field are plotted for various diffusion coefficients as a function of time. It is clearly seen in Figure 5–4 that the edge begins to be enhanced with an increasing diffusion coefficient up to a certain value ($D < 2.0 \times 10^{-3}$ cm^2/s) as time evolves. The peaks at the edges, however, begin to move inside with an increasing diffusion coefficient, and, with time, finally they merge to a single peak at the center in a manner similar to the motional narrowing in MR spectroscopy. This effect suggests that motional narrowing alone is not sufficient for the full explanation of edge enhancement, discussed by Lauterbur et al[14] and Pütz et al.[15]

Pulse Sequence-Dependent Selective Spectral Suppression Effect

In addition to possible edge enhancement due to the diffusion-dependent motional-narrowing effect discussed earlier, it is

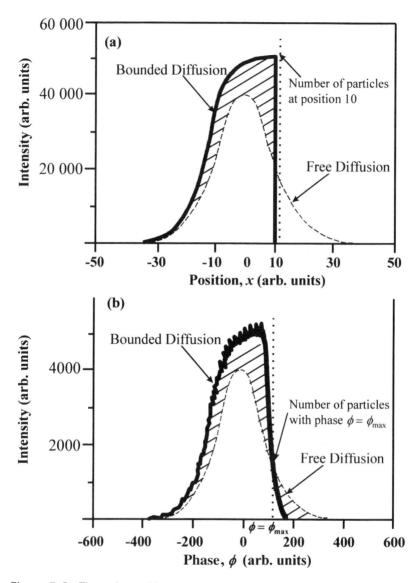

Figure 5–3. The spin position and the phase distributions of the free and bounded spins originated from $x = 0$ (at $T = 0$) observed at $T = 400\ \Delta t$. *(a)* The position spreads of the bounded spins limited at the wall (solid line), and the unbounded spins that follow the normal gaussian distribution (dotted line). *(b)* The phase distribution of the bounded spins. This distribution looks similar to the position distribution, but there is a difference. In the case of phase distribution, at $\phi \geq \phi_{max}$, the maximum phases of the bounded spins are spilled over the maximum phase value (ϕ_{max}) at and above the boundary.

Spin Evolution due to Motional Narrowing Effect

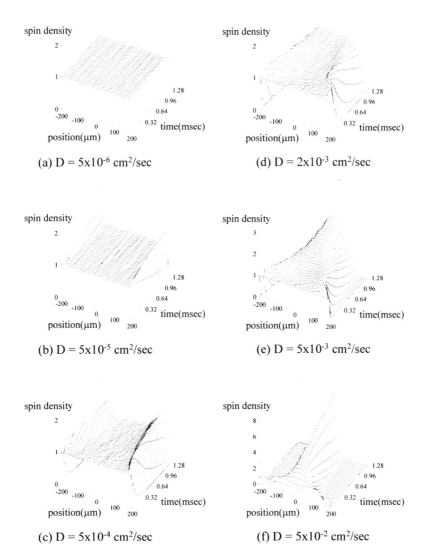

(a) D = 5x10⁻⁶ cm²/sec

(d) D = 2x10⁻³ cm²/sec

(b) D = 5x10⁻⁵ cm²/sec

(e) D = 5x10⁻³ cm²/sec

(c) D = 5x10⁻⁴ cm²/sec

(f) D = 5x10⁻² cm²/sec

Figure 5–4. Distributions of the instantaneous spin density due to the motional-narrowing effect over time for several values of the diffusion coefficients. The rate of diffusion increases from *(a)* to *(f)*. As shown, the edge enhancement effect occurs only on a few occasions, such as the cases with $D = 5 \times 10^{-5}$, to 5×10^{-4}cm²/s.

found that the edge enhancement effect can also result from the "spectral effect," as discussed later in this section. If spin distribution is translated into the NMR signal by solving the classical Bloch equation and using the imaging sequence shown in Figure 5–5, the following results are obtained. First, with the spin echo sequence shown in Figure 5–5(a), a typical echo signal is obtained as shown in Figure 5–5(b). In this case, the frequency distribution of the generated spin echo signal can be divided into three parts: one being the negative high-frequency components located at the left or the beginning of the echo, another being the direct current (DC) components at the center, and the last part being the positive high-frequency components located at the right, respectively. Another pulse sequence known as the diffusion-effect reduced gradient echo (DRG) sequence[6] is shown in Figure 5–5(c) with its signal shown in Figure 5–5(d). With the latter, as shown, one can obtain free induction decay (FID)-like echo signals.

In Figure 5–6(a), spin echo signals obtained with three different diffusion coefficients, namely $D = 10^{-6}$, 10^{-5}, and 2.0×10^{-5} cm^2/s, are shown. The diffusive motion of spins has two consequences, namely the diffusive motion that distorts the spin distribution from the original one and the spin phase dispersion that results in spin phase incoherency within a voxel that leads to signal attenuation. The latter, which is often referred to as diffusive attenuation, attenuates the signal similar to T_2^* attenuation.

The bounded spin case in Figure 5–6(a) shows how the spin echo signals are attenuated as a function of time due to the diffusion effect for several different values of the diffusion coefficients. Although it is difficult to visualize clearly from these figures, trends of unequal spectral attenuation are clearly visible; for example, the positive high-frequency parts and, to a lesser extent, the DC parts of each spectrum at $t = TE + \tau/2$ and $t \approx TE$ are severely attenuated compared with the negative high-frequency parts at $t = TE - \tau/2$, especially with large diffusion coefficients ($D = 2.0 \times 10^{-5}$ cm^2/s). Results of the reconstructed images are shown in Figure 5–6(b). As seen, the edge enhancement effect becomes more pronounced with an increasing diffusion coefficient while the attenuation of the DC components (middle part of the image) becomes more severe. Although some portion of edge enhancement could be due to motional narrowing, it seems to be mostly due to the **"selective spectral**

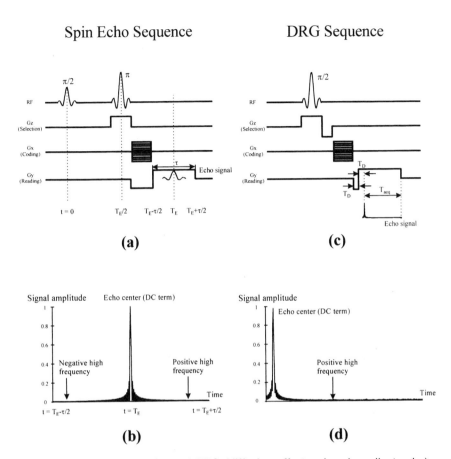

Figure 5–5. The spin echo and DRG (diffusion effect reduced gradient echo) pulse sequences used for the study and their typical nuclear signals. *(a).* The spin echo pulse sequence and *(b)* a typical echo signal. From the left, the negative high-frequency parts, the direct current (DC) parts at the center, and positive high-frequency part, respectively, are shown with arrows. As time progresses, diffusion attenuation becomes larger; that is, the negative high-frequency parts experience the least attenuation, whereas the DC and the positive high-frequency parts suffer the largest attenuation. *(c).* The DRG pulse sequence and *(d)* a typical free induction decay (FID)-like DRG echo signal. From the left, the DC parts and positive high-frequency parts are shown. As is known, there is only a small negative high-frequency part in the DRG pulse sequence.

suppression effect," that is, the effects of attenuations of the DC components and the positive high-frequency parts. It is not yet clear, however, from this study alone whether the edge enhancement is due to motional narrowing or selective spectral suppression since it is the case of bounded spins.

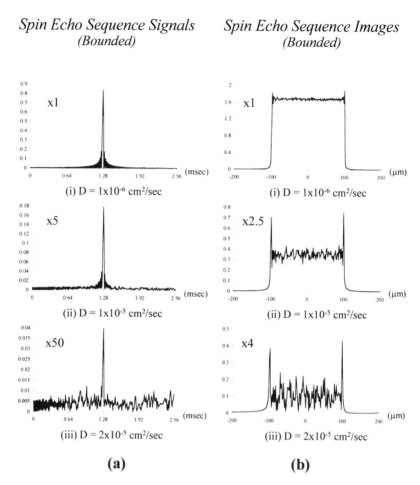

Spin Echo Sequence Signals
(Bounded)

Spin Echo Sequence Images
(Bounded)

(a)

(b)

Figure 5–6. The spin echo signals with selective spectral suppression effect and their corresponding one-dimensional (1-D) images for bounded spins. *(a).* The spin echo signals of different diffusion coefficients and *(b)* 1-D images reconstructed from the echo signals in part *(a).*

To clarify this edge enhancement effect, especially to determine whether it is due to motional narrowing or other factors, we simulated spin echo imaging with *unbounded* spins and obtained the results shown in Figure 5–7. To our surprise, nearly the same results as those observed with the bounded spin case were obtained (compare with Fig. 5–6). This led us to re-examine all the diffusion-dependent edge enhancement hypotheses,[14, 15] since edge enhancement still persists as shown in Figure 5–7(b), even when the spins are now no longer bounded **(unbounded).**

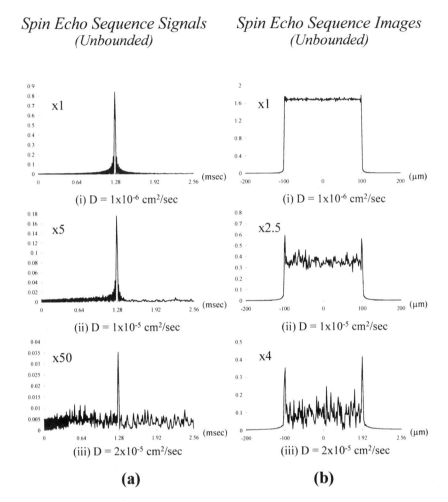

Spin Echo Sequence Signals
(Unbounded)

Spin Echo Sequence Images
(Unbounded)

(a)   (b)

Figure 5–7. Same as in Figure 6, but with unbounded spins. Although, in this case, we do not expect edge enhancement due to the absence of boundaries or walls, we still observe edge enhancements similar to the ones shown in Figure 5–6(b). This is believed to be due to the selective spectral suppression of the positive high frequency and the DC parts of the spin echo signal as discussed in the text. These results convince us that the edge enhancements are not entirely due to the diffusive motional-narrowing effect of the spins.

The latter cannot be explained by the motional-narrowing effect. The results of Figure 5–7, therefore, clearly imply that edge enhancement is due to some other effects, such as selective spectral suppression discussed by Cho and associates[16] and also implied by Callaghan and co-workers.[17] In other words, in spin echo sequences the DC parts at the center and the positive high-frequency parts of the echo signal are attenuated more severely by diffusion attenuation than by negative high-frequency parts. It is therefore clear that the remaining unattenuated negative high-frequency parts play major roles in edge enhancement.

Strictly speaking, spin density of the edge is not enhanced, but negative high-frequency terms are unattenuated and remain while the DC, and the positive high-frequency components are severely attenuated. Main edge enhancement is also due to the reduction of DC components, which in turn reduces the flat middle part of the image, resulting in an edge enhancement.

Selective spectral attenuation in the domain of the nuclear signal (in the echo signal as well as in FID) due to diffusion attenuation seems to be mostly responsible for edge enhancement in microscopic imaging rather than the motional-narrowing effect as previously thought. This is a new result not previously postulated by Pütz and co-workers,[15] Lauterbur and colleagues,[14] and Callaghan and co-workers.[17] Although Callaghan and co-workers postulated a diffusive relaxation effect, the specifics of the result were not discussed. To further prove that the spectral suppression effect plays the dominant role in edge enhancement, we tested a DRG sequence shown in Figure 5–5C. In this DRG sequence, positive high-frequency parts are always suppressed compared with DC parts, so edge enhancement is not expected, or at least should not dominate. In Figure 5–8A, as predicted, edges degrade in the case of unbounded spins, regardless of diffusion coefficient values. In the case of bounded spins, for high values of diffusion coefficients, some edge enhancement is seen, as shown in Figure 5–8B. This can be explained by the motional-narrowing effect as discussed earlier. A noticeable difference occurs compared with spin echo sequences; the DC components (the middle flat parts of the image data) remain high as expected in the DRG sequence. These observations confirm that the selective spectral suppression theory indeed dominates the edge enhancement in microscopic imaging.[16]

IMAGING TECHNIQUES

As discussed in the previous section, data acquisition time should be as short as possible to reduce the diffusion effect. Yet,

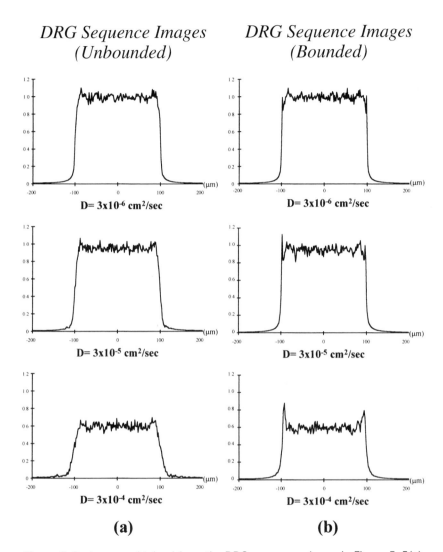

DRG Sequence Images (Unbounded)

DRG Sequence Images (Bounded)

(a)　　　　　　　　**(b)**

Figure 5–8. Images obtained from the DRG sequence shown in Figure 5–5(c). As expected, edge enhancement is no longer visible in the case of unbounded spins. The same trends are observed for the bounded spins, especially with small diffusion coefficient values ($D = 3 \times 10^{-6}$ cm2/s). Some edge enhancements are visible at the large diffusion coefficient values ($D > 3 \times 10^{-5}$ cm2/s). The latter is probably due to the classical motional-narrowing effect as discussed earlier.

it should be long enough to warrant the bandwidth-dependent resolution limit given in Equation 8. The DRG technique shown in Figure 5–5(c) is the sequence developed to satisfy both of these needs.[6,16] This scheme is a variation of the gradient echo imaging technique, using a short dephasing gradient pulse. As shown in Figure 5–5(c), the dephasing period is made short compared with the conventional gradient echo technique to reduce the signal attenuation due to the diffusion process. To compare the diffusion-dependent signal attenuation, signal amplitudes at the echo center are estimated for: (a) the spin echo technique, (b) the gradient echo technique, and (c) the DRG sequence, respectively. For a given set of parameters ($D = 10^{-5}$ cm^2/s, $G = 196$ G/cm, $TE = 4.0$ ms, $TD = T_x/4$, and $T_x = 1.5$ ms), the relative signal amplitudes calculated at centers are found to be 0.29, 0.54, and 0.99, respectively. Here TE, TD, and T_x represent the echo times of the conventional pulsed echo technique, the dephasing period in the DRG technique, and half of the data acquisition period in the conventional echo technique, respectively. The DRG sequence provides a substantially larger signal than the others and is almost twice as large as that of the conventional gradient echo sequence.[6] Since only half of the echo data is obtained in the DRG technique, compensation is required.[18,19] In the spatial frequency domain, half-echo data occupies only a small region of the four quadrants near the origin. The phase map necessary for whole-image reconstruction is derived from the data in the central square region. Phase information near the center is usually sufficient to estimate the phase in the whole-image domain. Another technique developed to avoid the diffusion effect due to long-readout gradient field duration is the k-space point mapping (KPM) technique and its variation, the multipoint k-space point mapping (MKPM) technique.[20] In MKPM, an extremely short-readout gradient is used for point mapping in k-space. K-space point mapping and MKPM require a long imaging time, but they can generate images that are free from the artifacts due to the effects of susceptibility, chemical shift, and diffusion.

One of the techniques most frequently used to improve SNR is the driven equilibrium Fourier transform (DEFT) technique.[21] The DEFT sequence is a sensitivity-enhanced data acquisition technique proposed by Becker and colleagues.[21] In spite of its obvious advantage, there are several difficulties in the application of this sequence to actual imaging experiments, especially in the area of conventional clinical imaging. Specifically, the RF deposition of the DEFT sequence is large compared with the spin echo sequence, and sensitivity improvement becomes less significant with longer repetition times. The DEFT sequence also requires exact 90° and 180° RF pulses and good homogeneity. Application of this method to whole-body imaging, therefore, has been limited. Nuclear magnetic resonance microscopy applications, however, are different. It is easy to fulfill the requirements discussed earlier in the case of microscopy with a small object; that is, it is easy to achieve uniform excitation over the whole volume. For this reason, a modified DEFT sequence is often used in NMR microscopy with a shorter repetition time and smaller flip angles.[22]

One of the promising application areas related to microscopic imaging is very high-resolution imaging of large objects in vivo, such as localized high-resolution imaging of a limited volume of the human body. Very high-resolution in vivo human body imaging has several interesting features, such as the possibility of observing fine anatomical details and pathological structures normally unavailable with conventional imaging techniques. In general, very high-resolution imaging has two important requirements, namely strong gradient fields and higher-sensitivity RF coils to compensate for the loss of SNR due to reduced voxel size. When we deal with high-resolution imaging of a large object, it is necessary to localize the region so that the size of the imaging matrix can be of a manageable size for image reconstruction. Software and hardware techniques are available that partially satisfy the requirements discussed. The gradient-subencoding technique[23] provides imaging of a localized region by a frequency-domain multiplication process, whereas the surface gradient coil provides localized imaging by forming a suitable field pattern produced from the coil characteristics.[24]

EXPERIMENTAL RESULTS

In NMR microscopy, the design of high-field gradient coils and the development of high-sensitivity RF coils are the two most important factors and are also the major instrumental difficulties. Since the solenoidal coil has good homogeneity and sensitivity, it seems to be the most natural choice as an RF probe for microscopy experiments. The important parameters deciding the Q factor of a small-sized solenoidal coil (1–5 mm in diameter) are coil diameter, coil height, diameter of wire, and number of turns. Although coil inductance can be increased to obtain a higher Q factor by increasing the number of turns, coil resistance also increases with the number of turns, thereby reducing the gain obtained by increasing inductance. The current density and the inductance of a coil can be increased by reducing the wire diameter and spacing. But, it is hindered by the proximity effect and increased coil resistance. The best conditions are usually found by experiment. For highest sensitivity, the diameter of a solenoidal coil is minimized to maximize the filling factor. In imaging of 4-μm resolution, a solenoidal coil of 1-mm diameter was used.[6,12] Golay-type gradient coils are used for high-field gradient generation sacrificing field homogeneity. For microscopic imaging with resolution less than 10 μm, Golay coils are used having an accessible bore size of about 1 cm with a gradient field of about 10^3 G/cm.

Figure 5–9 shows a sample image of 4-μm resolution obtained by using the gradient and RF coils described earlier.[6,12] The magnetic field is 2.0 T, and imaging time is about 1 h. The image in the figure is a cross section of a plant stem obtained with an optimized DRG sequence. It is interesting to note that the detailed inner structure of the plant is clearly visible; that is, the small holes surrounding the hollow region located at the

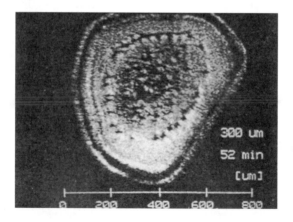

Figure 5–9. A cross-sectional image of a plant stem observed by NMR microscopic imaging of 4-μm resolution obtained by DRG sequence.

center are very clear. These small holes are 20 to 25 µm in diameter and observable by the NMR microscopy only when they are somewhat dried. In this image, the thickness of the slice was 100 µm, which is much thicker than the transverse resolution but acceptable for tomographic imaging if they are longitudinally invariant in shape. Many of the live embryo studies have been conducted using a somewhat higher magnetic field spectrometer modified for imaging; namely the 7.0 T Bruker spectrometer (MSL-300) has been employed for imaging. In Figure 5–10(b), an in-vivo microscopic imaging of an embryo is shown. Cell growth is observed between 1 h and 36 h, and an image at the stage of 36 (or 24 h after cell creation) is shown in Figure 5–10(a). One can observe the development of the neural tube. In Figure 5–11, a cell lineage study observing the pathway with a Gadolinium-diethylene-triaminepenta-acetic acid (Gd-DTPA) Gadolinium-diethylene-triaminepenta-acetic acid tracer injected into a cell at an early stage is shown.[12,13]

CONCLUSIONS

Principles, technical problems associated with NMR microscopy, and some experimental results obtained with currently available NMR microscopes are presented and reviewed, and future potentials are discussed. One of the most serious problems identified in NMR microscopy is poor SNR due to the reduced imaging volume and limited magnetic field strength available today. The much worried diffusion effects on NMR imaging are less severe than originally thought. The reasons may be twofold, namely, the diffusion-limited resolution due to spin phase dispersion and diffusion-dependent signal attenuation are both smaller than currently available resolution of the NMR microscope. The diffusion effect has an important consequence, namely, reduction of SNR due to signal attenuation. Regarding diffusion-dependent edge enhancement by the motional-narrowing effect originally conceived by Lauterbur and colleagues[14] and Pütz and co-workers,[15] one can only conclude that the idea is not yet concretely proven, and it is also difficult to prove experimentally with present technology. Although a number of papers have been reported on high-resolution NMR microscopy at or below 10 µm, practical use of the methods in this resolution range seems limited due to the poor SNR

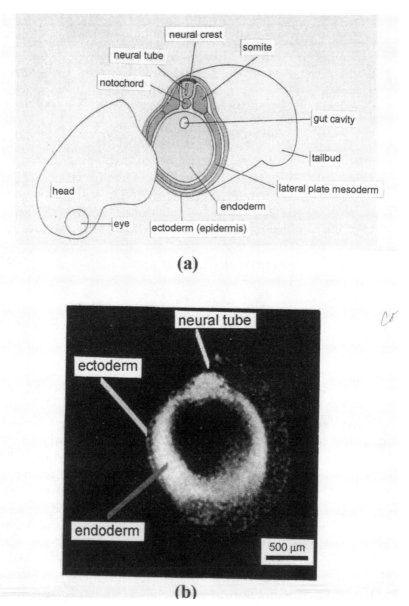

Figure 5–10. *(a)*. An illustration of a *Xenopus laevis* frog embryo at stage 36. *(b)*. An NMR image of an embryo in the early stages of neurulation.

or long imaging time usually required to obtain reasonable quality images in vivo. It appears that, for the time being, in vivo high-resolution imaging of live animals and small biological samples with resolution in the order of 10 to 20 μm appears

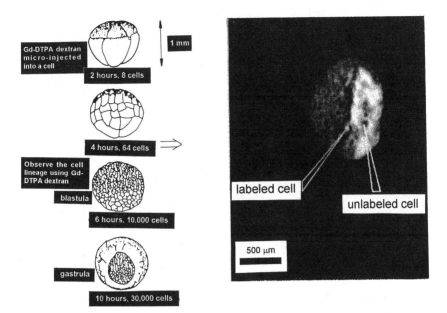

Figure 5–11. One-cell animal pole of this embryo was injected with a solution of Gd-DTPA dextran when it was at the eight-cell stage. This image was recorded at the 512-cell stage with the animal pole oriented to the right. Because this is a T_1-weighted image, significant intensity is to be expected only from regions in close proximity to the Gd ions. A somewhat blotchy image is observed, with most of the intensity sequestered in the rightmost third of the specimen (ie, the animal pole). This is precisely the expected result if the contrast agent remains inside the originally injected cell and its progeny. Moreover, the size of the isolated bright areas ("labeled cell") and isolated dark areas within the animal pole ("unlabeled cell") is of the size expected for cells at this stage of development. *Abbreviation:* Gd-DTPA = gadolinium-diethylenetri-aminepentaacetic acid.

very promising, but resolution beyond this limit seems difficult and probably will have to wait until some breakthroughs occur in the field of high-sensitivity RF coils, such as the superconducting RF coil proposed and developed by Black and Johnson [Private communication]. Another interesting avenue is the micro-detection coil under development by Magnin and Lauterbur at the University of Illinois at Urbana Champaign [Private communication]. With more refined detector assemblies and new pulse sequences, many new useful imaging researches can be carried out, such as micro-functional imaging of animals. Promising new avenues for the application of NMR microscopy include the study of plant physiology, which involves the study of the microscopic water transport phenomenon. Considering the fact that there are thousands of high-field NMR spectrometers all over the world (from chemistry to biophysics laboratories) and also that these spectrometers are relatively easy to modify for imaging purposes, it will not be difficult to imagine that application areas will grow continuously in the future. It should be emphasized that the potentials and the usefulness of NMR microscopy are unique compared with other microscopies in terms of its in vivo three-dimensional imaging capability thanks to the unusual contrast mechanisms that can be generated by T_1, T_2, flow, diffusion, and susceptibility variations, among others. It is obvious that a renaissance in research applications will result as the technology matures.

REFERENCES

1. Binnig G, Rohrer H: *Sci Am* 1985;253:50.
2. Lauterbur PC: *Nature* 1973;242:190.
3. Cho ZH, Kim HS, Song HB, et al: *Proc IEEE* 1982;70:1152.
4. Cho ZH: *Ency Phys Sci Tech* 1987;3:507.
5. Bihan DL, Breton E, Syrota A: *Abstract of 4th Soc. of Magn. Reson. Med.* 1985; 1238.
6. Cho ZH, Ahn CB, Juh SC, et al: *Med Phys* 1988;15:815; and also see Hoult DI, Lauterbur PC: *J Magn Reson* 1979;34:425.
7. Johnson GA, Thompson MB, Drayer BD: *Magn Reson Med* 1987;4:351.
8. Lauterbur PC: *IEEE Trans Nucl Sci* 1984;31:1010.
9. Aguayo JB, Blackband SJ, Schoeniger J, et al: *Nature* 1986;322:190.
10. Callaghan PT, Eccles CD: *J Magn Reson* 1988;78:1.
11. Blumich B, Kuhn W (eds): *VCH Publishers* 1992.
12. Cho ZH, Ahn CB, Juh SC, et al: *Philos Trans Royal Soc Lond [Biol]* 1990;A333: 469.
13. Jacobs RE, Fraser SE: *Science* 1994;264:681.
14. Lauterbur PC, Hyslop WB, Morris HD: *XIth Conference of the International Society of Magnetic Resonance,* Vancouver, BC, Canada, 19–24 July 1992, Abstract O-79.
15. Pütz B, Barsky D, Schulter K: *J Magn Reson* 1992;97:27.
16. Cho ZH, Hong IK, Ro YM: *Magn Reson Med* 1996;36:197.
17. Callaghan PT, Coy A, Forde LC, et al: *J Magn Reson Series A* 1993;101:347.
18. Oh CH, Hilal SK, Ra JB, et al: *Abstract of 6th Soc. of Magn. Reson. Med.,* 1987;455.
19. Margosian P, Lenz G: *Abstract of 6th Soc. of Magn. Reson. Med.,* 1987;446.
20. Cho ZH, Ro YM: *Magn Reson Med* 1994;32:258.
21. Becker ED, Ferretti JA, Farrar TC: *J Am Chem Soc* 1969;91:7784.
22. Tkach JA, Haacke EM: *Magn Reson Imaging* 1988;6:373.
23. Cho ZH, Jo JM: *Med Phys* 1991;18:350.
24. Cho ZH, Yi JH: *J Magn Reson* 1991;94:471.

CHAPTER SIX

REDUCED-SCAN IMAGING
Zhi-Pei Liang and Paul C. Lauterbur

Magnetic resonance imaging (MRI) is a relatively slow imaging technique. In practice, there are numerous motivations to acquire MR images more quickly. For example, in dynamic imaging applications, it is important that a data set be acquired in a short time interval so that high spatial and temporal resolution can be obtained. Over the last two decades, great effort has been made to develop fast imaging methods. Based on how the data space is scanned, these methods can be classified into two categories: fast-scan and reduced-scan imaging methods. Fast-scan methods, such as echo-planar methods,[1,2] and spiral-scan methods[3,4] achieve high-speed imaging by rapidly scanning the data space. Reduced-scan methods, on the other hand, shorten imaging time by reducing the number of encodings acquired. This chapter discusses reduced-scan imaging techniques. Emphasis is placed on the incorporation of a priori information into the imaging process so that image quality is not compromised significantly with a reduced number of encodings.

IMAGING EQUATIONS

Before we discuss reduced-encoding imaging methods in detail, it is useful to review some of the basic equations used for describing MR data acquisition and image reconstruction. In the popular k-space notation,[5] the imaging equation is given by the classic Fourier transform (FT)

$$S(\vec{k}) = \int_{\text{object}} \rho(\vec{x})e^{-i2\pi\vec{k}\vec{x}}d\vec{x} \qquad (1)$$

where $\rho(\vec{x})$ is the desired image function and $S(\vec{k})$ is the acquired signal. For the present chapter, it is convenient to limit our discussion to the phase-encoding direction only. Hence, we can rewrite the imaging equation as a 1-D FT

$$S(k) = \int_{-\infty}^{\infty} \rho(x)e^{-i2\pi kx}dx \qquad (2)$$

where k is a spatial frequency variable, whose value is determined by the phase-encoding gradient strength (G) and the duration (ΔT) for which the gradient is turned on. In practice, a set of N encodings is acquired at $k = n\Delta k = (\gamma/2\pi)n\Delta G\Delta T$, for $n = -N/2, \ldots, N/2 - 1$, where γ is the gyromagnetic ratio. The formula commonly used for image reconstruction is

$$\hat{\rho}(x) = \Delta k \sum_{n=\frac{-N}{2}}^{\frac{N}{2}-1} S(n\Delta k)e^{i2\pi n\Delta kx} \qquad (3)$$

which can be evaluated using a fast-Fourier transform (FFT) algorithm. This method is known as the Fourier, or FFT, reconstruction method.

DATA TRUNCATION ARTIFACTS

The total scan time for an imaging experiment with N phase encodings is

$$T = NT_R N_a \qquad (4)$$

where T_R is the pulse repetition time and N_a is the number of signal averages for each phase-encoded signal. To shorten data acquisition time, one can reduce the number of signal averages or the number of phase encodings (or both). Reducing the number of signal averages is at the price of the signal-to-noise ratio (SNR), and the absolute limit is reached when $N_a = 1$. The effects of reducing the number of phase encodings are discussed in this section.

From the well-known convolution theorem, it is easy to derive that the image reconstructed using Equation 3 is related to the true image function $\rho(x)$ by

$$\hat{\rho}(x) = \rho(x) * h(x) \qquad (5)$$

where * denotes the convolution operator and $h(x)$ is given by

$$h(x) = \Delta k \sum_{n=\frac{-N}{2}}^{\frac{N}{2}-1} e^{i2\pi n\Delta kx} = \Delta k \frac{\sin(\pi N\Delta kx)}{\sin(\pi \Delta kx)} e^{-i\pi \Delta kx} \qquad (6)$$

Since $\hat{\rho}(x) = h(x)$ for an idealized point object, $h(x)$ given in Equation 6 is often called the point-spread function of a Fourier imaging system. A typical $h(x)$ is shown in Figure 6–1. Due to the oscillatory nature of $h(x)$, the convolution in Equation 5 gives rise to spurious ringing in $\hat{\rho}(x)$, known as Gibbs ringing.[6] Some important characteristics of Gibbs ringing are

- The maximum undershoot or overshoot is about 9% of the intensity discontinuity in $\rho(x)$ and is independent of the number of data points used in the reconstruction.

- The frequency of oscillation increases with more data points since the widths of the main lobe and side lobes of $h(x)$ are equal to $2/(N\Delta k)$ and $1/(N\Delta k)$, respectively. Therefore, the distance over which Gibbs ringing is significant is reduced as resolution is increased so that it is often considered negligible in practice when a large number of data points are used.

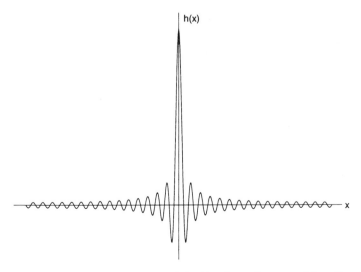

Figure 6–1. A plot of the amplitude of the Fourier point-spread function $h(x)$ for $N = 64$.

In addition to Gibbs ringing, data truncation also results in a loss of spatial resolution. The spatial resolution Δx of the resulting image is commonly characterized by the effective width of the point-spread function, which can be defined as the duration of the equivalent rectangular pulse approximating $h(x)$ in a cycle. More specifically,

$$\Delta x = \frac{1}{h(0)} \int_{-\frac{1}{2\Delta k}}^{\frac{1}{2\Delta k}} h(x)\, dx = \frac{1}{N\Delta k} \tag{7}$$

Therefore, the spatial resolution of a Fourier image reconstructed with N encodings is limited to $1/(N\Delta k)$. To demonstrate these data truncation artifacts, two images reconstructed from a phantom data set are shown in Figure 6–2. As can be seen, reducing N from 256 to 64 results in a significant loss resolution as well as spurious ringing from the sharp edges.

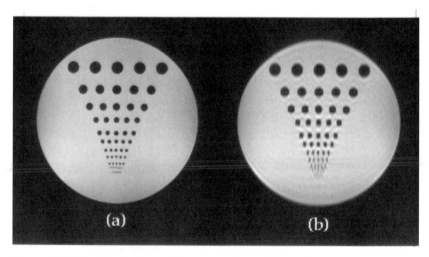

Figure 6–2. An illustration of the truncation artifact with the Fourier reconstruction method. Both images were reconstructed with 256 Fourier samples along the horizontal direction but with 256 samples in *(a)* and 64 samples in *(b)*, respectively, along the vertical direction.

HALF-FOURIER IMAGING

As a first example of reduced-scan imaging, we discuss half-Fourier imaging in this section. As the name implies, half-Fourier imaging methods reduce the number of encoding steps by almost half relative to the conventional full-scan Fourier imaging method. To understand how these methods work, consider the ideal case in which the image function $\rho(x)$ is a real function. In this case, the Fourier signal $S(k)$ has Hermitian symmetry, that is

$$S(-k) = S^*(k) \tag{8}$$

where the superscript * denotes the complex conjugate. The preceding equation suggests that if $S(k)$ is known for $k \geq 0$, then $S(-k)$ can be generated based on the Hermitian symmetry. This is the earliest form of half-Fourier imaging.[7] A practical limitation of this method is due to the fact that the realness constraint is often violated in practice because object motion and magnetic field inhomogeneity introduce a nonzero phase $\varphi(x)$ to the image function. This phase problem can lead to significant image artifacts if the Hermitian symmetry is blindly enforced. The usual approach to cope with this problem is to collect a few additional encodings across the center of k-space, as shown in Figure 6–3, so that k-space is symmetrically sampled in the central region to provide the necessary data to estimate the phase func-

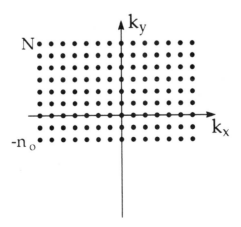

Figure 6–3. An illustration of k-space coverage by a half-Fourier imaging method.

tion. In the following discussion, we assume that the measured data $S(n\Delta k)$ are available for $-n_0 \le n < N$. Usually, n_0 is much smaller than N (typically, $n_0 = 16$ or 32). Therefore, one can still gain approximately a factor of 2 improvement in imaging time with this sampling scheme.

The key to the success of half-Fourier imaging lies in the image reconstruction step. Most existing half-Fourier reconstruction methods follow a two-step procedure. In the first step, a phase image is estimated. A common approach to phase estimation is to directly Fourier transform the central low-frequency data and then extract the phase image from the resulting low-resolution reconstruction. More specifically, $S(n\Delta k)$ for $-n_0 \le n < n_0$ are zero-filled to $-N \le n < N$ and Hamming-filtered to roll off the sharp transitions between the measured data and the padded zeros before they are Fourier transformed. Mathematically, this phase estimate can be formally written as

$$\hat{\varphi}(x) = \arg\left\{ \sum_{m=-N}^{N-1} \hat{S}(m\Delta k)e^{-i2\pi m\Delta kx}\right\} \tag{9}$$

where $\hat{S}(m\Delta k)$ are zero-padded and Hamming-filtered data given by

$$\hat{S}(m\Delta k) = \begin{cases} S(m\Delta k)\left[0.54 + 0.46\cos\left(\dfrac{2m\pi}{n_0}\right)\right] & -n_0 \le m \le n_0 \\ 0 & \text{otherwise} \end{cases} \tag{10}$$

In the second step, the phase image is used as a constraint to reconstruct the final image. With $\hat{\varphi}(x)$ and the asymmetrically sampled k-space data, a number of methods exist to carry out the phase-constrained reconstruction. The method devised by Margosian and co-workers is one of the early but rather successful methods for half-Fourier reconstruction in spin echo imaging applications.[8] A similar method has also been proposed by Noll and Macorski[9] based on homodyne detection theory. The central idea of the Margosian method lies in the observation that the FT reconstruction from a half-echo, denoted here by $\rho_h(x)$, is related to the true image function $\rho(x)$ by the following convolution (in the continuous case):

$$\rho_h(x) = \rho(x) * \left[\frac{1}{2}\delta(x) + i\frac{1}{2\pi x}\right] \tag{11}$$

$$= \frac{1}{2} \rho(x) + i\rho(x) * \frac{1}{2\pi x}$$

Phase-shifting $\rho_h(x)$ by $- \varphi(x)$ yields

$$\rho_h(x)e^{-i\hat{\varphi}(x)} = \frac{1}{2}|\rho(x)|e^{-i[\varphi - \hat{\varphi}(x)]} + i\left[\rho(x) * \frac{1}{2\pi x}\right]e^{-i\hat{\varphi}(x)} \qquad (12)$$

where $\varphi(x)$ is the true phase function of $\rho(x)$. Inspection of Equation 12 shows that if $\hat{\varphi}(x)$ is close to $\varphi(x)$, the first term gives the desired reconstruction. In practice, instead of obtaining $\rho_h(x)$ from the half-echoes as described earlier, the n_0 data points before the echo are also used to avoid the data discontinuity at $k = 0$. This asymmetrical data set is zero-filled to $-N$, and the central $2n_0$ data points are filtered with an asymmetrical Hamming filter to roll off the sharp transition between the zeros and the measured data,[6] after which a standard FFT reconstruction is carried out.

A limitation of the Margosian reconstruction method is its sensitivity to phase errors. Notably, the reconstruction is proportional to

$$\cos[\varphi(x) - \hat{\varphi}(x)]\,|\rho(x)| \qquad (13)$$

This cosine modulation can be significant in regions where large phase errors exist. Additionally, when the true image phase variations are large, as is often the case in gradient echo imaging, this method cannot guarantee a perfect reconstruction even if the exact phase function $\varphi(x)$ is available. This is because the real part of the second term in Equation 12 is significant when $\varphi(x)$, as well as $\hat{\varphi}(x)$, is not small. This term can contribute serious artifacts in the form of geometric distortions to the final image.[6]

In an attempt to overcome the problems with the Margosian method, Cuppen and Van Est[10] proposed an iterative extrapolation method that generates a full symmetrical data set for use with the conventional Fourier reconstruction method. Conceptually, it is similar to the conjugate symmetrization method. Unlike the simple conjugate symmetrization method, however, this method uses $\hat{\varphi}(x)$ to constrain the symmetrization process. In this way, if $\hat{\varphi}(x)$ is accurate, one can potentially recover the symmetrical data set exactly. On the other hand, if $\hat{\varphi}(x)$ deviates significantly from the true phase $\varphi(x)$, exaggeration of the phase errors can be avoided by terminating the iterative process early.

The original phase-constrained symmetrization method proposed by Cuppen and Van Est[10] enforces the phase constraints by setting $\hat{\rho}_l(x)$ to $\hat{\rho}^*_{l-1}(x)e^{i2\hat{\varphi}(x)}$ in the lth iteration. This image is then Fourier transformed to create a pseudo data set $\tilde{S}_l(k)$ that provides data points for symmetrizing $S(k)$. This procedure, however, may not converge to a symmetrized data set with the required phase since $\hat{\rho}_l(x)$ is not constrained to have the required phase $\hat{\varphi}(x)$.

Another iterative scheme is based on the mathematical framework of projection onto convex sets (POCS).[6] In this scheme, the phase constraint $\hat{\varphi}_l(x)$ is applied as follows:

$$\hat{\rho}_l(x) = \left| \hat{\rho}_{l-1}(x) \right| e^{i\hat{\varphi}(x)} \tag{14}$$

The resulting image $\hat{\rho}_l(x)$ is Fourier transformed to the data domain to provide the necessary data points to symmetrize $S(k)$. The symmetrized data set is then used to obtain a new reconstruction to be used in the next iteration of the algorithm. This iterative scheme converges very quickly; in many practical situations, two to four iterations appear to be sufficient.[6]

In general, the quality of the final half-Fourier reconstruction depends on the phase constraint $\hat{\varphi}(x)$. If $\hat{\varphi}(x) = \varphi(x)$, the half-Fourier image can be as good as would be obtained from a symmetrical data set. When the phase estimate is poor, however, image artifacts may result. In addition, a loss in SNR is expected for half-Fourier images because noise in the extrapolated data is correlated with noise in the measured data. Specifically, as compared with the corresponding full-scan images, half-Fourier images suffer a factor $\sqrt{2}$ loss in SNR. Some examples of half-Fourier reconstruction are presented in Figures 6–4 and 6–5.

Figure 6–4 shows a set of reconstructions from a phantom data set acquired using a gradient echo sequence. The imaging parameters were $T_R = 45$ ms and $T_E = 12$ ms and the matrix size of the raw data was 256×256. Reconstruction along the horizontal direction was first performed using the standard Fourier method on the full echoes, but the vertical direction was reconstructed with different levels of truncation. Specifically, the images in Figures 6–4a and b were reconstructed by conventional Fourier method from symmetrical echo data of 256 and 128 points, respectively, whereas images in Figures 4c–f were reconstructed using the half-Fourier reconstruction method using 128 asymmetrical data points. As can be seen, all of the half-Fourier

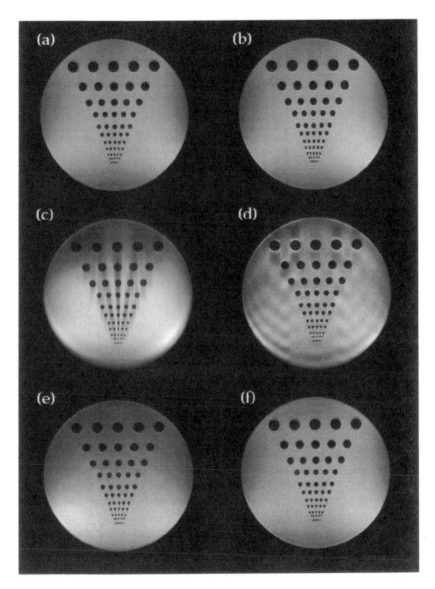

Figure 6–4. Phantom images reconstructed from an experimental data set. The horizontal direction of all images was reconstructed from 256 symmetrical echo data points, and the vertical direction was reconstructed using different methods. Images *(a)* and *(b)* were reconstructed from symmetrical echo data of 256 and 128 points, respectively. Images *(c)–(f)* were reconstructed from asymmetrical echo data of 128 points. Specifically, $-8 \le n < 112$ for *(c)* and *(d)*, and $-32 \le n < 96$ for *(e)* and *(f)*. Images in *(c)* and *(e)* were reconstructed using the Margosian method, and images in *(d)* and *(f)* were reconstructed by the POCS method.

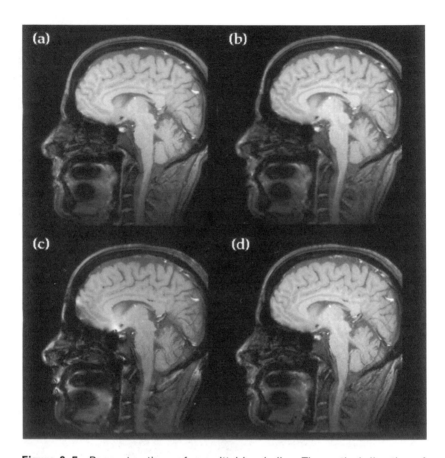

Figure 6–5. Reconstructions of a sagittal head slice. The vertical direction of all images was reconstructed using the Fourier method from full echoes of 256 data points. The horizontal direction was reconstructed using different methods. Specifically, images *(a)* and *(b)* were reconstructed from 256 and 128 symmetrical data points, respectively, whereas images *(c)* and *(d)* were reconstructed from 128 asymmetrical data points ($-32 \le n < 96$) using the Margosian and POCS methods. Notice the phase artifacts in *(c)* and the resolution improvement of image *(d)* over image *(b)*.

reconstructions have better spatial resolution than the Fourier image in (b), which was reconstructed using the same number of data points distributed symmetrically in k-space. The half-Fourier images in (c) and (d), however, contain serious artifacts. These artifacts arose because the phase function $\hat{\varphi}(x)$ estimated from 16 data points in the central k-space was a poor constraint for both the Margosian and POCS half-Fourier reconstruction methods. When the phase constraint was estimated from 64 central k-space data points as in (e) and (f), the half-Fourier reconstructions improved considerably. These results demonstrate that the quality of half-Fourier reconstructions is closely related to the quality of the phase constraint, as discussed earlier. In practice, a simple way to improve the phase estimate is to use a large n_0. This, however, reduces the number of high-frequency encodings if the total number of encodings is fixed, thus sacrificing the spatial resolution of the final image. In practice, one may therefore have to balance resolution and image artifacts in order to get the optimal results from half-Fourier imaging for a given application. It should also be noted that the image artifacts in half-Fourier reconstructions manifest themselves differently for different reconstruction methods. As can be seen, phase errors result in geometric distortions and a "shadowing artifact" in Margosian images but in spurious ringing in POCS images.

Figure 6–5 shows the results from another experimental data set obtained from a sagittal head slice using a gradient echo sequence with $T_E = 10$ ms and $T_R = 200$ ms. This data set has rapid phase changes and is a good test of the practical utility of half-Fourier imaging methods. For comparison, Figures 6–5a and 6–5b show the reconstruction results from symmetric k-space data of 256 and 128 points, respectively. The images in Figures 6–5c and 6–5d were reconstructed from 128 asymmetrical data points ($-32 \leq n < 96$) using the Margosian method and POCS method, respectively. As can be seen, both half-Fourier images have better resolution than the Fourier image with an equal number of encodings in (b). Although the Margosian reconstruction suffers from serious phase errors in the form of signal cancellation (signal voids) in regions near the pituitary gland, mouth cavity, and spinal cord where large phase variations exist, the POCS method overcomes this problem effectively. This suggests that with an appropriate image reconstruction method, half-Fourier imaging is practically useful.

Although the "one-sided" data acquisition scheme is most popular in half-Fourier imaging, there are many other ways in which one can acquire the half-Fourier data. One that is of particular interest collects the high spatial-frequency data from both sides of k-space, with one side being covered on the odd encoding lines and the other side on the even encoding lines. Such a data acquisition scheme could reduce half-Fourier image blurring due to magnetic field inhomogeneities.[11]

REDUCED-SCAN DYNAMIC IMAGING

To further demonstrate the concept of reduced-scan imaging, in this section we discuss its application to dynamic imaging applications. Dynamic imaging experiments are characterized by the acquisition of a time series of images, $\rho_1(x)$, $\rho_2(x)$, . . . , from the same anatomical site. These images are useful for a number of applications, including functional MRI (fMRI), MR mammography, and interventional MRI, as well as for the measurement of relaxation time constants and diffusion coefficients. The challenge with such an imaging experiment is to obtain both high spatial and temporal resolutions simultaneously. Conventional Fourier imaging methods acquire each of these images independently, leading to a trade-off between spatial resolution and temporal resolution. Specifically, if N encodings are collected for each image, the spatial and temporal resolutions available are given, respectively, by

$$\Delta x = \frac{1}{N \Delta k} \tag{15}$$

and

$$\Delta t = N T_R \tag{16}$$

Therefore, if a large N is used to obtain high spatial resolution, temporal resolution is compromised accordingly.

To overcome this problem, several reduced-scan imaging methods have been proposed in the last few years.[12–21] A common feature of these methods is that a high-resolution reference image is obtained first, which is followed by the collection of a sequence of dynamic data sets with a small number of encodings. One example of such data acquisition schemes is shown in Figure 6–6. Assuming that N encodings are collected for the reference image and M encodings for each dynamic data set, a factor of N/M improvement in temporal resolution (or imaging efficiency) is gained with this data acquisition scheme compared with the conventional full-scan imaging method. This section discusses some of the relevant concepts for this type of reduced-scan dynamic imaging method.

Data Acquisition

Most of the existing reduced-scan dynamic imaging methods collect the high-resolution image using the conventional Fourier

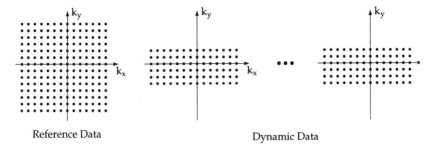

Figure 6–6. Sampling scheme for a reduced-scan dynamic imaging method with Fourier encodings.

imaging method. Acquisition of the dynamic data sets, however, differs considerably in different imaging methods. Based on how spatial information is encoded in the data, we may classify these methods into three classes: (1) Fourier encoding methods, (2) wavelet-encoding methods, and (3) singular value decomposition (SVD)-encoding methods.

Most generally, spatial information encoding in MRI can be expressed as the inner product of the object function $\rho(x)$ and an encoding function $\xi_m(x)$

$$d(m) = \int \rho(x)\xi_m(x)\,dx \qquad (17)$$

where $d(m)$ is the measured data. For Fourier encoding, $\xi_m(x) = e^{-i2\pi m\Delta kx}$. If $\xi_m(x)$ is taken to be a wavelet function or an eigenfunction of the SVD representation of $\rho(x)$, the data acquisition method is called the wavelet-encoding method or SVD-encoding method, respectively. The popular Fourier encoding can be easily realized because of the nature of nuclear magnetic resonance (NMR) signals. Wavelet-encoding and SVD-encoding methods have recently been proposed as an alternative to the Fourier encoding method, but they often need special selective RF pulses, which can pose technical problems if high accuracy of implementation is desired. Another difficulty with both wavelet- and SVD-encoding methods lies in the selection of a reduced set of most "significant" encoding vectors. These encoding functions are usually chosen based on the reference image, and they may not be the most significant ones with respect to the dynamic images. As a result, these encoding vectors could bias the data acquisition step toward reproducing the dominant features in the reference image,[22] thus undermining the optimality of these mathematical models.

Image Reconstruction

The key image reconstruction issue in reduced-scan dynamic imaging methods is how to effectively use the reference data for reconstruction of the dynamic images so as to minimize data truncation artifacts due to the reduced encodings. The most straightforward approach to this problem is to replace the un-measured encodings of each dynamic data set with the corre-sponding data from the reference data set and then process the "extrapolated" data set with the conventional reconstruction method. This approach is called the data-replacement recon-struction method and is applicable to any encoding method. For example, with Fourier encoding, suppose that $S_r(n)$, $-N/2 \leq n < N/2$ is the high-resolution reference data set and $S_d(n)$, $-M/2 \leq n < M/2$ is a dynamic data set. Then, an extrapolated data set $\hat{S}_d(k)$ can be formed as

$$\hat{S}_d(n) = \begin{cases} S_d(n) & -\dfrac{M}{2} \leq n < \dfrac{M}{2} \\ S_r(n) & -\dfrac{N}{2} \leq n < \dfrac{-M}{2} \text{ and } \dfrac{M}{2} \leq n < \dfrac{N}{2} \end{cases} \tag{18}$$

from which the final image is obtained using the conventional Fourier reconstruction method. With wavelet- or SVD-encoded data, signal extrapolation can be done similarly. Specifically, as-sume that the high-resolution reference image $\rho_r(x)$ has the fol-lowing SVD representation:

$$\rho_r = U\Sigma V^H \tag{19}$$

where U, Σ, and V are matrices containing the left singular vec-tors, singular values, and right singular vectors, respectively, and superscript H represents the complex transpose operation. Data from M SVD encodings along the vertical direction of a dy-namic image ρ_d are given by

$$S_d = U_M^H \rho_d \tag{20}$$

where U_M is the matrix constructed from the M most significant left singular vectors. Direct SVD reconstruction of the dynamic image from S_d can be done using the following formula:

$$\hat{\rho}_d = U_M S_d \tag{21}$$

Using the data-replacement method, the missing "high-frequency" dynamic data must be first generated from the reference image as

$$\widetilde{S}_r = \widetilde{U}_{N-M} \rho_r \tag{22}$$

where $\widetilde{U}_{N-M}$ is formed from the $N - M$ least significant left singular vectors, such that

$$[U_M \widetilde{U}_{N-M}] = U \tag{23}$$

These data are then appended to the measured data S_d to give a full data set from which the dynamic image is reconstructed as follows:

$$\hat{\rho}_d = U \begin{bmatrix} S_d \\ \widetilde{S}_r \end{bmatrix} \tag{24}$$

A weakness of data-replacement methods, in general, is that any data inconsistency between the dynamic data and the reference data results in data truncation artifacts, and, therefore, dynamic image features may be produced only at low resolution depending on the number of dynamic encodings. In the case of Fourier encodings, a generalized series-based method has been proposed to alleviate this problem.[13,14] This method, referred to as reduced-encoding imaging by generalized series reconstruction (RIGR), expresses a dynamic image in terms of a generalized series as

$$\rho_d(x) = \sum_{n=\frac{-M}{2}}^{\frac{M}{2}-1} c_n \varphi_n(x) \tag{25}$$

where the basis functions $\varphi_n(x)$ are given, according to the maximum cross-entropy principle, by

$$\varphi_n(x) = |\rho_r(x)| e^{i2\pi n \Delta kx} \tag{26}$$

The M model parameters c_n are determined based on the data-consistency constraint between the reconstructed image and the measured dynamic data, which can be expressed as

$$S_d(m) = \sum_{n=\frac{-M}{2}}^{\frac{M}{2}-1} c_n \hat{S}_r(m-n) \quad -\frac{M}{2} \le m \le \frac{M}{2} - 1 \tag{27}$$

where

$$\hat{S}_r(m-n) = \int_{-\infty}^{\infty} |\rho_r(x)| e^{-i2\pi(m-n)\Delta kx} dx \tag{28}$$

Substituting the resulting coefficients into Equation 25 yields the desired dynamic image.

The spatial resolution of the resulting generalized series image depends on both the dynamic and reference data sets. If well-defined boundaries for a feature exist in the reference image, it is reconstructed with the spatial resolution of the reference image. If the dynamic changes introduce new edges to the image, however, the spatial resolution of these features are limited by the number of dynamic encodings available. This property of reduced-scan dynamic imaging can be appreciated from the examples presented in the ensuing section.

Examples

Some examples in this section demonstrate the practical utility of reduced-scan dynamic imaging. The first example involves monitoring the wash-in/wash-out process of an injected contrast agent in a biological system, which is important for determining areas of altered blood flow and leakage from capillaries. This problem often requires fast data acquisition to provide adequate temporal and spatial resolution. The images in Figure 6–7 were obtained from a dynamic study of an injected contrast agent (Magnevist) in a rat. In this experiment, a time series of data sets with 128 phase encodings was obtained before and after the injection of the contrast agent. The high-resolution pre-injection image and one of the post-injection images are shown in the top row of this figure. When the high-resolution pre-injection image and a subset of eight encodings from the post-injection data set were fed into the reduced-scan imaging schemes, the images in the second and third rows were obtained. As can be seen, the data-replacement method appeared to reconstruct the post-injection image in (d) nicely, but the difference image in (e) suffers from the usual data truncation artifact. This means that the high-resolution post-injection image produced by the data replacement method has captured only the low-resolution dynamic variations.[23] This problem is significantly reduced with the generalized series reconstruction method since the dynamic image variations are produced at a much higher resolution. As can be seen, however, the difference image in (g) is not at the resolution of the reference image either. This is because dynamic information in the generalized series model is contained exclusively in the series coefficients c_n. Since this model has only as many terms as the number of dynamic encodings, the dynamic information

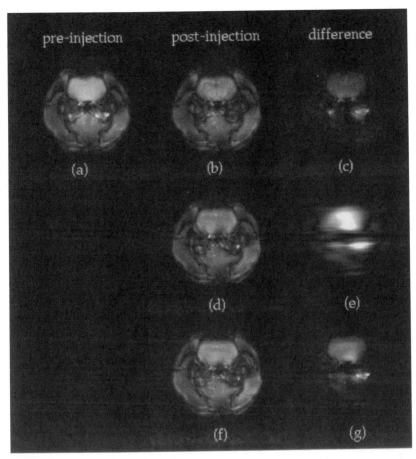

Figure 6–7. Cross-sectional images obtained from a rat during a dynamic study of an injected contrast agent. The top row shows the high-resolution Fourier images reconstructed with 128 encodings along each direction. The post-injection images in *(d)* and *(f)* were reconstructed with eight post-injection encodings and the pre-injection image as the reference. The images in *(c)*, *(e)*, and *(g)* show the dynamic variations between the pre-injection image and the corresponding post-injection image.

"registered" on the reference image may not have the same spatial resolution. This limitation can be alleviated by further improving the data acquisition and image reconstruction steps. For example, in some dynamic imaging applications, it is possible to acquire two high-resolution images at different times of the dynamic imaging process such that their difference reflects the dynamic signal changes. By building this difference image into the basis functions, one can reproduce the inter-image variations at the resolution of the reference images.[24] In the processing step, one can also further improve the reconstruction results by segmenting the reference image into different regions and directly building region boundaries into the basis functions of the generalized series. Liang and Lauterbur[25] show that, even with one reference image, this method can reproduce dynamic signal changes at a resolution close to that of the high-resolution image.

The second example is an application to diffusion-weighted imaging. Studies[26–28] have shown that diffusion-weighted imaging is a useful tool for early detection of ischemia and stroke, among many other applications. Its widespread use, however, is hindered by some practical difficulties. For example, in the classic Stejskal-Tanner pulse sequence,[29,30] long echo times (≈ 100 ms) are needed to avoid the use of very large diffusion gradients and the associated eddy current problems. This long echo time requirement can lead to a substantial loss of signal from biological samples with comparable or shorter T_2 values. To circumvent this problem, signal averaging and a long T_R are used, both leading to increased imaging time and, hence, lower temporal resolution in dynamic studies. This problem becomes more acute when multiple diffusion-weighted images are taken to calculate the diffusion map. To overcome this problem, RIGR has been applied to reconstruct dynamic image contrast changes introduced by variable diffusion weightings. A typical set of results is shown in Figure 6–8. For comparison, the high-resolution Fourier diffusion-weighted images obtained with 128 encodings are shown in (a). The RIGR images in (b) were reconstructed using the first high-resolution Fourier image as the reference and a subset of 32 encodings from the rest of the data sets. As can be seen, the quality of both sets of images is comparable, with a saving in imaging time of a factor of 4 for the RIGR images. The corresponding diffusion maps generated by fitting the data with a single exponential curve are presented in (c) and (d), respectively. Again, their difference is minimal, demonstrating the ability of RIGR to capture practical dynamic image contrast changes with only a small number of dynamic encodings.

As a last example, a set of simulation results is shown in Figure 6–9 comparing the performance of SVD encoding with Fourier encoding for reduced-scan dynamic imaging applications. Specifically, a needle biopsy simulation was used in which Figures 6–9a and b are the high-resolution reference and dynamic images, respectively. As can be seen, the ideal dynamic feature is a narrow

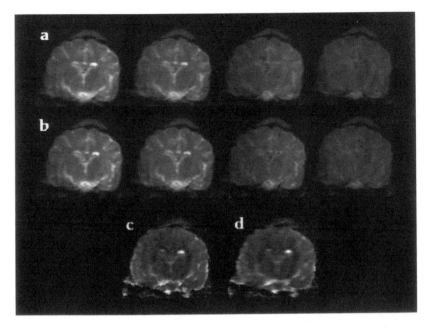

Figure 6–8. Diffusion-weighted images reconstructed using: *(a)* the Fourier method with 128 encodings and *(b)* the RIGR method using a subset of 32 encodings with the first image as the reference. The diffusion maps in *(c)–(d)* were obtained by fitting the diffusion curve pixel by pixel through the images in *(a)* and *(b)*, respectively.

dark line through the object, supposedly created by the insertion of the needle. With 32 SVD dynamic encodings generated according to Equation 20, images (c) and (d) were obtained using the direct SVD reconstruction method and the data-replacement SVD reconstruction method, respectively. For comparison, the dynamic image reconstructed with 32 Fourier encodings using RIGR is shown in (e). As can be seen, the dynamic feature is better reproduced in the RIGR image than in the SVD images. The reason for this is that the SVD encoding vectors, was chosen with respect to the dynamic image. A more detailed discussion of these issues can be found in Hanson et al.[22]

CONCLUSION

Reduced-scan imaging, like fast-scan imaging, is motivated primarily by the need to acquire an image quickly. Unlike fast-scan

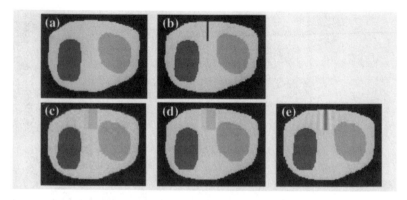

Figure 6–9. Computer simulation results: *(a)* and *(b).* High-resolution reference and dynamic images. Note that the dynamic feature is the dark line through the image supposedly created by the insertion of a needle in an interventional MRI experiment. *(c)* and *(d).* Dynamic images reconstructed with 32 SVD encodings along the horizontal direction, using the direct and data-replacement SVD reconstruction methods, respectively. *(e).* Dynamic image reconstructed with 32 Fourier encodings using the RIGR method.

methods, however, which achieve high-speed imaging by scanning through data space very quickly, reduced-scan imaging methods shorten imaging time by reducing the number of encodings acquired. In many practical situations, in fact, reduced-scan imaging techniques are used in combination with fast-scan techniques to achieve even higher imaging speed. The general concept of reduced-scan imaging, as described in this chapter, is applicable to both slow-scan and fast-scan imaging methods. Two examples are discussed in detail to illustrate the feasibility and usefulness of reduced-scan imaging. The first example is half-Fourier imaging, in which the number of encodings is reduced to about half compared with the usual full-scan imaging techniques, giving rise to about a twofold reduction in imaging time. The second example is dynamic imaging, in which the reduced-scan approach makes it possible to obtain a time series of images with both high spatial and temporal resolution while keeping the total number of excitations small. These reduced-scan imaging techniques may find useful application in fMRI, dynamic studies of injected contrast agents, interventional MRI, and spectroscopic imaging.

REFERENCES

1. Wehrli FW: *Fast-Scan Magnetic Resonance: Principles and Applications.* New York: Raven Press, 1991.
2. Mansfield P: Multi-planar image formation using NMR spin echoes. *J Phys C: Solid State Phys* 1977;10:L55–L58.
3. Ahn CB, Kim JH, Cho ZH: High-speed spiral-scan echo-planar NMR imaging, I. *IEEE Trans Med Imaging* 1986;MI-5:2–7.
4. Macovski A, Meyer C: A novel fast-scanning system. Work-in-Progress Proceeding of the Society for Magnetic Resonance in Medicine 8th Annual Meeting, 1989, p. 362.
5. Twieg DB: The *k*-trajectory formulation of the NMR imaging process with applications in analysis and synthesis of imaging methods. *Med Phys* 1983;10:610–621.
6. Liang Z-P, Boada F, Constable T, et al: Constrained reconstruction methods in MR imaging. *Rev Magn Reson Med* 1992;4:67–185.
7. Feinberg DA, Hale JD, Watts JC, et al: Halving MR imaging time by conjugation: Demonstration at 3.5 KG. *Radiology* 1986;161:527–531.
8. Margosian P, Schmitt F, Purdy DE: Faster MR imaging: Imaging with half the data. *Health Care Instru* 1986;1:195–197.
9. Noll DC, Nishimura DG, Macovski A: Homodyne detection in magnetic resonance imaging. *IEEE Trans Med Imaging* 1991;MI-10:154–163.
10. Cuppen JJ, Van Est A: Reducing MR imaging time by one-sided reconstruction. *Topical Conference Fast MRI Techniques.* Cleveland, Ohio, May 15–17, 1987.
11. National Research Council and Institute of Medicine: *Mathematics and Physics of Emerging Biomedical Imaging.* Washington, DC: National Academy Press, 1996.
12. Plevritis SK, Macovski A: "Spectral extrapolation of spatially bounded images." *IEEE Trans Med Imaging* 1995;14:487–497.
13. Liang ZP, Lauterbur PC: An efficient method for dynamic magnetic resonance imaging." *IEEE Trans Med Imaging* 1994;13:677–686.
14. Webb AG, Liang Z-P, Magin R-L, et al: Reduced encoding imaging by generalized series reconstruction (RIGR): Applications to biological MRI. *J Magn Reson Imaging* 1993;3:925–928.
15. Chandra S, Liang Z-P, Webb A, et al: Application of reduced-encoding imaging with generalized-series reconstruction (RIGR) in dynamic MR imaging. *J Magn Reson Imaging* 1996;6:783–797.
16. Jones RA, Haraldseth O, Muller TB, et al: *k*-Space substitution: A novel dynamic imaging technique. *Magn Reson Med* 1993;29:830–834.
17. van Vaals JJ, Brummer ME, Dixon WT, et al: Keyhole method for accelerating imaging of contrast agent uptake. *J Magn Reson Imaging* 1993;3:671–675.
18. Cao Y, Levin DN: Feature-recognizing MRI. *Magn Reson Med* 1993;30:305–317.
19. Zientara GP, Panych LP, Jolesz FA: Dynamically adaptive MRI with encoding by singular value decomposition. *Magn Reson Med* 1994;32:268–274.
20. Weaver JB, Xu Y, Healy DM, et al: Wavelet-encoded MR imaging. *Magn Reson Med* 1992;24:275–287.
21. Panych LP, Jakab PD, Jolesz FA: An implementation of wavelet encoded MRI. *J Magn Reson Imaging* 1993;3:649–655.
22. Hanson JM, Liang Z-P, Magin RL, et al: A comparison of RIGR and SVD dynamic imaging methods. Vol. 38, 1997, pp. 161–167.

23. Spraggins TA: Simulation of spatial and contrast distortions in keyhole imaging. *Magn Reson Med* 1994;31:320–322.

24. Hanson JM, Liang Z-P, Wiener EC, et al: Fast dynamic imaging using two reference images. *Magn Reson Med* 1996;36:172–175.

25. Liang Z-P, Lauterbur PC: Efficient high-resolution dynamic imaging with explicit boundary constraints. *Proceedings of the Annual Meeting of the Society for Magnetic Resonance.* 1994, p. 53.

26. Doran M, Hajnal JV, Young IR, et al: Diffusion-weighted MRI reveals white matter tracts. *Diagn Imaging* January, 1991;50–55.

27. Le Bihan D, Lallemand D, Grenier P, et al: MR imaging of intravoxel incoherent motions: Application to diffusion and perfusion in neurologic disorders. *Radiology* 1986;161:401–407.

28. Le Bihan D: Molecular diffusion nuclear magnetic resonance imaging. *Magn Reson Q* 1991;7(1):1–30.

29. Stejskal EO, Tanner JE: Spin diffusion measurements: Spin echoes in the presence of a time dependent field gradient. *J Chem Phys* 1965;42:288–292.

30. Stejskal EO, Tanner JE: Use of spin echo in pulsed magnetic field gradient to study anisotropic restricted diffusion and flow. *J Chem Phys* 1965;43:3579–3603.

ESSENTIALS OF MR ANGIOGRAPHY

John A. Markisz, Joseph P. Comunale, Jr., and Patrick T. Cahill

Very rarely does a technology move so rapidly that techniques introduced fewer than 15 years ago are deemed archaic. This is, however, the situation now prevailing with the use of magnetic resonance imaging (MRI) techniques to study the vascular system. Initially the flow void phenomenon— that is, the lack of signal within blood vessels on spin echo images, due primarily to the lack of dephasing of flowing blood within the slice-selection gradient—was thought to herald a new era in noninvasive angiography. Under the proper conditions, that is, with cooperative patients, regular cardiac rhythms, and lack of artifacts, a significant amount of angiographic information could and can be obtained from spin echo images. Detection of aneurysms, dissections, coarctations, and vascular malformations and evaluation of tumor thrombus, varices, and extrinsic compression can routinely be done (Figs. 7–1 through 7–4). The absence of a thrombus can be confirmed by a normal scan, but a relatively high number of vascular artifacts often introduce an uncertainty into the study that precludes a definitive answer to the clinical question. Signal can be introduced into the lumen of a normal blood vessel on a spin echo image by irregular flow, even echo rephasing, diastolic pseudogating, slow flow within a vessel, and also by partial volume averaging (Figs. 7–5 to 7–7).

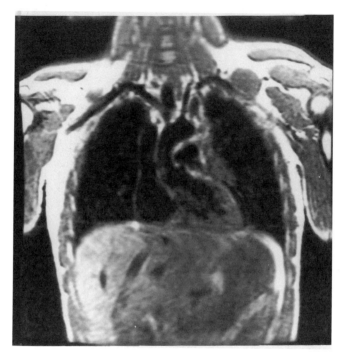

Figure 7–1. Coronal T_1-weighted image through the chest. Flow void in the heart and great vessels allows visualization of normal structures.

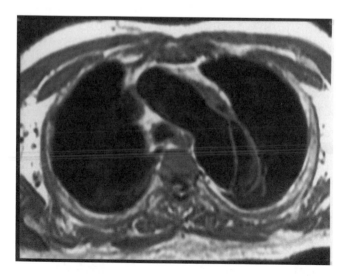

Figure 7–2. The intimal flap of a large dissection of the distal aortic arch can be well visualized on this axial image.

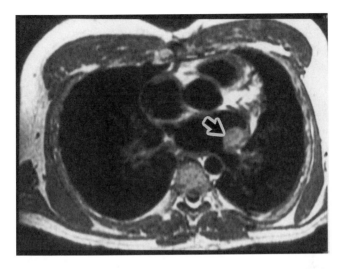

Figure 7–3. Flow void in the heart and major vessels allows evaluation of narrowing of left pulmonary inflow tract by a left atrial myxoma (arrow).

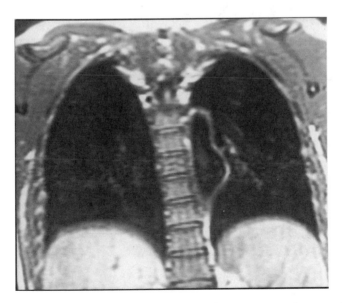

Figure 7–4. A focal aneurysm of the descending aorta can be seen in this coronal image.

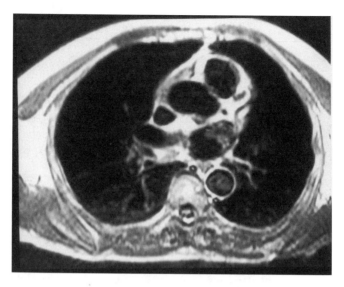

Figure 7–5. Axial section through the chest obtained during diastole. Signal within the lumen of a normal descending aorta is caused by diastolic pseudo-gating.

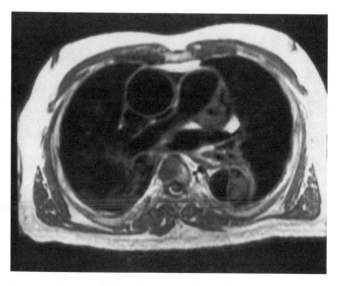

Figure 7–6. Axial section through the chest shows a dissection of the descending aorta. The true lumen is noted to be medial, with blood flow producing the signal void. Absence of continual flow produces signal within the false lumen.

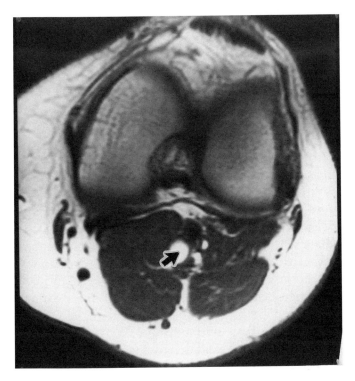

Figure 7–7. The most inferior axial section of a multislice acquisition of a T_1-weighted sequence through the knee. Notice the bright signal within the lumen of the popliteal vein. Blood from within this vein is entering the imaging volume from below (lower leg), causing this entry phenomenon artifact.

The normal, or expected, appearance of blood on a spin echo image is a region devoid of signal due to the loss of signal as the protons fail to remain within the slice being excited long enough to acquire both 90° and 180° pulses, required to form a spin echo. This phenomenon is directly related to the magnitude of the velocity: the greater the velocity, the greater the number of protons in blood that will move through the slice without being pulsed to produce a signal. If the anatomical slice is thick enough and/or the flow velocity slow, some protons may remain long enough to produce a signal. In this case, the relative flow void (loss of signal) will depend upon the actual number of protons producing a signal.

Neglecting pulsatile effects, flow through a blood vessel is laminar, producing smooth flow, faster at the center than at the edges, but constantly directed along the axis of the vessel. During laminar flow, blood at the edges of a vessel moves more slowly than that at the center, so that blood at the circumference is more likely to remain within the slice long enough to produce a signal. Turbulence involves a randomized motion of blood cells as they move through the vessel, and can be caused by tortuosity in vessels producing abrupt changes in direction, changes in vessel diameter (either abrupt narrowing or enlargement), or irregularities in the contour of the vessel. The irregularities of the artifacts produced by turbulent flow can cause either increased or decreased signal, thus either underestimating or overestimating abnormalities.

Images obtained by using cardiac-gating techniques can produce artifactual signal within the lumen on images obtained during the diastolic portion of the cardiac cycle. Because blood flow is rapid through arteries during systole and significantly decreased, or sometimes absent, during diastole, those sections imaged during diastole will have blood within the lumen that is relatively motionless and capable of producing a signal. This is referred to as **diastolic pseudogating.**

Although the signal void of flowing blood can be helpful in detecting certain abnormalities, there are too many artifacts to make spin echo imaging a routine, reliable angiographic imaging modality. A positive signal, such as produced in conventional angiography, would be much more useful to establish a diagnosis. Within all blood vessels there is a wide range of velocities of individual blood cells, and this plus local variations in magnetic field homogeneity, usually due to susceptibility effects, is the cause of significant signal loss, called intravoxel spin-phase dispersion. Protons that remain within a voxel but are moving with different velocities will change their phase differently. This difference in phase of these protons results in a lack of phase coherence and therefore a loss of signal. During symmetric multi-echo acquisitions, a second echo (or any even-numbered echo) can sometimes demonstrate signal within the lumen of a normal vessel, although the normal flow void is seen on the first echo. This "even echo rephasing" is a result of a reconstituting of the signal lost due to dephasing at the time of the first (or odd) echo. Although this can often simulate an intraluminal mass or thrombus, comparison to the odd echoes will verify the artifact.

Another important flow effect is the so-called entry phenomenon. Although only a small portion of the patient may be being imaged, it is important to keep in mind that most of the body is within a high magnetic field and therefore blood away from the imaging volume will become magnetized. During a multislice acquisition, slow-flowing blood that is entering the first slice (entry slice) being imaged is totally unsaturated. This blood will move into the imaging volume (first slice) fully magnetized, replacing partially saturated blood, and will have greater signal than the partially saturated stationary tissue around the vessel. The strength of the resulting signal from within the lumen is dependent upon the velocity of flow, the slice thickness, and the repetition time (*TR*) (Fig. 7–7).

All of these various types of signal aberrations described can occur simultaneously and in various combinations. It should be no surprise, then, that a precise evaluation of the vascular system by the spin echo techniques, used for many years to evaluate other organ systems, would be inadequate, and other techniques would have to be found before MR became a major force in angiography. Fortunately, several different approaches are now available that overcome many of the deficiencies mentioned.

TIME-OF-FLIGHT ANGIOGRAPHY

Time-of-flight (TOF) imaging can be performed as either a 2-D or 3-D acquisition in a plane perpendicular to the direction of flow. It is based upon the contrast that is provided by fully relaxed material, blood that has had no prior excitation, entering into the volume that is being imaged. These unsaturated, fully relaxed protons produce a much higher signal than tissue that is stationary and has been excited by very rapid radio frequency (RF) imaging pulses. The normal alignment of the magnetic fields of protons will align with the direction of the field, arbitrarily the z-axis (Fig. 7–8A). When an RF pulse is applied, the magnetic vector of the tissue is tipped in the direction of the transverse plane (Fig. 7–8B). This vector can be considered to have two components: the M_z vector, which is its component along the z-axis; and the M_{xy} vector, which is the component in the transverse (xy) plane (Figs. 7–8C and 7–8D). The greater the magnitude of the RF pulse, the larger the flip angle produced and the greater the component of the magnetic vector in the transverse plane (M_{xy}). The signal that will be produced is proportional to the size of the M_{xy} vector.

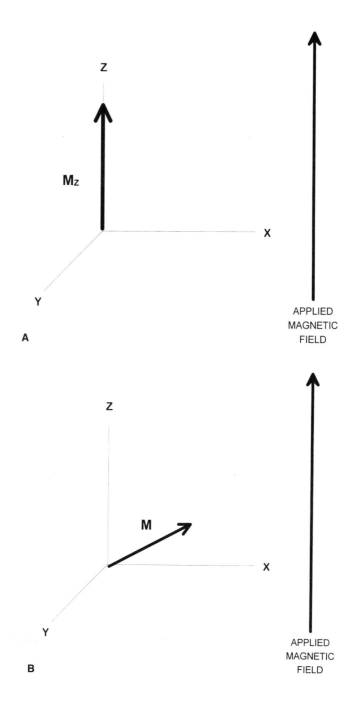

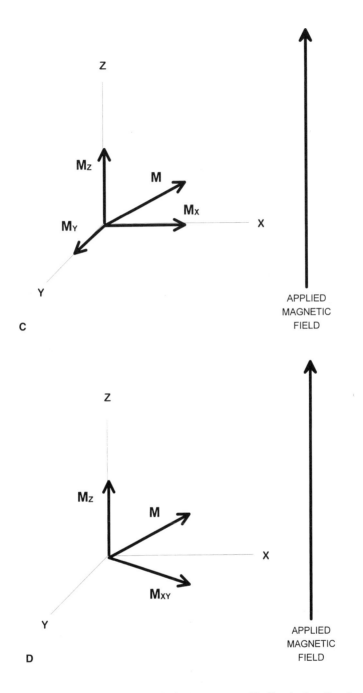

Figure 7–8. **A.** The magnetic vector **(M)** of a proton will align in the direction of the applied magnetic field. **B.** Application of an RF field will tip the magnetic vector **(M)** away from the z-axis, towards the xy plane. **C.** The tipped magnetic vector **(M)** can be considered as the result of individual components along each of the three axes. **D.** The tipped magnetic vector **(M)** can alternately be considered to be the resultant of two vectors, one along the z-axis and one in the xy plane.

Within a short time the magnetic moment of the excited tissue will eventually "relax," or return to equilibrium, continually increasing the magnitude of the M_z vector while decreasing the size of the M_{xy} vector. The relaxation along the z-axis is referred to as longitudinal relaxation and is dependent upon the T_1 value of the tissue; the relaxation within the transverse plane is referred to as transverse relaxation and is dependent upon the T_2 value of the tissue.

T_2 values for most tissues are relatively short (30 to 60 ms), while the T_2 value of arterial blood is significantly longer (about 190 ms). On a practical basis, this means that blood will continue to give off a strong signal long after signal from other tissues has disappeared. The T_1 value for blood is on the order of 1 second, very long compared to fat (240 ms) and somewhat longer than muscle (800 ms). The longitudinal relaxation of blood therefore takes much longer than that of fat, which relaxes much more rapidly. Both of these relaxation values, along with the TR and echo time (TE), determine the values of the magnetic vectors:

$$M_z \text{ is proportional to exp } (T_1/TR)$$

$$M_{xy} \text{ is proportional to exp } (-TE/T_2)$$

The shorter the value of TR, the greater the saturation of stationary tissues. The greater the flip angle, the larger the value of M_{xy} and the longer it takes to return to equilibrium. In TOF imaging, short TR values on the order of 10 to 70 ms are used, along with large flip angles from 20 to 90°.

Before the initial RF pulse, all tissues are at their maximum values of longitudinal magnetization, M_z, which is dependent upon the concentration of mobile protons and the magnetic field strength. After the application of the first RF pulse, there is a decrease in the value of M_z (Fig. 7–9), followed by a slow increase toward the equilibrium value. A second RF pulse is applied before M_z can increase too much, and a further decrease occurs, again followed by a slow increase after the pulse is turned off. Continual rapid application of RF pulses to a slice, using short TR values, eventually leads to the steady-state equilibrium seen in Figure 7–10, during which time there is very little change in the magnetic vector and therefore no signal from the tissues within the slice being pulsed. Blood that is flowing into the slice, however, is not at a steady state and will produce a bright signal. Because the blood will reach a steady state if it remains in the tissue for too long a time, the faster the blood is

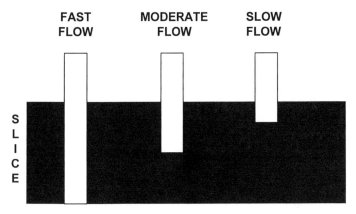

Figure 7–9. The longer that blood remains within the slice being imaged, the greater the chance that it will become saturated and give no signal. Fast-flowing blood will produce a bright signal through almost the entire slice depicted here, while a blood vessel with moderate flow will "penetrate" the slice only partially, and a slow-flowing vessel will only produce signal during its initial entry into the slice.

flowing, the further into the slice it will penetrate before it reaches a steady state. At that time, the blood will no longer produce a bright signal (Fig. 7–11).

Acquisition can be obtained in either 2-D or 3-D modes. Two-dimensional studies are acquired as a stack of slices, which when taken together produce a volume image. Three-dimensional imaging obtains data from a complete volume at one time. Although it may appear that these methods result in equivalent images, there are significant differences in practice that make them useful for different clinical applications. Although imaging parameters will vary somewhat, 2-D TOF imaging uses the shortest *TE* available. A single slice is saturated using short *TR* RF pulses and the flip angle is adjusted so that background is suppressed to the maximum, while artifact due to pulsation is minimized. An image is produced that has a dark background and bright circular regions from the flowing blood. Once this image has been obtained, the adjacent section is imaged, and then the next, and so on, until the entire volume has been sequentially imaged by a stack of slices. Presaturation bands are used parallel and adjacent to the slice being acquired in order to saturate blood flowing into the slice from the opposite direction and thus eliminate any signal from these vessels.

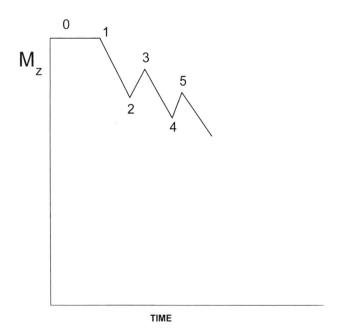

Figure 7–10. Graph of the changes in longitudinal magnetization, **M**$_z$, with time. Initially, at equilibrium, the value of the vector is indicated by point 0. After application of a single RF pulse at point 1, the value drops as the vector is tipped toward the xy plane. At point 2, the RF pulse has been stopped and the vector begins to rise toward its equilibrium value. Before it can reach equilibrium, however, another RF pulse is applied at point 3, at which time the value of the vector **M**$_z$ again decreases to point 4, with another RF pulse applied at point 5. This process is continually repeated.

The 2-D TOF techniques are particularly sensitive to vessels with slow flow, because blood only has to travel a short distance through the slice, and there is little chance that it will become saturated and lose its ability to produce a signal. Once the volume image is produced, projections from any direction are obtained using maximum intensity pixel (MIP) methods.

Three-dimensional TOF images are obtained by exciting a large volume, which is divided into multiple partitions (usually 32 or 64), making resolution potentially much higher than can be obtained by 2-D TOF techniques. It is also sensitive to blood flowing in three dimensions, rather than just through the imaged section. The major disadvantage is that blood can become saturated much more easily unless it is flowing very rapidly, because it is remaining within the excited volume for a much

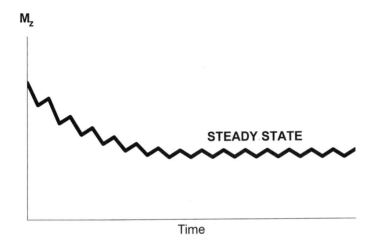

Figure 7–11. After the continued rapid application of RF pulses, a time is reached after which time the signal decrease due to the pulse is equal to the signal increase due to recovery, leading to a stationary, or steady, state.

longer period of time. Vessels that have slow flow will only be visible at the edges of the volume, and even moderate flow may only be seen in a portion of the blood vessel, especially if it is tortuous within the imaged volume.

In order to compensate for this major disadvantage, an alternative to simple 3-D TOF imaging has been developed. This technique employs a combination of 2-D and 3-D methods to obtain the sensitivity to slow flow of 2-D and the inherent increased resolution of 3-D. Termed MOTSA (multiple overlapping thick-slab angiography), as its name implies, it uses thick slabs instead of large volumes but acquires them sequentially, as in the 2-D method (Fig. 7–12). To eliminate the loss of signal from saturation as blood remains within the imaged volume, these slabs are overlapped—usually 25% on both the top and bottom. Using this technique, regions of potentially lost signal at the edges of the slabs are compensated for. The "far" region of one slab, in which there is a loss of signal, is counterbalanced by the next slab, in which this same section is the "near" region, in which all flowing blood is bright. Increased imaging time is the major disadvantage to this technique. Time-of-flight imaging of the head and neck are of relatively high quality, while images of the body suffer from artifacts caused by physiological motion. Even slight patient motion will cause a misregistration

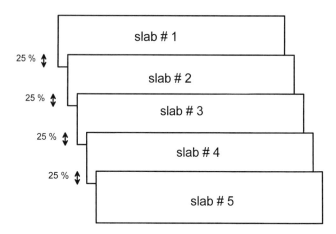

Figure 7–12. MOTSA representation, whereby multiple slabs are imaged, with each slab overlapping each of the adjacent slabs, usually by about 25%.

of adjacent sections, making interpretation potentially difficult (Figs. 7–13 and 7–14).

Compared to 2-D TOF images, the advantages of 3-D TOF imaging include high spatial resolution, sensitivity to fast and medium flow rates, and the use of very short *TE* values. Scan times are relatively short and high-signal, high-contrast images can be produced. The method is relatively insensitive to slow flow, and venous structures cannot be reliably imaged by this technique. There is less of a potential for overestimating stenosis than with 2-D TOF.

PHASE CONTRAST

Phase contrast (PC) angiography employs direct visualization of motion to produce images of the velocity of flow. Using this technique, static tissues are suppressed because there is no motion, and only moving protons contribute to the image. In order to produce a PC image, a bipolar gradient is used to determine the velocity of the moving proton in terms of a change in phase. The phase shift is proportional to the gyromagnetic ratio, the time interval between applications of the gradient, the area of each gradient lobe, and the component of velocity of the direction of the applied gradient. A bipolar gradient in-

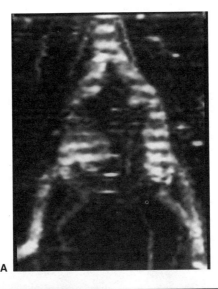

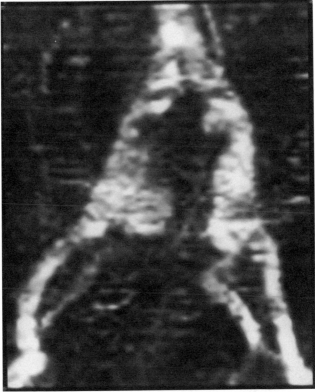

Figure 7–13. *A.* Two-dimensional TOF image of the iliac arteries shows significant misregistration due to patient motion. Strong suggestion of bilateral iliac artery aneurysms can be seen. ***B.*** Next acquisition on the same patient as in ***A,*** with better cooperation from the patient, demonstrates the aneurysms more clearly.

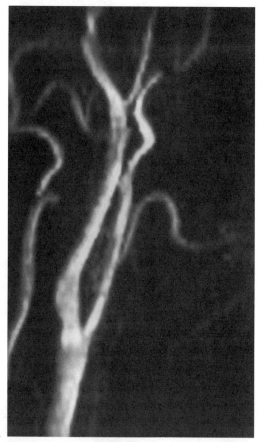

A

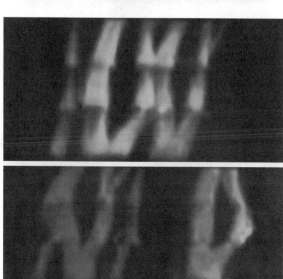

B

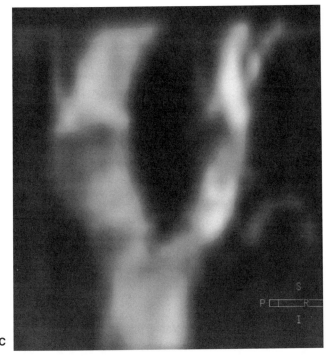

C

Figure 7–14. Normal carotid arteries obtained by *(A)* 2-D TOF, *(B)* 3-D TOF (two rotated views), and *(C)* MOTSA techniques.

volves applying a gradient at a specific point, followed by a second gradient equal in magnitude but opposite in direction. The magnitude of these applied gradients is different at different points. In such a situation, stationary tissues do not experience any net changes since the magnitude of the applied gradients at each point are equal and opposite in sign (Fig. 7–15) and will not, therefore, produce any data. A moving proton, however, will experience a net accumulation of phase because it will experience a net gradient effect (Fig. 7–16). The only data, therefore, when the two images are subtracted from one another, are from flowing material. In practice, five complete data sets are acquired: one velocity set in each of the three orthogonal axes, one speed (magnitude) image, and one complex image. Although the combination of the three velocity sets to produce a 3-D angiogram is most often used for diagnostic purposes, individual directional images can be useful. Along a given axis, flow is seen as bright in the positive direction, while reverse flow is dark.

Perceived Gradients for Stationary Tissues

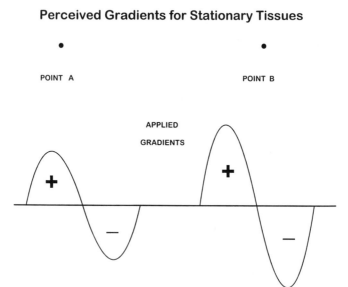

Figure 7–15. Effect of applied bipolar gradients in PC imaging on stationary tissues. Tissues at point **A** initially experience a positive gradient, and then a negative gradient of equal magnitude. Therefore, no net change in phase is observed on any of the stationary tissues at point **A.** A similar situation exists at point **B,** except that the magnitude of the bipolar gradient is different.

Aliasing can be a major problem in PC angiography. To minimize aliasing artifact, a velocity-encoding (VENC) value is chosen. The precise value depends upon the region being imaged. The VENC determines the amplitude of the applied gradients, so that all velocities up to and including the VENC will be imaged and the aliasing will be eliminated (Fig. 7–17). As an approximation, 80 cm/s can be used for the carotid arteries, and 40 cm/s in the pelvis, as these values represent the usual peak velocities in these areas. Selecting the VENC is often not routine, and 2-D PC imaging is used to optimize the value of the velocity chosen.

Two-dimensional PC imaging allows a single projection through a volume to be obtained. The major advantage of this method is that it is very fast and several VENC values can be examined in a few minutes, prior to the 3-D PC acquisition. It also permits an examination of slow flow rates in areas that

Perceived Gradient of Moving Proton

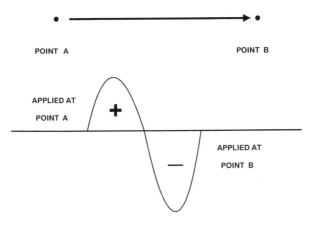

NET GRADIENT = NON-ZERO (NEGATIVE)

Figure 7–16. Effect of applied bipolar gradients in PC imaging on a moving proton. The positive gradient experienced when the proton is at point **A** is different in magnitude from the negative gradient that the proton experiences when it has reached point **B**. The proton thus experiences a change in phase due to its motion.

may be difficult to analyze, such as venous occlusions or vascular malformations.

Recently, a significant amount of work has been performed to study the effects of using intravascular magnetic contrast to further increase the quality of MR angiograms. These have been particularly successful in the body, where respiratory and cardiac motion cause misregistration artifacts in both TOF and PC images (Fig. 7–18). The use of 3-D TOF techniques using breath-holding techniques has started to gain rapid acceptance in visualizing the aortic arch, renal arteries, and peripheral arteries. A

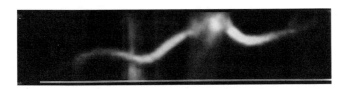

Figure 7–17. Phase contrast image of the renal arteries, using a VENC of 60 cm/s.

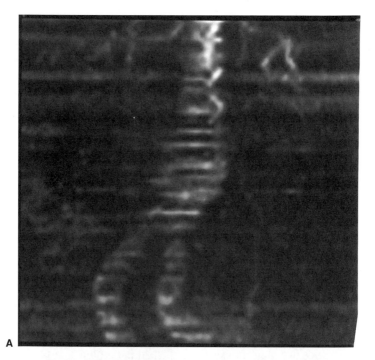

A

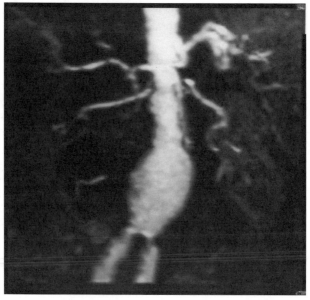

B

Figure 7–18. ***A.*** Three-dimensional TOF image through the abdomen and pelvis. Severe misregistration artifact caused by exaggerated respiration makes the image almost uninterpretable. Imaging time was 9 minutes. ***B.*** Three-dimensional TOF on the same patient as in ***A,*** using contrast enhancement. The large aneurysm, barely visible in the previous image, is clearly visible. Imaging time was 40 seconds.

bolus injection of gadolinium contrast agent is injected and the patient instructed to hold his or her breath. Typical acquisition times are between 30 and 60 seconds, so that breath holding is possible, depending upon the physical state of the patient. Additional techniques are being designed to significantly decrease these times. As an adjunct to these contrast-enhanced images, both 2-D and 3-D digital subtraction techniques have been employed as additional methods of decreasing imaging times and increasing quality of imaging. Examples of these techniques are presented in Figures 7–19 and 7–20.

Continued improvements in MR angiography are reported almost continuously in successive issues of the major journals. Decreased imaging time, use of intravenous contrast, and improved hardware and software indicate that the state-of-the-art image in magnetic resonance angiography (MRA) will continue to improve in the foreseeable future. Rather than replace conventional angiography, which will continue to be the gold stan-

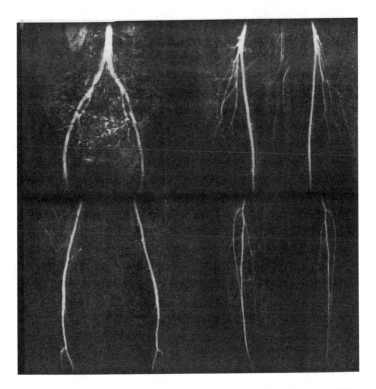

Figure 7–19. Contrast-enhanced 2-D digital subtraction images of the pelvis and lower extremities are of excellent quality.

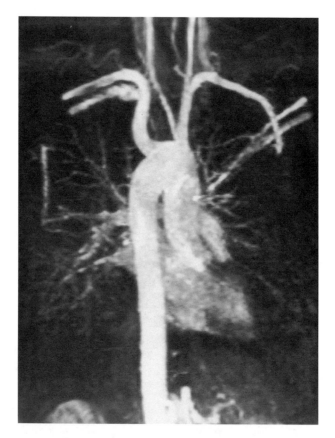

Figure 7–20. Contrast-enhanced 3-D TOF image of the aortic arch showing an anomalous right subclavian artery arising from the posterior portion of the arch.

dard, MRA would appear to offer a diagnostic approach to clinicians for their patients who may not be candidates for angiogram, or for whom clinical suspicion is not high enough for them to be subjected to angiography. MRA is currently an excellent adjunct to interventional techniques and is certain to continue to improve.

SUMMARY OF VASCULAR IMAGING SEQUENCES

Technique	Advantages	Disadvantages	Applications
2-D TOF	• sensitive to slow flow • minimal saturation effects • short imaging times • asymmetric echoes increase signal, decrease artifacts • presaturation bands allow selective arterial or venous imaging	• poor visualization of in-plane flow • overestimates stenoses • minimum TE values larger • flow compensation critical • artifactual flow in hematomas • misregistration artifacts common	• cartoid stenosis • extremities: arteries or veins • intracranial thrombosis • occlusive disease • selective arterial or venous imaging
3-D TOF	• increased resolution • decreased acquisition times • minimal echo times possible • high contrast and SNR	• effective for small volumes • artifactual flow enhancement by short T1 substances • slow flow poorly visualized • unreliable for venous structures	• intracranial aneurysms • carotid occlusion • arteriovenous malformations
2-D PC	• very rapid imaging • flow proportional to signal intensity • determines encoding velocity	• decreased resolution • small voxels not possible • increased intravoxel dephasing • only single plane images possible	• evaluate proper encoding velocity • portal venous system • AVM and venous occlusion evaluation
3-D PC	• quantitative flow measurements possible • background suppression • minimal saturation effects • variable velocity encoding • magnitude and phase images can be obtained • increased SNR • large volumes can be imaged • decreased intravoxel dephasing	• increased imaging times • sensitive to turbulence • 2-D PC needed to determine encoding velocity	• renal artery stenosis • intracranial aneurysms • congenital malformations
Contrast Enhanced TOF	• enables use of breath-hold techniques • extremely short acquisition times • increased signal from contrast produces very high SNR • eliminates breathing artifacts • high resolution images	• relatively high contrast volumes utilized • repeat studies impractical if initial study fails	• renal artery stenosis • aortic arch studies • thoracic outlet syndrome • peripheral arteries

BIBLIOGRAPHY

Anderson CM, Saloner D, Tsuruda JS, et al., Artifacts in Maximum Intensity Projection Display of MR Angiograms. AJR, 1990; 154:623–629

Borrello JA, Li D, Vesely TM, Vining EP, Brown JJ, Haacke EM, Renal arteries: Clinical comparison of three dimensional time-of-flight MR angiographic sequences and radiographic angiography. Radiology, 1995; 197:793–799

Bradley WG, Basic Flow Phenomena, MRI Clin North Am, 1995; 3:375–390

Bradley WG, Waluch V, Blood flow magnetic resonance imaging. Radiology, 1985; 154:443–450

Bradley, Jr. WG, Flow Phenomena in MR Imaging. AJR, 1988; 150:983–994

Creasy JL, Price RR, Presbrey T, Goins D, Partain CL, Kessler RM, Gadolinium-enhanced MR angiography. Radiology, 1990; 175:545–552

Davis CP, Hany TF, Wildermugh S, Schmidt M, Debatin JF, Postprocessing techniques for gadolinium enhanced three dimensional MR angiography. Radiographics, 1997; 17:1061–1077

De Cobelli F, Vanzulli A, Sironi S, et al., Renal artery stenosis: Evaluation with breath-hold, three-dimensional, dynamic gadolinium-enhanced versus three-dimensional phase-contrast MR angiography. Radiology, 1997; 205:689–695

Dumoulin CL, Souza SP, Walker MR, et al., Three-dimensional phase-contrast angiography. Magn Reson Med, 1989; 9:139–149

Dumoulin CL, Phase Contrast MR angiography techniques. MRI Clin North Am, 1995; 3:399–412

Edelman R, Ahn S, Chien D, et al., Improved time-of-flight MR angiography of the brain with magnetization transfer contrast. Radiology, 1992; 184:395–399

Haacke EM, Masaryk TJ, Wielopolski PA, et al., Optimizing blood vessel contrast in fast three-dimensional MRI. Magn Reson Med, 1990; 14:202–221

Heiserman J, Drayer B, Fram E, et al., Carotid artery stenosis: clinical efficacy of two-dimensional time-of-flight angiography. Radiology, 1992; 182:761–768

Ho KY, deHaan MW, Oei TK, et al., MR angiography of the iliac and upper femoral arteries using four different inflow techniques. AJR, 1997; 169:45–53

Huston III J, Rufenacht DA, Ehman RL, Wiebers DO, Intracranial aneurysms and vascular malformations: comparison of time-of-flight and phase-contrast MR angiography. Radiology, 1991; 181:721–730

Itai Y, Matsui O, Blood flow and liver imaging. Radiology, 1997; 202:306–314

Kim D, Edelman RR, Kent KC, Porter DH, Skillman JJ, Abdominal Aorta and Renal Artery Stenosis: Evaluation with MR Angiography. Radiology, 1990; 174:727–731

Kopka L, Vosshenrich R, Rodenwaldt J, Grabbe E, Differences in Injection Rates on Contrast-Enhanced Breath-hold Three-Dimensional MR Angiography. AJR, 1998; 170:345–348

Laissy JP, Schoman-Claeys E, Time-of-flight magnetic resonance angiography of aorta and renal arteries: state-of-the-art. Eur J Radiol, 1996;21:201–211

Laub GA, Time-of-flight method of MR angiography. MRI Clin North Am, 1995; 3:391–398

Pelc NJ, Bernstein MA, Shimakawa A, Glover GH, Encoding strategies for three-dimension phase-contrast MR imaging of flow. J Magn Reson Imaging, 1991;1:405–413

Pernicone JR, Siebert JE, Potchen EJ, et al., Three-dimensional phase-contrast MR angiography in the head and neck: preliminary report. AJNR, 1990;11:457–466

Prince MR, Schoenberg SO, Ward JS, et al., Hemodynamically significant atherosclerotic renal artery stenosis: MR angiographic features. Radiology, 1997; 205:128

Rosovsky MA, Litt AW, MR Angiography of the extracranial carotid arteries. MRI Clin North Am 1995; 3:439–454

Siegelman ES, Gilfeather M, Holland GA, et al., Breath-hold Ultrafast Three-dimensional Gadolinium-enhanced MR Angiography of the Renovascular System. AJR, 1997; 168:1035–1040

Slossman F, Stolpen AH, Lexa FJ, et al., Extracranial Atherosclerotic Carotid Artery Disease: Evaluation of Non-Breath-hold Three-Dimensional Gadolinium-Enhanced MR Angiography. AJR, 1998; 170:489–495

Swan S, Weber D, Grist T, Wojtowycz M, Korosec F, Mistretta CA, Peripheral MR angiography with variable velocity encoding. Radiology, 1992; 184:813–817

Valk PE, Hale JD, Crooks LE, et al., MRI of blood flow: Correlation of image appearance with spin echo phase shift and signal intensity. AJR, 1981; 146:931–939

INDEX

Page numbers followed by *t* or *f* refer to
tables and figures, respectively.

Page numbers followed by *t* or *f* refer to
tables and figures, respectively.

Page numbers followed by *t* or *f* refer to
tables and figures, respectively.

3